It's the ultimate teen information guide! Kandias gives teens and the adults who support them comprehensive information sources to help them meet the challenges that they face. She delivers the same dynamic nurturing messages that she delivers to her own successful teenager. This book is a source to be treasured for years to come. It should be added to homes and libraries across the country.

~Nicole Cabell-Pope, Host of the Mahogany Blue Show WVON AM 1450, Professional Speaker, Founder, Build Today, Lead Tomorrow Teen Communications.

A great introduction to entrepreneurship for teenagers! I have known Kandi for over 15 years. She has taught entrepreneurship and life skills to hundreds of teens. She's charismatic, energetic and teenagers love her enthusiasm. Kandi has now authored three books, and this is by far her most important, most needed work. Every school and organization should have this informational resource guide.

~ Ida Manning, Exec. Director, Illinois Institute for Entrepreneurship Education.

What a dynamic resource for teenagers! I started working with Kandi many years ago through the Chicago Bulls/Chicago Park District Late Nite Basketball League where she taught life skills to the athletes. Her knowledge and passion in this field has allowed us to continue working together on numerous other programs to enhance the life experiences of young adults. She is a very dynamic trainer for youth and young adults and now adds this 270 page resource guide to her repertoire of Life Skills information. This book will surely enhance programs for teens across the country.

~ Michelle Ruscitti, VIP Marketing & Entertainment, Former Coordinator of Community Relations for the Chicago Bulls

This book is a must-have for teenagers! Kandi taught Life Skills to our transitioning DCFS youth at Transitional Living. We relished her creativity and delivery to our teens and young adults. This book will only be an asset to any program, organization or home. It's armed with Life Skills, Survival Techniques and much more.

~ LaConda Mines, Resident Services Administrator, Transitional Living Career Institute.

For Teens Who "Think" They Know Everything

For Teens Who "Think" They Know Everything

For Teens Who "Think" They Know Everything!

12 Tips for Teens On: Life Skills, Sex, Parents, Peer Pressure, Health & Everything Else

Life Skills and Survival Techniques for Today's Teenagers

By: Kandias Conda

GSW Publishing Company
Chicago, IL

For Teens Who "Think" They Know Everything!
12 Tips for Teens On: Life Skills, Sex, Parents, Peer Pressure, Health & Everything Else

Life Skills and Survival Techniques for Today's Teenagers

By Kandias Conda

Published by: GSW Publishing
3400 W. 111th, Suite #142, Chicago, IL 60655
Email:ForTeenz@aol.com/www.forteens.biz

ISBN# 1933556-10-2

Library of Congress Cataloging-in-Publication Date PCN
Conda, Kandias
For Teens Who "Think" They Know Everything!
12 Tips for Teens On: Life Skills, Sex, Parents, Peer Pressure, Health & Everything Else
1.)Teenagers 2. Life Skills 3. Juvenile Literature
Library # 2005937715

Table of Contents

Acknowledgements

This book is a project that has been in the long time making. One of the most important moments for an author, is this point. It usually means that you have arrived to the party. As you climb to your summit, you couldn't have arrived without help from some very important people. They held your hand, pulled you up and sometimes just gave a few encouraging words. Your utopia signals that you have completed your journey. Now you must thank those who held you during the process. Without God this book would not be possible. My thanks is to God for giving me the strength to keep going, and then to my daughter Deminique who also gave me day-to-day encouragement and inspiration.

An extra special thanks to Brian JA Kelley of Psychodrama, for designing the cover of this book. He's talented and dynamite. This book would not be possible without Sean Hicks of Gargoyle Creative Services. Thank you Sean and God Bless You!!

I'd like to give a high five and special thanks to my great friend Michelle Ruscitti for the final editing. She understood the project in it's entirety, she has a creative eye and became my right and left hand in the final stages of the book. Thanks to authors in music, hip-hop and sports chapters; Michelle Ruscitti and Dr. Angela Wheeler.

To the beautiful book models and teen authors; Demi Lobo (Cover Model and Author), April Miller (Model and Author), Dominique Jones (Cover Model and Author), Darius Williams, Brittany Johnson, Nakiah Robinson, Dominique Davis, and Stacy Council. A very warm thanks to them and their parents.

A wondrous thanks to Cedric Pope, aka Pharoah of 360Beyond Photography who provided the stunning cover photo of Demi Lobo. And, an extra special hug and "thank you" to Ida Manning and Nicole Cabell Pope, who both provided me with additional motivation and strength that writers, speakers and creative minds need to get to the top of the mountain. It's a different kind of journey.

A special thanks to my "focus group", the ones that kept me in check, that helped me to stay encouraged and focused on my project. This group would endearingly ask me "what's the status, and how is the progress coming?" They are; Angel Smiley, Hazel King, Dr. Zira Smith, Maxine Washington, Betty Jones and Joe Gray. Also a thanks to all of my friends and clients that I have taught Life Skills and Entrepreneurship to; LaConda Mines, TLCI, Tim Benson for his interview and all other students that provided me with research information for this project.

Finally, I have one of the most supportive families in the world. My father William Conda, who provides consistent wisdom and encouragement beyond my years I say "thanks and send him 12 pounds of love." Smile. I also like to thank my sister Patrice Conda and all of my cousins, the entire Conda Clan! But, a most significant and loving thank you, and the Thanks Award" goes to my cousins Theresa Miller and Beverly Taylor. They are on the forefront of my cheering squad with every project. It's almost as if they are writing with me. I love them they are the ultimate definition of family support.

Thanks to Deborah Evans of DAE Communications, she was the first line editor and was instrumental in providing our initial direction. Lastly; I'd like to give a big hug to all my Life Skills and Entrepreneur students across the City of Chicago and other states.

How To Use This Book

This book is a one-stop-shop for teenagers. A special guide designed with you in mind. During these challenging and difficult years, you need a book in your own language, which deals with the real life choices you have to make. ***"For Teens Who Think They Know Everything"*** is a cutting edge resource guide that deals with *parent-teen communication, school, teachers, peer pressure, music Hip-Hop, etiquette, homeless teens, piercing, tattoos, dating, job readiness, entrepreneurship, sex, health, dieting, finding a job, keeping a job, college scholarships, proms, money management, college preparation, conflict resolution, friendship, teen testimonials and much more.* It is written in an easy read format, with 12 tips on each subject. The tips are explained so that you will gain maximum understanding. This is your own special resource guide to use when you have no one to ask or the subject is too sensitive. This book will help you to understand the life changes, hormonal changes, growing pains and your transition to young adult hood. Teens are now inundated with personal choices about Hip-Hop, videos, technology, along with trying to juggle school, work and life. When you add social and peer issues to the pot - you have much to do. Use this resource and all of its information to help you in your transition to you a positive young adult. Get ahead of your peers! After reading each chapter, there is a journal for you to write down what you learned from it.

You don't' have to buy different books; you have over 55 subjects and 1000 web resources in this one important book. Many teens are raising themselves and need to know what to do next. Many teens go through high school and miss the experience. Either because they may have just been unaware of some things that are available and others because no one told them. This book will encourage teens to engage in programs, self assuredness, confidence and team building. Life is yours for the taking. Get into the experience!

TEENAGERS will enjoy having their very own resource guide at their fingertips. It's easy to read and written in your own language. This book is for your own personal growth and enrichment. Learn how to grow and transition into a positive young adult person.

SCHOOLS, TEACHERS and **EDUCATORS** can use this book in classrooms to deliver life skills to students. This is a great way to introduce subjects such as etiquette, music, Hip-Hop, teachers, prom, graduation, college, sex and health just to name a few. Schools can also use this book in their after-school or regular school programs. This book will help you to train students on job readiness skills, how to keep a job and give them real life answers to challenging scenarios they will face as they transition into young adults. We have included the hard to discuss subjects such as; homeless teens, homosexual teens and sex. Teachers will be able to use the 55 life subjects for discussions and to help teenagers with life enrichment.

PARENTS and **GRANDPARENTS** finally have the life skills book they've always wanted. A book to change your teens! How many times have you said, "mind your manners" or "when we were young we had more respect." Finally, here's every subject you always wanted to discuss with your teenager and more. AND..an extra added value is the chapter "For Parent's Only" and more "Parent's Secret Weapons."

CHURCHES, YOUTH GROUPS & COMMUNITY ORGANIZATIONS will have 55 life skills subjects to institute into their programs. "For Teens" will help you engage your teenagers in workshop discussions regarding their everyday lives. Youth leaders can help them with conflict resolution, anger management, gangs as well as personal life choices.

Introduction

What is Life Skills? Why Life Skills? Life Skills are the basic qualities and survival skills that pre-teens, teens and young adults need to work, live and operate in society. Life Skills are needed because although you may have some of these qualities, it's rare that you have all of them. Life Skills training comes into the picture to fill the gap and help to enrich your life. Since we all come from different back grounds we are not always able to explore and perfect every aspect of life's demands. After working in high schools and meeting with hundreds of teenagers over the past years, I have also realized that; many teens are raising themselves, have issues with their parents, have limited or no parental communication, are homeless or have situations at home that force different types of misunderstood behavior coupled with the other unique challenges of the world.

Also, I am the parent of a wonderful, talented, busy, creative teenager that is an athlete, and an entertainer which gives me plenty of insight to how you think. I have to remain focused on the needs of teenagers and young adults. It's how I give back. Now you must educate yourself in the world, which is why this book is so instrumental with 55 life subjects and 1000 web resources to get you started. Use them both to familiarize yourself about the things you don't know. Your very own resource guide will to introduce you to the basics about; money, sex, health, diet, jobs, entrepreneurship, parents, communication, dating, relationships and much more. You will need all or some of the information, at one time or another. Life isn't something you "go through", it's something you "grow through". You are responsible for the outcome of your life, it's your show. This guide will help you to navigate through some life challenges and situations. It's like having a big sister, brother or parent with you when those certain subjects come up and you need advice. Those subjects, some of which are listed below, are a preview to the book. This intro will give some insight into why this book was necessary and why it was written.

On Real Life Issues – You only get one chance in life to do things right. This is not a practice run. Do it right as much as possible. Don't let others talk you into unnecessary behavior. Live each day to the fullest and enjoy it within reason. Never at the expense of others! This book will help you understand positive ways to live life, love and stay healthy emotionally.

On Parents – Your parents are the heart of your life. Negative or positive, you can't give them back. If you know the secret password, we will do just about anything for you. You have to bring your 40% to the table. This usually means honesty, good behavior, grades, clean your room some of the time and respect us, and mind curfew ..for starters. We bring the big end; money, the transportation, the love and everything else you may need. This chapter will help to build your parent-teen communication.

On Friends – Friends unlike family are of your own choice. The key to friendship is having good friends, keeping good friends and being a good friend. You will always need a shoulder to cry on. Even the best of us have one bad day. The friendship chapter will guide you on making friendships, mending friendships and being a best friend. This doesn't come easy for everyone, some teens are shy or have trouble making friends.

On Communication – Communication is a very important tool for teenagers. It's how we interact with parents, friends, family, teachers' and at school. When you get a job, your communication will be the one of the most important things you are judged on. You must have good verbal and non-verbal communication skills. Speaking properly is not phony. Learn to adapt to your surroundings, how you present yourself may be worth a job or important event in your life one day.

Music, Videos & Hip-Hop – The new culture, Hip-Hop has taken over and crossed all ages, genres' and races. It is one of the most controversial topics of conversation in regards to youth. It's the music we love to hate. We love the beat, the creative lyrics that are so questionable and dynamic video' s that give ideas to impressionable youth. This is any industry that eats its young. With that being said, they key is to admire the creativity of these artists and their art, without mimicking the bad behavior and language. Being a mature young adult means you know the difference and where to draw the line. The video's and the people in it are for entertainment purposes only. They aren't all rich, and acting like them won't make you rich. This chapter discusses positive ways to enjoy your Hip-Hop experience.

School – School is an important part of your teenage life. Many of you will go through high school and then to college or trade school. Make the most of it and do your best from day one. It will go so quickly. You will be a happy new freshman just entering and the next thing you know you'll be will be applying to colleges and stressing out over entrance exams, essays and scholarships. Once you get over the excitement, join your sports and clubs, then get down to business. Academic Business. We'll show you how to have fun, study, and what to do if you don't mix immediately with the "in crowd".

Peer Pressure – Peer Pressure is that anxiety you feel in the pit of your stomach. It's the when you feel pressured to do something your friends or peers ask you to do. If they tease you or make you feel like you're not cool, that's when the peer pressure comes into play. You have to stay focused, grounded and keep your eye on the prize. Never let anyone else decide what's best for you. If you know it's not right, stand up for yourself. This chapter shows you how to be a leader and head off peer pressure in areas dealing with body image, clothes, smoking, drinking, drugs and school.

Health – Health is important for teenagers. We explore healthy eating and suggestions and advice from our doctor on how to stay healthy. Also, we have a chapter for athletes, on how to avoid injury and stay healthy. In a time where fast food is king, teenagers are becoming more aware of what they must do to stay healthy.

Sex – Sex, abstinence and STD's are difficult decisions in the life of a teenager. Starting as early as fifth grade, sex seems to be the hot curiosity. While we parents are close to heart attacks, the world is desperately trying to give you more safe sex and education. Sex has many consequences attached to it. Some people have emotional effects after having sexual contact too young, and others get pregnant on the first time. Some individuals contract STD's from sexual relations that may cause further physical damage. You must be informed as to your options on not having sex-abstinence, safe sex and birth control. It is important to know how you can get pregnant or contract an STD.

Jobs & Entrepreneurship – Some teenagers will leave high school and go to college or trade school. Teens will soon start to look for summer jobs and evening jobs and they will need an edge as to how to get started. To help you make these important decisions we have included sections on how to get a job and how to keep a job. We also give you advice on how to start a small business, business plans and suggestions of several home based businesses that can be started for under $100.

Race – Each day as we live, we experience racism and prejudice when dealing with people. A new milenium didn't guarentee new people, that we can gain a new attitude, new thought, and renew our inner selves. We may never elliminate segregation, but we can do our part in the world by changing one person at a time. In the end, we are all part of one race "the Human Race".

Chapter One:
What's
Happening
Now!

PARENTS

MANAGING YOUR PARENTS AND STAYING OUT OF THE PARENT TRAP!

Parents are very important because without them you would not be here. Make sure you respect your parents because this is the most unconditional love you will ever have. That's right, they (we) love you no matter what. This is a tough one! Parents are the ones you love, the ones who take care of you and who you go to when you need advice. As you enter into "Teenagehood" it seems that you have less time for your parents. All of a sudden, you have "business" and you don't want us in it. It's just as well because we really don't want to be in it. However, you must still include us in the process because if you stray in any way, we don't want to be the last to know.

Keep in mind, we've been there. The plan is to keep you from going through the fires we've already been burned from. Some teenagers just have to find out things the hard way, by trial and error. Experience can sometimes be the best lesson. So when parents give you advice, please, please give us the benefit of the doubt. Go out of your way to show your parents that you respect them and their values. No reason - just because you're their kid.

12 TIPS FOR TEENS ON MANAGING YOUR PARENTS:

1. Parents Just Don't Understand

You are absolutely right! You speak teenager - we speak Mom & Dad, you say party, we say curfew. Get the idea? This is not true in every case. Some of us parents actually understand better than you think. Give us a little credit, we just know better. However, if you really think we are "not getting it," THEN break it down for us. Draw pictures, color them in, or do whatever you need, because we want to be on the same page with you. We want to understand and communicate with you. This is a growth period for both of us so we will have a better relationship. We usually lose you when we are telling you something that is wise, responsible or good parental advice and you go against us. Then you use a shabby excuse to follow and that's when we want to skin your scalp! Let's communicate regularly, try to understand each other and bring pictures when necessary.

2. What To Do When You Disagree With Your Parents

Simply put, disagreements occur when two or more individuals disagree or do not see eye-to-eye on a subject, topic or idea. There are several ways of handling disagreements. As you become teenagers and you uh... smell yourself as we say, you will start to disagree with us. Guess what? Sometimes you will be right. But - that doesn't mean we will always give in, hey we're parents. Here are a couple of suggestions when dealing with disagreements; *(1) You can "agree to disagree"* (Note: this one usually does not work well with parents). *(2) You can sit down with your parents in a mature manner and present your case.* We will listen to your point. If you have witnesses to support your argument bring them (this is where dads, aunts and siblings are usually very helpful). Remember: We will not always agree, your teachers, friends and employers will not always agree with you either, but demonstrate good solid points and you may be surprised.

3. Healthy Relationships

Parents are your world from birth until eternity. A healthy relationship is when we trust you, love you and want only the best for you. You should always feel comfortable and safe with your parents. You should be able to call them or talk to them about anything - no matter what. I know that we parents are sometimes difficult to communicate with but we try very hard, you must meet us half way. Your parental experience should be a good, healthy one. This does not mean we aren't occasionally hollering, or that our heads aren't spinning around and spitting up green stuff. This just means we're having a fairly normal family experience. Healthy relationships consist of support, fun, life exposure, family time, open communication and love. A healthy relationship should be a positive family experience that is free from dysfunction and negativity. If your family is having problems, first try family meetings where you can *air the laundry.* If that doesn't work, you may want to ask your parents or school counselor to arrange for family therapy.

4. Unhealthy Relationships

Unhealthy relationships are when we are not experiencing the love in #3. You may be the product of an unhealthy relationship with "a" particular parent or both parents. This does not have to be your biological parents; it could be extended, blended or adoptive parental situations. An unhealthy relationship can stem from personality problems and misunderstandings to dysfunctional family environments. You must also take responsibility for your part, meaning, if things aren't going well, you must take inventory of your own life. You must recognize the factors that feel negative and try to do something about it. Strive to have the best childhood experience that you possibly can and don't let anyone take that away from you. If you and your parent or guardians are not getting along, try sitting down to have some discussions that directly tackle the problem at hand. Try to find the source of the problem, if you can, or suggest family counseling. If that doesn't work, then try to change your attitude to adjust to the situation. You can't change others, but you can change yourself. When all else fails, remember time heals all wounds and the situation will look better in the morning. Family counseling, mediation or therapy is also available to help get your family back on track.

5. Living with an Alcohol/Drug Addicted Parent

This is a very difficult topic to discuss because this hits very close to home. Rule number one is - please refuse to be in denial. If you realize that you are living with a parent that has a problem, counseling would be the best bet. If that doesn't happen, attempt to keep YOU focused in the meantime while you are going through life. Read books on Al-Anon/Al-Ateen or join one of these organizations (they are free support groups that specialize in counseling and meetings for children and families of alcoholic parents). Parents that are addicted to substances are much more common today and there are many counseling groups, books and websites dedicated to the subject. If you are not ready to share your personal life with others, you may want to do some research first then, prepare for the next step. As a teen I lived in a household with an alcoholic parent. I worked, studied and kept myself busy so I didn't have to deal with it. When I became seventeen I left home to go to the military. I experienced some traumatic moments, outbursts and cursing that were painful, but I was strong and I lived through it. Like the saying goes, if it doesn't kill you, it will make you stronger. For me, I became stronger by refusing to repeat the cycle of violence and dysfunction with my teen.

6. Single Parents – Teenager's Responsibilities

Today there are millions of single parents raising children alone. Whether it's a mom or a dad, it's your responsibility to help out around the house and help with younger siblings. Here are a few things you can do to make their job easier; wash your own clothes, keep your room clean and pick up behind yourself without being told. If you see the dishes or laundry piling up, throw in a load and see it through to the dryer and the folding. If you see the garbage overflowing take it out without being told. When you get home, start your siblings on their homework and chores. A single parent has a lot of responsibility being both mom and dad; add work and raising kids to the equation and that is a full plate. You are a teenager on your way to becoming a young adult. Any experience you can get at home now will help when you go away to college or leave home. What's really neat is once they see how mature you are, they will give you more responsibility, trust you more, and next thing you know you'll be driving the truck!!! This will help you to have a more harmonious home environment and teach you about family commitment and loyalty. Being responsible means you know to come straight home and do your homework before you get on the phone, turn on the television or go outside.

7. Blended Families Are Today's Growing Families

The definition of a blended family is when a marriage brings together separate families from both mom and dad; you now have instant brothers and sisters from the previous marriages. They move in together and share the same household environment. This usually takes some getting used to, especially if your household and living arrangements have to be altered or changed. If you've watched the Brady Bunch you know this is a challenge. You have individuals that may be resentful because their living space has been invaded, or upset because they have a new step-mom or step-dad. If the house is large enough to accommodate everyone, this can usually work once all of the personalities have adjusted. If you are living in a blended family environment and there is tension, sit down with your parent first and tell them your issues privately, then put the problem on the table with both parents. Hopefully, you will be able to work this out for a happy family lifestyle.

8. Coping with Divorced Parents

Divorce and separation can be very painful. Parents usually go the extra distance to make sure that their children are comfortably dealing with it. However, this can really be challenging in long distance relationships or argumentative families. Some suggestions include setting a regular date to visit the other parent, working as hard as you can to spend equal time with both and sharing your accomplishments with both parents. They should work equally as hard to not put you in the middle of any disputes or disagreements they may have. If holidays become a concern, you may want to suggest that you split and alternate them. This way everyone gets a turn at each holiday. Divorce and separation will only be successful if all parties work together.

9. Communication and Attitude

You must communicate with your parents. "My parents just don't understand!" *Yes they do* - we understand plenty. We are the piece to the puzzle when you are trying to understand the complexities of life. Your parents have been around the block a few times, and they know how to communicate to get what they need. Regardless if it's about school, boys, girls, teachers, friends, family or something very personal, you should be able to share with your parents. As you mature, you are starting to discuss, debate and even disagree with your parents. Get advice from your older siblings, they are usually very helpful in these situations. You'll start to have more adult conversations, and sometimes disagreements. Make sure that you respect your parents with your grown up attitude, they will always be there for you. Weigh your decisions carefully and include your parents, in most cases, they won't steer you wrong. Put your cards on the table, be honest and be as open as you can. No problem or situation is without a solution, and you shouldn't carry any load on your shoulder that's too heavy for you to handle.

10. Why Did You Go Through My Stuff?

Occasionally, you will find that your parents have gone through a pocket, purse or drawer in your room. Your response will be "this is my stuff, what about my privacy?" There are two sides to this story. Some parents respect your right to privacy; other parents feel like *"it's all my stuff until you start paying for it."* Regardless of which mom or dad is yours, if it's something you don't want anyone to see, you should put it away. Secondly, if you are doing something illegal such as; drugs, alcohol or underage sexual activity – your parent should call you on it. If a parent can't do it, who can? Although you have a right to your privacy, your parents have a duty to make sure you're safe and using good judgment. If that means an occasional pocket check every now and then… oh well.

11. Abuse

If you are in an abusive household you must first recognize the signs. There are several different types of abuse; verbal abuse – where someone consistently calls you out of your name or screams degrading obscenities at you. *Verbal abuse* leads to emotional abuse, when your inner core and self-esteem is breaking down. *Physical abuse* is when someone is putting their hands on you, slapping, hitting or beating you. This is illegal and adults can be punished and in some cases jailed for physically abusing their children. *Sexual abuse* is when someone is touching you in private places that you know are inappropriate or wrong. It is illegal and adults can be punished for inappropriate touching or having sex with a minor. If you are feeling any type of pressure from any type of abuse, please contact authorities, a school counselor, nurse or let other family members know immediately.

12. Where's the Love?

Affection varies between individuals and families. Our immediate family is a touchy feely type of family. We hug when we see each other and when we depart. Many times we kiss each other on the cheek as well. However, some of our other family and friends don't like the PDA (Public Display of Affection). Smile. There's something to be said about a child that never receives a hug. Sometimes you ought to get one whether you need it or not, just to know you're loved. I have found that some kids have never had a hug. Everyone has a day when they need to feel that someone cares, or need the comfort of a human touch. This provides reassurance that things are going to be alright. *Moral:* it's ok to hug your parents, friends and family or show affection and let them know you care. I love when my teenage daughter gives me a big wet one on the jaw or the forehead. She still doesn't think it's too corny to give me a kiss or hug. It's a wonderful feeling to know someone genuinely loves you and cares.

MY JOURNAL ENTRY

List 5 things that you learned after reading the chapter on ***parents.*** Discuss them with a parent, teacher, mentor or friends.

FRIENDSHIPS

Everyone should have a friend, even if it's just one good one. You need that special friend to bounce things off of or share those personal thoughts with. That someone, to sit by your side through the good times and the bad. In my research I have learned that girls have special friendships between each other, boys have special friendships between them, and then there are just all kinds of friendships spread between school and sports. Just make sure the person you choose is a friend that gives back what you give to them, emotionally. Friends are an extension of your family. On that note, here are some tips to consider when choosing or making friends.

3 Rules for Friendship: (1) Be a good friend. (2) Learn how to keep a good friend. (3) Don't be afraid to make new friends. We all know you can't choose your family, but you can certainly choose your friends.

12 TIPS FOR TEENS ON MAKING, HAVING AND KEEPING GOOD FRIENDS:

1. What Is A Good Friend?

A relationship between two or more people that builds over time through trust and loyalty is a true friendship. A friend is someone that has your back! Someone who will be an ally, (on your side) someone who will take the time to listen, support and sympathize with you. A good friend is that person who will really give you the shirt off their back, even if it has a name brand or logo on it. Smile. Finding that special friend can be a challenge, especially when you start a new school or move to a new neighborhood. Suggestions on easy ways to make new friends range from joining organizations, clubs, dance groups or sports teams. A good friend has the following qualities; they are positive, fun, trustworthy, loyal and supportive. Everyone you meet will not automatically become a friend. Don't force it, let it happen and watch the good relationships turn into great friends over time.

2. Keeping and Mending Friendships

Friends can be fickle, moody, and give us challenges that we may not be up to. If they are a *good friend*, maintaining the friendship should not feel like a job. Conflicts should be addressed and resolved in order for friendships to continue. If talking does not work, get a third party to mediate (listen and judge). Yes, there will be times when you question yourself because friends just take you there. If you and your friends have a disagreement, you will have to learn how to get past it. You can't get to the bottom of every problem. Sometimes in a friendship, a simple "I'm sorry" is worth a million dollars. Sometimes you may have to agree to disagree. Keep good friends you can trust at the top your list. You'll need them on your *"blue day,"* a day when your parents, teachers, and everybody else has gotten on your nerves.

3. Positive Friends

Positive friends are the ones that can see a fight or problem escalating and diffuse (stop) it before it happens. Positive friends say positive things and uplift you when you are down. They sense when you need them and they are there. They may not be perfect; however they are the ones that you can go to on a real bad day. You can always count on them to be funny or say something to cheer you up. I love positive friends because they are "just necessary human beings." The universe smiles on them and they smile back at us. If you have a positive upbeat friend, then by all means keep them around as long as possible.

4. Negative Friends. Kaboom!

Negative friends are always drama and never satisfied no matter what you do or say. Negative friends are emotional drains. Know who they are and be able to spot them. If necessary, you may need to distance yourself from them. They are the ones who never have any good news. A negative friend may not even know they are being negative. If they are close to you and you want to salvage (save) the friendship, have *"the talk"* and let them know how you feel. If they don't get the hint, you may need to start spending less time around them so they don't eventually drag you down. They may say things that hurt your feelings and because you are close to them, you let them off the hook. This will most likely end with you disliking and resenting them. Finally one day, the relationship will blow up and the friendship will end up in smoke.

5. Having "NO FRIENDS"

Not having any friends can sometimes feel just as bad as having negative friends. But if you are a teen without any friends, you "can" do something to change it. It is not the end of the world. Just make sure the ones you do have are *good ones.* I would rather have one good, dependable, loyal friend than a lot of people around me that I don't trust. Hopefully you've already read "Good Friends" a few sections up. If those ideas didn't work, you may want to look in your circles of interest or activities. Look for kids that have something in common with you and start your own club. Teens have been known to be ostracized (left out) because they are loners, smart, not-so-smart, quiet, dress or look different. It happens all the time in teen worlds across the planet so just be patient. Everyone you come across doesn't have to instantly be your friend; it's ok to have associates.

6. The "CLIQUE" Is Everywhere. ***Not The Clique Again!***

Let's be honest, cliques are everywhere. "Popular cliques, drama/arts cliques, sports cliques, nerd cliques," the cliques go on and on. Most times they are harmless and we don't care that they exist… until we want to get into one of them. This is fine as long as you know where to draw the clique-line. This means if you are having trouble getting into what you think is your *dream clique*, maybe that's because it's not for you. If they are doing things they shouldn't be doing like making fun of others, pranks or hurting people, that's not good either. If their clique looks, smells and acts like a secret club, maybe they don't deserve to have you. Be careful of being a part of something unhealthy that could be worse than not having any friends.

7. What to Do When You Have 2 Or 3 *Different Sets of Friends*?
When you have two different posse's, someone usually doesn't like someone else and they put you in the middle. If this happens, you'll have to keep the groups separate and it will be difficult to have outings will all of them together. Just don't let them pull and tug at you, make you feel uncomfortable or feel like you have choose. That kind of pressure you can do without. Explain to them how this makes you feel and that you would like to have more events where they can mingle together. If none of this works, go out with them on separate days but make sure it works for you.

8. Gossip Is A Nasty No-No
Have you ever wondered why gossip is juicy as long as it's not about you? If it is about you, then for some reason it's not funny anymore. Matter of fact, when they finally get around to you, it's something really personal, that will hit very close to home. Most gossip is not true or it's embellished (added on) to make it sound more exciting. Hope that the next juicy story you hear is not about you. The less you gossip about others, the less you'll be gossiped about.

9. Best Friends are a "MUST HAVE"
Best friends are like good friends with a gold star. Everyone should have at least one best friend – but feel free to have as many as you can stand. Best friends are an extension of your family, ones that you actually pick yourself. How cool is that! Some best friends are the friends you will keep throughout your lifetime. Your sister, brother, or other family member can be your best friend. They listen to you when no one else will, they listen to you cry and listen to you laugh. The challenge is being a good best friend in return to this person. If you have a best friend, you should sign them on for life… besides, they know too much of your personal business to let them go.

10. For Boys Only
All you guys, young men, caballeros, amigos want a girl friend. Why? Your friends have one, you're curious or you think it's cool. Let's learn a few things first. You can have a friend-girl without making them a girlfriend. Next, always treat girls/young women like ladies, always. This is something you definitely won't learn from a music video or from friends. Respect for women includes; never calling a girl or young woman out of her name, never hit or curse at them and never, never use the "B" word. Open doors and pull out chairs, especially on a date or at a formal event. Be a gentleman and always consider the feelings of others. Respect their family and household wishes by calling during designated hours, usually not later than 9-9:30 p.m. on weekdays and 10-11:00 p.m. on weekends. Always announce yourself when calling, and go to the house and meet the parents before you pick up your date. This is also expected for prom or special event dates.

11. For Girls Only

Young ladies, ok let's talk. Realistically you start to look at boys seriously when you're in about 5th & 6th grade. However, this can vary because some girls still think boys are aliens. You are still quite young, and really shouldn't be in a hurry to get a serious boyfriend. Why? Several reasons; your school work and studies should come first and this boy thing can be very distracting. Some parents let their young ladies date with a chaperone or let their teens date in groups. I have witnessed girl's that are way too young saying things like *"that's my man."* This is the sign of misguided identity issues and self-esteem problems; it means we have a lot of work to do. Are you taking notes? Boys do not stay with girls because they get sex. This is a curiosity that destroys and mixes up your inner emotions. If you give up your virginity and the boy doesn't come back, or he tells his friend - then you'll be embarrassed. You could get pregnant and a baby would complicate your life and future plans. Some boys will not accept the responsibility and then blame you for changing their life. The list is endless and the best decision is to stay abstinate (don't have sex)!

12. Drama Kings & Queens

There's really no place for drama in a friendship. But, there are some girls and guys that like to keep bringing stuff up. If you recognize these kinds of people, keep your distance. Here's what they act like; they are liked by some and hated by others, they seem to need attention 24/7 and are mixed up in everything that happens. Keep in mind that they are mostly caught up in the excitement of all the drama. They eat, sleep and drink gossip and just when the last scandal is ending, they have landed a new eagle, at the other end of the hall. They frequently jump from clique to clique and can always be found right in the middle. Matter of fact, it's not happening without them. When you see these Drama Kings and Drama Queens, help them to find a new hobby. Leave them alone and make them stay out of your business.

MY JOURNAL ENTRY

List things you have learned about your ***friendships***. Discuss them with a parent, teacher, mentor or friends.

____

____

____

____

____

____

____

HIP-HOP HYPE & MASS MEDIA

Mass media engages as much as a third of most people's lives. News, magazines, films, music, television and the internet are, for most people, the major source of information about their world. Few can dispute the impact of mass media on your lives, whether the power in its messages can be used for good or bad reasons. In this media driven world, entertainers have a significant influence on your cultural identity, norms and beliefs. Music and videos can be even more influential for pre-teens and teens your age.

The Hip-Hop culture encompasses one of the most popular forms of music today. This music speaks to youth through experiences, challenges, passions, fears and hopes. Over the past 30 years, hip-hop has seen many new styles evolve; giving us the "Hip-Hop nation" we live in today. Hip-Hop can be viewed as the most significant cultural symbol of today's youth. It not only informs our musical tastes, it also encompasses everything from fashion and film to religion and politics. We took notice when rappers started voting drives.

In the 21st century, we realize Hip-Hop music is the representative voice of youth, since the genre was created by you and for you. However, we also realize that rap music and the media are highly accused for teens gone bad. This chapter will discuss ways to embrace this culture in a positive way. *Written by: Kandias Conda & Michelle Ruscitti.*

12 TIPS FOR TEENS ON HOW TO POSITIVELY EMBRACE THE HIP-HOP CULTURE:

1. Know Your Culture... What is Hip-Hop?
Hip-Hop culture can consist of thoughts and beliefs or, material things such as gear, language, behaviors, music, symbols, art/style including graffiti, jewelry and other possessions. The language can be verbal or nonverbal consisting of rhyme, rhythm, timing, syntax and word structure. The different beliefs, values and norms found within the Hip-Hop culture are the aspects that give a culture its energy and dynamics. The impact of Hip-Hop music seems to transcend race, as Hip-Hop is composed of individuals from diverse racial, ethnic, social and economic backgrounds. The culture of Hip-Hop seems to be adopted by youth through its different, yet similar, forms of communication, dress and musical identity.

2. What's the Hype?
Many people want to know why rap music and Hip-Hop have captured youth and adults for so many years. There are several reasons; the music sounds good, we can relate our personal experiences to the lyrics, it's entertaining and we love watching it all come together. The cable shows play music videos that emulate behavior of rich and famous lifestyles. Great cribs, fabulous rides and fresh clothes. These videos have gorgeous men and women, exotic dancers and elaborate themes. Rap artists often make appearances on television, radio and in movies. It is a multi-billion dollar industry that has turned rappers into businessmen with clothing lines, record labels and dozens of other business ventures. Their allure, bodacious attitudes, smart lyrics and

savvy business skills has turned this into years of successful bliss between teens and their music.

3. Learn and Study Your Craft

We know a lot of you out there want to be in the entertainment business. Whether you are a singer, dancer, musician, actor, writer or producer you will want to know every aspect of the game. You may be one of those naturally talented and gifted individuals however, you must study those who came before you and learn from their experiences. Your knowledge will only go so far. Expand your strengths by taking classes, practicing, listening, watching, and learning. You don't want to just be good - you want to be great *and* make money. Be prepared to spend many days, nights and years pitching your songs, ideas or your specialty. Not everyone knows someone or gets lucky. The majority of successful entertainers were in the grind long before anyone knew their name; working regular 9 to 5 jobs, networking, hustling 24 hours a day while waiting and hoping to be discovered.

4. Embrace the Diversity of Hip-Hop

While the aesthetic of the Hip-Hop culture is still primarily rooted in the African and Caribbean-American experience, Hip-Hop and rap music now influence people from virtually every social environment. Statistically speaking, non-minorities purchase the largest amount of rap music. This is an important point to know because society is under the impression that minorities are the only ones that purchase and listen to rap music. The point is not *who* listens to the music, but *how they listen* and *how they interpret it*. Use Hip-Hop to embrace other cultures and other people's point of view.

5. Don't Act a Fool… Be Yourself

Many youth want to emulate music artists because they think that it will make them rich. Although this industry looks glamorous, it doesn't come without hard work and a high price. Music artists do not achieve overnight success and neither will you. This book will help you to understand the *reality* of what it really takes to make it big. All is not glamorous in the entertainment world, they are real people who have struggles and make mistakes just like you. Have your own style, don't dress and act like someone you're not. I see many people changing their hair, teeth and dressing like rap stars and music artists. Be your own person. If you make a major change in your appearance and the fad changes, you're stuck with it forever. Be careful who you copy, gold fronts don't look good on many people.

6. Rap it Positive!

Everyone should take pride in listening to positive music. If you're a rapper or singer, you should also commit to making positive music. Your audience should be able to listen to your music on the radio without getting "bleeped." Do not be afraid to stick with your beliefs. Try to make a conscious effort to support rappers that don't curse or make degrading music. Positive music breeds positive minds.

7. Parental Advisory / Ratings

Due to politicians and watch groups that govern the music and media industry, a censor system has been devised to rate music CD's and DVD's for youth. Adults feel that there is some content that is not appropriate for children of all ages. CD's of concern will be labeled "Parental Advisory." These have curse words and explicit messages not intended for youth. Your parents are concerned with what you are listening to. Respect them when you buy your music and movies; after all, you're going to be listening to and watching them in their home. We're not saying you can't get these CD's or movies, just get the censored version with the radio cuts and edits.

8. That "B" Better Stand for Beautiful!

My number one goal is to have young ladies understand that the "B" and "H" words aren't cute. We understand sex and gangsta attitudes sell, but those words are musical lyrics that an artist gets paid hundreds of thousands of dollars to sing. This seems to be a part of everyday language, but that doesn't make it appropriate in the real world. The women portrayed in these songs get paid to "act" this role, but I bet if they get called these names after the gig is over, they will be like "I don't think so." Despite how many songs you hear it in, or how many videos you see it in, don't be a "B" or "H." You have a name and are a special princess, and everyone must know it. Respect yourself and demand respect from others.

9. Slow Down Shorty .....Someone's Watching You.

America's youth have become extremely invested in the culture of the mass media, especially Hip-Hop. When two and three year olds can sing the words to songs before they can read and do a booty shake that will put adults to shame, this is a major problem. What's the lesson here? When we first see it, we all think it's cute. The world has gotten away from discipline and respect; this is the same world that is now setting standards and raising our children. Be a role model for your younger siblings. If you find yourself watching or listening to grown up things, don't do it in front of them. You know they look up to you and will try and copy your every move, literally.

10. I Want My Own Hip-Hop Clothing Line or Record Label

Many music moguls have crossed over into these areas and these are great ambitions to have. In anything that you do, make sure you are in it for the right reason. You should have a passion for your work because it will make it that much more rewarding. It would be great if we could all get our name on a clothing line or record label. But, there are many components that go into these business ventures; production costs, financial backing, marketing, and advertising for starters. These are competitive businesses and you will have to be extremely dedicated to your craft. In the beginning, you will have to spend all of your time and money to be successful. And through it all, you will need to network, network and network some more with everyone you know in the business. You will have to dog this day and night and leave no stone unturned. There's always someone out there who thinks they are better than you – "the best." Keep good contacts and relationships, you never know who will be calling you or who you will need to call.

11. Ways You Can Make Hip-Hop a Positive Experience

Organize a focus group to discuss the history of Hip-Hop and its impact on society. Write your own song or poems to express your feelings or struggles. Rewrite a negative song with a positive spin. Read a Hip-Hop magazine and take note of the positive stories featured. Conduct an interview with a positive Hip-Hop professional and share it with your classmates and friends or in your school paper. Research the Hip-Hop artists who have foundations and give back to their communities.

12. How Can I Get My Parents to Accept Hip-Hop?

First you must realize that the media industry eats its young. It preys on impressionable minds with its lure of the bling. You and your parents must not alienate each other when it comes to your interest in Hip-Hop; have an open line of communication. We know even if we tell you not to listen or watch it, you're going to find a way to do it anyway. So, let's compromise a bit. Let them run a little interference and together you can decide what is appropriate and take it from there. Your parents are just trying to protect you, but they are probably going to try and set some guidelines for your music and television. After all, you do live under their roof and if they don't want you to listen to explicit music, respect their decision. Don't get mad if they find inappropriate CD's or movies and get rid of them. If it offends them, it's probably offending others around you while you are listening to it.

MY JOURNAL ENTRY

List 5 positive changes about your ***Hip-Hop*** experience that you would like to make. Discuss them with a parent, teacher, mentor or friends.

____

____

____

____

____

____

____

____

____

EVERYDAY ETIQUETTE & MANNERS 101 – AKA THE PARENT'S HIT LIST

This chapter is a personal favorite. It is a collaboration of ideas from parents that includes a few tips about everyday manners for the personal enrichment of today's teenagers. It includes some behaviors that teens (and also some adults) are known to perform. That does not make it appropriate. Now that you are a young adult, you must be careful how you act in public and how your actions affect others. Someone is always watching you and people react to you by how you act. If you are a smart aleck – they talk to you that way. If you are pleasant and well-mannered – people will treat you with respect. Your actions = reactions. You are officially a young adult in the making; you have to be more responsible, well-mannered, use good judgment and have good behavior. Everyone will know you have had some "home training."

12 TIPS FOR TEENS ON EVERYDAY ETIQUETTE & MANNERS:

1. Always say "Thank You, Excuse Me, Yes Sir/Ma'am, No Sir/Ma'am"
Probably sounds corny, but today's teens should have that level of respect we grew up with. Just think how would you feel if it was your mom or dad - you wouldn't want a teenager or someone to walk up to them and say yo' yo' what's up. This is disrespectful and it's not cool. When you say yes Sir/Ma'am it makes adults look up and take notice. Say thank you without being told, it's a simple form of respect. Hold the door or help someone just because, for no other reason than it's a nice thing to do.

2. R-E-S-P-E-C-T ELDERS
You must respect your elders (adults, people older than you). To fully understand respect, you must respect yourself first. If you see adults, curb your language, and read number #3, there will be a test afterwards. In our generation, our parents would clock us out if we disrespected adults. Society is presenting bad language through music and TV and we have become numb to it. Teens talk back to adults without a second thought. If you are upset with an adult, communicate with them, plan to sit and talk with them in a mature manner.

3. Cursing & Name Calling
"Cussing" as it is also called, is unfortunately very common among teens. It doesn't make you sound intelligent so try to avoid it and use other words to express yourself. Cursing is what you do when you have a lack of vocabulary. With music and daily influences I know this may be hard to stop. If you just can't help yourself, try to curb it a little, especially around adults and in public. If you and your friends are on the bus saying those REAL bad words and daring adults to look at you and say something, please don't do it. You will be the same teen that may need help from one of these adults in a time of trouble. Teenagers need to spare those MF and F-U words in public areas. Name calling is an unnecessary evil. If you see other kids in the mall, at school or on the bus, don't call them out of their names. It may hurt someone's feelings or start an altercation that could have been avoided.

4. Curfew & Calling Home

Every city has a curfew and most teens have a curfew their parent's set. Missing curfew or calling home late may not seem serious to you, but it is. We know this already, because you have told us before. We want to trust you, and you must keep your word. If you are going to be late, you must call so that we know you're ok. If your cell battery dies out, borrow your friend's phone, use a pay phone if you have to – make it happen. Speaking of curfew; if you are a teenager under 17 and you're out driving past your curfew, it makes your driver's license invalid and you could get arrested.

5. Restaurants, Formal Affairs & Cell Phone Etiquette

You will find out more about this in detail in the Advanced Etiquette chapter, but here are a few basic tips for now:

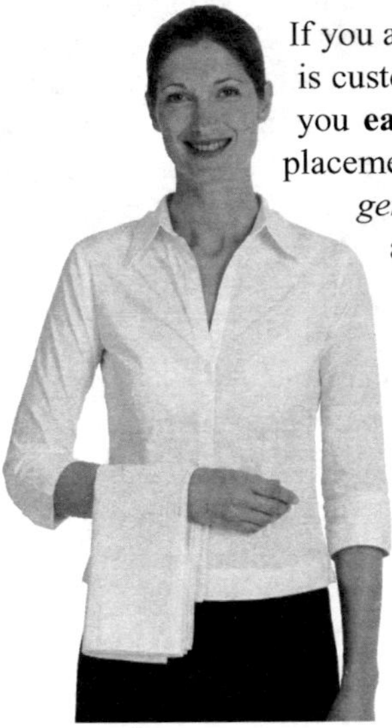

If you are invited to a **wedding or formal affair**, dress accordingly. It is customary to ask in advance what kind of attire is expected. When you **eat at a restaurant** make sure you pay attention to silverware placement, napkins and glassware. **Signal the waiter** *with your fingers never snap your fingers* or clap, and please be respectful at all times. **Tip the waiter/waitress** accordingly for their service – an average tip is approximately **15%** of the check. Guys should take off their hats when inside and pull out the chairs for all of the women at their table. When they leave the table, stand up and again when they return. **Check your coats, umbrellas and bags**. **Cell Phones**; Now illegal in many states to use while driving unless you are using a hands free device. Hands free devices such as earpieces are plugged into your phone, speaker phones may also be used as hands free. If you are having reception problems, don't holler; take your call outside or in a secluded area. **You should turn your phone OFF** *or on vibrate while at church, restaurants, events, class or meetings*. Practice cell phone etiquette and keep the noise to a comfortable level when in a group.

6. Safety, Strangers, Beggars & Con Artists

When shopping and traveling don't be too friendly with strangers. Watch all of your bags that you've purchased and keep them with you at all times. Watch behind you and look around at all times. You would be surprised how many people are waiting for you to lay your bag or purse/wallet down in a store. They are calculated, organized and will have your money spent before you realize it's gone. The *street beggars* are more prevalent and you have the unpleasant task of trying to figure out who's really needy and who's not. If you're not sure, or don't have any spare change, be polite and keep going. The next person or set of persons to watch out for are the *con artists*. They come in all shapes, forms and sizes and are not always easy to recognize. They may be well dressed or bummy looking and you can't recognize them by clothes or their actions. Con artists pull several different scams and usually work in pairs or small groups. It depends on how elaborate their scheme is. The cons that play "3 Card Monte" on the bus have two to three players, which usually are the players that are losing so badly at first. You decide you can play better, and they may even let you win once. After that you will lose your shirt. If someone comes up to you with a line about finding some money that they want to split with you, or if it just sounds too good to be true, let your inner voice and common sense take over and walk away. They usually approach you around malls, banks or places where you may have cash. It's just like they say, if it sounds too good to be true, it probably is.

7. Clothes, Combs, Rollers & Wave Caps

We have already covered clothes in our chapter on Peer Pressure. We are now referring to *clothes etiquette*. Everyone has their own fashion faux pas (FO'PAAS) that make them crazy; for example, those pants that show the crack of your butt – it is not cute or sexy, it actually looks nasty. Keep that one away, ok? Thanks. If you are interviewing for a job, wear your Sunday outfit, jacket, blazer, khakis or white shirt and pants/skirt. Do not wear jeans or your brand name sweat suit no matter how sharp you think it is. Business casual is a nice white shirt and a dress or khakis pants or a skirt. Do not wear hats indoors. No exceptions. Combs, rollers and wave caps are products used to help your daily grooming. They should not be worn in public. We have come to accept wave caps like hats, but even if your hair is still in wave motion these caps certainly aren't meant to be worn at formal events or in restaurants.

8. Drinking, Smoking & Drugs

If you are underage, it is illegal to drink and smoke. Drugs are illegal under all circumstances and should not be consumed or used in public or private. Smoking has become such a health concern that it is not allowed in many public places, it provides health risks for others because they are exposed to second hand smoke. If there is a *"no smoking sign"* posted it means do not smoke. Don't sucker someone else in a crime by asking them to get liquor for you if you are underage. Once you are 21 and can drink legally, you should never drink and drive - it will put you and others in danger. Drugs ruin your body and your mind, if not today…eventually. Remember you only have one body and one life, protect it.

9. Belching, Passing Gas, Coughing, Picking Your Nose and Sneezing

We've gotta go here people. Belching and passing gas should not be done in mixed company. If you cough or sneeze near people make sure you always cover your mouth so that you don't spread germs around. Picking your nose is also something no one wants to see you do. If this behavior is absolutely necessary in public, you should try your best to excuse yourself to a bathroom or area where you can have privacy.

10. Cheating/Lying/Stealing

These subjects are covered in detail in the chapter on Peer Pressure. However, they are worth another mention because they are also a part of your daily behavior. This is part of your personal character building. Cheating, lying and stealing are detrimental characteristics and will not get you ahead in the world. Don't cheat on tests in school, don't lie to your friends or family and don't take things that don't belong to you. If you practice these principles you will be building the character of a mature young adult.

11. Quit The Spit

I know this appears to be cool, but… it really looks nasty. Especially for girls and young ladies, this is a nasty No-No. Don't spit in the street or in public. It is very unhealthy and you are spreading germs when you spit with others close by. It's like someone sneezing in your face. If you know adults who spit outside all the time, do not follow their bad habits… they can't teach what they haven't learned themselves.

12. Fighting & Violence

High school teens are fighting in school and beating each other within inches of their lives. There is a new trend of violence sweeping through schools and neighborhoods across the country. This along with senseless gun violence is unforgivable. Learn to walk away from a fight or altercation. It will show how much class you have and how strong you are. You don't have to put your life on the line to prove anything to anyone; this includes friends, family or associates. These actions often lead to injuring a person or worse, taking a life. The thought that you are infallible (can't be hurt) is completely wrong. It may be you or your family that gets hurt in the process. Defending yourself in a fight is legal, but if someone loses an eye, limb or dies, you will be missing mom's home cooking and wearing your county's orange jumpsuit.

MY JOURNAL ENTRY

List 5 positive changes about your ***everyday etiquette or manners*** that you would like to make. Discuss them with a parent, teacher, mentor or friends.

COMMUNICATION

Communication is one of the most important experiences of our every day lives. We communicate everyday through verbal and non-verbal communication. Many times we are judged on our ability to communicate. In some cases this is our scorecard when we are in interviews, meetings, giving speeches, or making presentations - *and we may not even know it.* Whenever you speak, you should be doing your very best. How you communicate determines the outcome of the message you are trying to deliver.

We also use technology to communicate; the telephone, pagers, cell phones, Internet, fax machines and Email. In this century of advancing technology, it is also important to know how to use electronic media to communicate with each other. Communication skills are so important, that athletes and entertainers often hire publicists, speech writers, speech therapists and public relations personnel to make sure they are appearing, speaking and sounding their very best in public. The rest of us can not afford this expense and must do this on our own, which is why we have included ways to help improve your communication skills.

12 TIPS FOR TEENS TO COMMUNICATE EFFECTIVELY:

1. Verbal Communication
Verbal communication is when you use words to speak. Positive verbal communication consists of positive uplifting words, a nice voice tone and words that make you smile or feel good. *Example*: "You look nice today." Negative verbal communication would be someone speaking loud, hollering at you, using derogatory language, words that make you angry or curse words. *Example*: "Having another bad hair day?"

2. Non-Verbal Communication
Non-Verbal communication is when you communicate by using body language through actions and gestures. You may use your hands, eyes, arms and facial expressions to deliver a message to others. Individuals that are hearing impaired use sign language (words and letters that are made with your hands) to communicate. Positive non-verbal communication would be smiling. Negative non-verbal communication would be frowning, putting your hands on your hips or flipping someone off with your hand or fingers to imply negative words.

3. Tips for Teen-Parent Communication
Parents are easier to manage than you think. Respect should be the first part of any teen-parent communication. Be honest, express your feelings and keep the conversation direct and to the point. The tone and gesture someone uses while talking determines how much you will listen. With teen-parent communication, trust and non-judgment are very encouraging parts of the process. Be specific about the subject you want to discuss. If your feelings are hurt, tell your parents or whomever you are talking to. If you are confused about a subject, ask them to explain before emotions or attitudes get out of control or you get angry. Also remember, the parent or adult that is talking to you has feelings also. Teenagers often express moodiness and unpredictable behavior while growing toward the young adult phase. When parents and

teens are communicating, the feelings and the subject must come to the forefront, this is more important than the behavior. Your body and society is saying that you that you are older, but emotionally and mentally you are still in transition. Always keep the lines of communication open, so that you can discuss any subject with us. If you do this, we usually give you anything you want. We just want to know that you are including us. Your parents are learning also.

4. Speaking Properly

Effective communication includes speaking properly and presenting yourself well. This includes proper enunciation (speech and pronunciation) of words. You must also choose the correct verbiage (right words at the right time) when speaking. Speak slow enough to be understood, if you speak too fast you will have to repeat most of your conversation. Speak with a clear concise voice so that everyone will always be able to understand everything you say.

5. Words That Hurt, Criticize or Blame

We must stay away from words that hurt, criticize or blame. These negative words hurt you and make you feel bad. If you talk this way, others will feel like its ok to say them back to you. Taunting each other with names like, "stupid, fool, dumb" and other expletives seem funny at first, but after a while it gets old. Someone will call you a name when you're not in a playful mood or in front of a particular person and your feelings may get hurt. Words that feel good or praise, help to encourage support and give positive outlooks to everyone.

6. Encouragement

This is the greatest form of positive communication. You need to be encouraged and supported as much as possible. When you feel encouraged by teachers, parents, peers and family you strive to do better. Encouragement can come in the form of words, money, letters, praise and attendance to an event or important achievement in your life. Whoever is around you should be a positive supportive network. If the individuals that are in your close circle of direct contact are not supportive, you must find a new circle. If you are an athlete and want to take care of your body you should spend time with others that want to work out. If you are into computers, music or you want to be an entrepreneur, join clubs or organizations with teens that enjoy the same passion. When your friends and family aren't on the same page with you or reading from your book - they are not encouraging your plan.

7. Hard or Difficult Subjects; Sex, Drugs, & Drinking

Parents and adults aren't always easy to talk to, especially when the subjects are personal or difficult. An easy way to communicate with parents is to have continuous open dialogue on a regular basis. When a problem or situation comes up, discuss it right on the spot. Teens sometimes think parents are aliens, but we've been there... everywhere you're going. If you need to talk to your parents or an adult about sex, drugs or drinking, find a quiet time to sit down and discuss the subject openly. It's better to get it out of the way as soon as you can. Don't avoid it and let a potential situation brew out of control because you were too scared to discuss it. You may feel the need to have a family friend or older sibling attend the discussion, this is perfectly fine, just make it happen.

8. Speaking on the Phone – Voice is Important

How you speak on the phone can get your foot in the door for an interview or have them hang up on you. This is, sometimes your first contact with an organization or company and it's important to make a good impression. This may also be the voice you use at your job when you answer the phone. You are representing the company that is paying you. Again, you are the first voice they hear when they call which can lead them to an opinion about your company. When using your voice inflection (tone), it's ok to have your "friends and family voice," and your corporate "impressive voice." It should be clear, concise and sharp – this voice should be confident. Here's the key - *know when to use the proper voice*. If you are trying to get hired at a job, they want to know that you can speak properly and effectively communicate with others. Speaking professional is not phony.

9. Listening

Listening is harder than speaking. You should listen as much as you talk. It takes discipline to listen. Stay attentive; give your dedicated attention to whatever is being said and to whoever is speaking. This is one of the most important components of any conversation. If you don't listen you can't hear. While listening you should also look at the person's body language, tone, gestures and expression. This will better help you to understand the message they are trying to get across.

10. Wireless Communication

Wireless communication refers to cell phones, pagers, palm pilots and computers. We are now totally wireless and very excited about it. *Cell Phones*; the million-dollar question continually springs up, "At what age should pre-teens/teens get a cell phone?" The safe rule of thumb for some parents is; if you are a pre-teen you can have a cell phone if you are walking home in case of an emergency. For teens, cell phones are necessary so you can keep up with your parents and they can keep up with you. It is also helpful if you need a ride, you're driving or when going out late, you will have 24 hour contact in case of an emergency. Try not to misuse your cell phone, always be responsible and don't go over your minutes. If you are on a family share plan – take others into consideration. Be respectful and try not to talk while in restaurants. If you're driving, it is mandatory in most states to use a "hands free" device (earpiece) or speaker phone. While communicating via computer, e-mail and chat rooms on the Internet, you must also think safety and responsibility at all times. Never give out your personal information, credit card information, passwords or talk to strangers online. Respect others; don't send mean or anonymous E-mails to others that start arguments or wars between friends. Try to go to safe chat rooms and websites.

11. Why Are You Yelling at Your Parents?

You are coming into your own personality now. You are torn between still being a teenager, mom's little kid and growing up into young adulthood. To really win your parents over, act like the best kid in town as much as you can. There's no need to raise your voice when talking to your parents. Don't embarrass them in front of their friends or other adults. It always seems as though stuff breaks out or you have a misunderstanding when company is present. Due to the media and the acceptance of bad language, we've accustomed ourselves to back talk and disrespectful attitudes. Try to use your "back talk coupons" when it's really important. This should not be on a regular basis. When you debate an issue, make sure it's something worth your time and energy, not just to be obstinate (argumentative). Keep your voice down, unless it's absolutely necessary. You soon will be a young adult and young people will be looking up to you, no more complaints, shouting or pouting.

12. I Curse A Lot And Just Can't Help It

Using bad words doesn't make you cool. Actually, studies find that people who curse all the time aren't able to speak properly or have a limited vocabulary. Find substitute words for your everyday "cuss" words. If you are using music lyrics as your excuse, maybe you're listening to the wrong music. Your peers and younger siblings listen and repeat everything you say. If you do it they will emulate (copy) your behavior regardless of whether it's good or bad. Yes, parents should make better role models, we usually say we've earned the right to do and say what we want, but well, we know better.

MY JOURNAL ENTRY

List 5 positive changes about your ***communication*** that you would like to make. Discuss them with a parent, teacher, mentor or friends.

CONFLICT RESOLUTION

A number of schools and communities are attempting to reduce teen violence by using conflict resolution programs. Conflict resolution programs are put in place to stop youth violence and broaden awareness and sensitivity to situations that may quickly escalate. This chapter is strictly designed to prevent violent acts from brewing. These tools are to be used in case you find yourself upset, mad or in conflict. If you are extra sensitive, always mad at friends, parents and peers or find yourself always ready to fight, you may need mediation or conflict resolution. The more positive control you have over the conflict in your life, the happier your life will be.

12 TIPS FOR TEENS ON CONFLICT RESOLUTION AND PROBLEM SOLVING:

1. Is Conflict Resolution Necessary?
Yes. Conflict resolution limits unnecessary arguments and fights. Conflict resolution will show you positive ways to deal with challenges and problems between friends and peers. When arguments or disagreements start brewing, sometimes it's ok to *"agree to disagree"* on a subject. You will never agree with everyone about everything. If you are discussing a subject and you're probably right as usual, don't lose a friend over a silly disagreement. Conflict resolution will show you how to understand people, turn negatives into positives and change your behavior. When things get too hot, don't waste your energy, just move on.

2. THIN SKIN!
Most arguments and fights develop because someone has very thin skin. If you are a person that gets upset over little things, cries a lot, or your nickname is "Sensitive Sam or Sandy" - stop it! Quit taking life so seriously, it's too stressful and you're still young. If you stay mad all day over small disagreements, you may want to reevaluate if it's really them, or you who's causing the problem. Take "self inventory" and ask yourself what you can do differently. Start laughing some of it off. Tell the person what you think of their actions and move on.

3. Gang Conflict
Gangs fight over disrespect or because their homies are fighting. Once a war gets started, it's on until it's over. If you are a gang member, you should not want unnecessary bloodshed or harm done to your friends or family. Find a way to be mature, put away the guns and try to resolve matters amicably and without violence.

4. Don't Be a "Sore Loser"
Do you know someone that always loses games and always gets mad? If you are in a close competitive game, don't be a sore loser. You should have left that attitude in the 3rd grade. Equivalent to a tantrum, a close game or sports disagreement can quickly escalate to a fight if taunting and trash talking is going on. Accept a loss graciously - shake hands - and offer a challenge or rematch. This is called "good sportsmanship."

5. Angry Parents & Angry Kids

Many parents are raising angry, violent kids that fight at a moment's notice. The sad part of this is that the parents are encouraging this behavior, making you feel insecure if you don't fight back. Parents are also helping and encouraging their teens to fight other teens. Yep, for real! There is a difference between self defense (which is protecting yourself against someone who has provoked you first) and taking on every altercation that comes your way. This is how you lose a limb or a life. If you are the victim of violence in your home, tell someone such as a; doctor, police officer, teacher or family friend. If your parent is encouraging you or a sibling to fight someone, don't do it, report it to a school official. Some parents don't teach better because they don't know any better. This is your life and you should know better. Pass up an opportunity to fight, and walk away.

6. Random Acts of Kindness

This is when you choose to be nice for no reason. The nicer you are to people and the more goodwill you put in the universe, the more positive karma will come back to you. So the next chance you get, say thanks to someone, pick up something that someone has dropped or hold a door open for someone without asking. You will be surprised how others will step up and help you unconditionally.

7. Resolving Arguments

When you see a problem brewing between you and someone else, check it at the door. If you can, pull them to the side and have a face- to- face discussion. This will squash any "he said - she said." If you are having trouble with another individual or a group of individuals, try a group discussion with a mediator or person that you trust. Arguments that seem playful or harmless can quickly escalate. When an argument is budding, state your case and let the other person state their case without fingers in the face or waving hands. Discuss your disagreement without accusing anyone and encourage them to do the same. School counselors are good resources when solving disagreements. You may even just decide to use a parent or big brother/sister to intervene. Invest your time not in arguing, but in resolution early on before things escalate or get out of control. The next step is fight, the step after that is suspension or jail.

8. Jump in Every Fight

What do you do when a fight breaks out? Many teens stand around and watch, jump in or encourage others. You are being an accessory to violent behavior. I am not saying don't help your friend if they need help, but I am saying you don't have to be a part of every fight. This is how innocent bystanders get into trouble and get hurt. Leave the scene of an out of control situation. Pass up the opportunity to be a witness, this way when the police get there, you can say you weren't involved.

9. Weapons Check

There has been an increase in the use of weapons to solve minor arguments and altercations. Myself and other parents have personally witnessed the use of bats, window poles, shanks, knives, box cutters, drills and BB guns, just to name a few. BB guns and look-a-like guns can now get you up to five years in prison, even if you're kidding around. Thousands of people have lost an eye to BB gun incidents, they are also illegal on school campuses.

10. Options for Arresting Youth

There are many other ways to punish or teach youth without arresting them. Every teen in the nation may not have access to these programs but they include; boot camps, alternative schools and state juvenile programs. In the mean time, teenagers must start to make mature positive decisions. Try to stay away from senseless acts of violence. If a situation arises, ask your counselor refer you to someone that can help talk you through it. You may just need one time counseling, therapy or maybe you can get together with a group and work it out. Don't get caught up in the jail system, you must protect your future.

11. It's Nothing But a Girls' Thang Baby!

I have discussed this **"Girl Thing"** throughout the book on several occasions. For whatever reasons, girls are getting involved in more fights and altercations than ever before. It's not cute or funny. It's certainly not ladylike and I hate to think that young ladies are being raised to fight and disfigure each other. In a few short years, you will look back and realize how silly and insignificant it was, and if you could change it, you would. Let's not forget to mention you could end up with a criminal record that will follow you to every future job that you apply for. You are responsible for raising the next generation of children, and I don't think you want them to copy your bad behavior. So change any wicked ways you have now, while you can.

12. Murder One

At the end of every conflict could be the big one - death. Even if you were with someone and didn't know they had a gun, it was an accident or retaliation, you could still go to jail. Jail is no fun - ask anyone you know that's been there. Ask them about the fun and freedom, their hard cot and delicious meals. Life isn't a game and there's no "back button" like on a computer.

MY JOURNAL ENTRY

List 5 things about ***conflict resolution*** that you learned from this chapter. Discuss them with a parent, teacher, mentor or friends.

____

____

____

____

____

INTERNET WORLD

The Internet was originally designed for military intelligence, which allowed them to exchange information with other international support groups. Additionally, the Internet was used for the high end physics community to collaborate internationally. Most people use the terms Internet and World Wide Web interchangeably and synonymously, *but they are not*. They are separate but related. The Internet is a networking infrastructure that connects to millions of computers that communicate with each other. The World Wide Web is a way of accessing information over the medium of the Internet. It is built on top of the Internet, thanks to Tim Berners-Lee, an English computer scientist for the Nuclear Research physics lab in Geneva Switzerland. He wrote the Web software in 1990, which made the Internet popular and easier to use.

The Internet is second nature to us, and we must stay safe as possible while online. Most teens already know much of the information in this chapter. It is the new Internet users that may need a little refresher course. We need to be cautious of who we talk to, chat with, and to whom we give our personal and financial information. Below are tips and suggestions on how to stay safe while enjoying and using the World Wide Web.

12 THINGS TEENS SHOULD KNOW ABOUT STAYING SAFE WHILE ONLINE:

1. Never Give Out Any Personal Information

Never give out personal information or tell anyone anything about you. Do not give out your name, address, credit card number, bank information, social security number or phone numbers. If anyone asks for your screen name or password, do not give it to them under any circumstances. If they access your account, they could possibly use your e-mail for suspicious or illegal behavior. Although shopping on the Internet should be safe, many instances have been reported where information has been stolen or misused. Only use your credit card on secure shopping sites. You should never use credit cards or do any financial transactions without your parents' permission.

2. Chat Rooms & Web Surfing

There is really no way of knowing who you are chatting with inside of a chat room. Unless it's someone you know personally, you have no way of knowing if people are actually who they claim to be. If you are a preteen you really should stay out of chat rooms. If you are older and have your parent's consent for you to be in chat rooms, beware of the individuals you are talking to. There have been instances where people have had strangers they met on the Internet appear at their house. *Surfing the web is harmless most of the time*. Be careful not to visit x-rated or adult sites. Do not download games or sign up for services that charge fees without your parent's approval. You should get advice from your parents on which rooms and sites are safe for you to chat in.

3. Personal Ads

Teens are too young to be participating in online personal ads. Although it is a common occurrence among young people today, this does not make it right. These ads may seem harmless because many of the sites are featuring all teenagers, but you are putting your life into the universe for all "freaks" at large. You may encounter stalking or other deceptive practices. The best chance you have is possibly a *"school only"* or *"teen only"* website. Any site has the potential to be dangerous. Don't post your picture unless you are sure of the security of where it will be posted or distributed. Be cautious and extremely careful at all times.

4. Do Not Ever Meet Anyone Alone That You've Met Online

A screen name is just that. A name without any knowledge as to who they really are. You don't know who's behind the name regardless of what they tell you. They could be untruthful about their age or intentions. Individuals have put themselves in life threatening situations by meeting strangers. If you decide for some reason to meet someone off the Internet, make sure you are in a group setting, public place and that you have told several people know who you are meeting and where. Just in case.

5. What To Do If Someone Makes You Feel Uncomfortable

If someone makes you feel uncomfortable, or upsets you, ignore them and sign off immediately. Most ISP's (Internet Service Providers) have areas where you can report individuals that are acting suspicious online. Do not be scared to report them if you feel threatened.

6. Viruses

The Internet has numerous viruses that can destroy the hard drive on your computer. This is caused by downloading programs, games, and opening e-mails that are suspicious and possibly carrying a virus. Make sure you have a virus protection program installed on your computer system and a firewall. If you don't recognize the e-mail or it looks suspicious - delete it. Curiosity can cost you a bundle later when you are trying to clear a virus from your computer. You can also pass viruses to others via e-mail.

7. ISP's are Internet Service Providers

ISP's are companies such as; AOL (America Online), Yahoo, Netscape and Wide Open West just to name a few. These companies allow you to sign up for their service and sign onto to the Internet. There is a fee to use their services, some of them have free e-mail service.

8. Internet Acronyms

FAQ (means Q & A, Facts or information), HTML (Hypertext Markup Language used to create documents), IM (Instant Message, text where you can communicate instantly), LOL (means laughing out loud). There are tons of acronyms and abbreviations that are used to communicate online. You can actually download them to familiarize yourself with them. ;) = **a wink!**

9. E-mail

We all love e-mail, it's quick and can be used for business, pleasure and a few things in-between. Most importantly its available 24 hours. Use e-mail wisely and for all intended legal purposes. E-mail should be used for fun, business and contacting friends and family. Before sending an e-mail, use the spelling feature and check the content of your e-mail. Do not send derogatory e-mails and double check to make sure you are sending the e-mail to the correct person before you push the send button. Make sure you know who you are e-mailing.

10. What is SPAM?

We hear so much about SPAM, the hundreds of pieces of junk e-mail that bombard our mailbox that we can't control. When SPAM hits your e-mail your first instinct is to look, and sometimes act on what's in it. Most of it is junk and you should delete it. SPAM can occasionally carry viruses. When you sign on to your computer, activate your SPAM blocking mechanism that will catch unwanted mail and give you the opportunity to delete it before opening it.

11. Have A Life!

Have a life and don't let the Internet consume all of your time. Regardless if you're surfing the web, playing Internet games, downloading music or watching videos. Some teens spend so much time in front of their computer and have no time for themselves, to exercise or to interact with other teens. This can be unhealthy, because the computer, the Internet and Web can be addictive and time consuming. You must have a social life and that's an order!

12. Regulations & Illegal Activities:

Internet activity is regulated by the federal government. Identity theft, illegal activities, SPAM and improper solicitation are all governed and individuals can be prosecuted. Internet crimes are punishable by law and individuals can receive life sentences.

MY JOURNAL ENTRY

List 5 things you learned in this chapter about ***internet surfing & chatting***. Discuss them with a parent, teacher, mentor or friends.

____

____

____

____

____

____

____

PRE-TEENS ONLY

Preteen Life Preparation is just in case you don't read the rest of this book. This chapter is designed for ***pre-teens only***. Life is so short and it will fly by so very fast. After grammar school it will be four short years in high school and then off to college. Before you know it you'll be all grown up and paying for your own gym shoes. Smile. Start making plans now to save your money and think about your future. Take school seriously now, and keep your grades up now – later is too late! Be nice to your teachers and treat them with respect, even the ones that you don't like. Remember, this is your education not a personality contest, take what you need and throw the rest away. Be respectful of parents and all adults, they've earned the right.

Your body is your temple and you must take care of it. Don't abuse your body with drugs, tobacco, food or alcohol. Eat as many fruits and vegetables as you can stand, and exercise at least three times a week, even it it's just walking. Joining organizations, sports teams, dance groups, school clubs, and church organizations are a must. It will help you to build self-esteem, character and confidence. The recipe for life is to meet new people, get out of your neighborhood, visit museums, theatres and attend cultural events. Explore and research spirituality, religions, politics, races and cultures. Investigate life for yourself, even though others will give you their colorful version.

12 LIFE TIPS FOR PRE-TEENS ONLY!:

1. Middle & Grammar Schools 6th – 8th
During these years you realize that your school life is changing. Your friends are maturing, acting differently and peer pressure is looming high over you. You have figured out by now that your 7th grade competency test scores will have an affect on what high school you will be accepted to. It's time to buckle down and get serious about your education. You and your friends have figured out that you may be separating and going to different schools. You are preparing for high school through tests, grades, sports, educational clubs and affiliations. You are now becoming your own person, as you grow into puberty. If you are in 8th grade you are also preparing for graduation and that comes with an entirely different set of responsibilities. Start thinking about high school, saving for college and preparing for your future educational goals and career. Think about entrepreneurship, you can also start and own your own business.

2. Peer Pressure
You will always have peer pressure as a pre-teen. Just be your own person. Don't let anyone dictate what you should wear or what you should do. If you are self-confident, your peers will be following you as a leader and not a follower. This is how you can be in control of your world. Your peers will try guilt trips, games and challenges to

get you to do things you know are wrong. Your inner voice usually tells you that smoking, drinking, sex or drugs is wrong and not allowed on the school property. You know that cutting class or picking on other kids is not good behavior. Your parents, teachers and school counselors will not steer you wrong, they are trying to prepare you for high school and for life. Be true to yourself, it's time for you to step up.

3. Grooming & Clothing

Your grooming and clothing should be top notch at all times. Take care of your personal hygiene, hair, nails and clothes on a regular basis. You don't have to buy all name brand clothing, regardless of what your friends are wearing. You can buy discount clothing or find sales at your favorite store. Get creative, mix, match and make sure you look good in whatever clothes you buy. The key is to make sure your body is clean, you are well groomed and your clothes are clean and neat. Don't wait on your parents to wash your clothes. Ask them how to sort clothes and which temperatures to use and set your own schedule to wash. If you can't go to the barber or hairdresser every week, learn how to take care of your hair and nails in between shop visits. Make sure your shoes aren't scuffed up or worn. If you notice some of the athletes and actresses that aren't really that attractive – basic grooming is the key that takes them over the top.

4. Acne

Teens will have acne, which is only one of several changes that will occur as you switch over to being a real full-fledged teenager. There are many myths about what causes acne such as; diet, stress, chocolate and other factors. There are many solutions to what supposedly cures acne problems, from over the counter medicines to prescribed medication. The best thing to do is to go to a dermatologist (doctor that specializes in skin problems) so that they can test your skin, get to the root of the problem and help you clear it up. In the meantime you must not let it determine who you are. Some teens let acne problems affect their self-esteem and their lifestyle. Don't let acne control you - you must control it. Most kids will experience acne and other forms of puberty; you're not the only one.

5. Your Money

Many teens have their own bank accounts, save money and know more about Money Markets and CD's than adults. If you are one of these teens, we are taking off our hats in praise and practically bowing at your feet. If not, then this is a perfect time to start by encouraging you to open up your own bank account. Depending on your age, you may need a parent, but once you start seeing the money building up you will want to save more. As you start working summer jobs or working your summer business, you will need a bank account. Save money now in preparation and training for college. In a few short years you will be budgeting and operating your own finances each month. It's never too early to get started.

6. Safe Sex/STD's (Sexually Transmitted Diseases)

Know the best prevention is abstinence. Safe sex and STD's are discussed thoroughly in chapter four. It is important to know that STD's can be contracted through sexual contact if condoms are not used. STD's can also cause health problems, AIDS and other severe diseases. It is important to practice safe sex to prevent pregnancy. All of your friends and peers will be discussing sex, and some will be practicing sex. That does not mean that you have to do it. It's ok to say NO. You must be your own person; you know when and when NOT to do something. Sex is not to be taken lightly; it will change your life forever. Once you commit the act, you can't take it back. Many pre-teens that have sex too early regret it later. Your decisions regarding sex will affect you mentally, physically and emotionally.

7. To High School and Beyond

As you prepare for high school, it's time to get all your ducks in a row. Start helping your parents find a high school that fits into your overall plan. Factors to consider when selecting a high school; academic focus, college preparatory, location, sports and traveling distance. Catholic and private schools have great benefits, but the tuition costs must be considered in the family budget. Hopefully, you will be able to participate in the same sports and activities once you get to high school. You will be meeting new friends and joining different clubs and organizations. Make your experience fun, educational and meet new challenges head on. You may want to give a little thought about the occupation you want to explore. In some cases, it will reflect the high school you choose. The school may have a science, math or special focus. Some kids will follow in the footsteps of their family of doctors, lawyers or business owners. Although, you are not expected to decide to make a final decision at 13 years old, you can start thinking of what kind of career or job you would like to have. You will probably change your mind several times. Job shadowing programs allow you to go to work with a professional and spend a few hours a day learning about their job. The earlier you start, the more prepared and focused you will be when you get to high school.

8. Etiquette

You will start going to school banquets, formal lunches and upscale restaurants that serve seven course meals. Chapter three has an Advanced Etiquette section that will go into detail about which knife or which fork should be used for which foods. There are a few basic tips to know about proper etiquette. If you are at a formal event the following attire is appropriate; a tuxedo, formal dress, suit, matching outfit, nice shirt, blouse, slacks or skirt. Males should remove their hats and pull out chairs for females at their table. If there is a coat checkroom, hang your coat up, umbrella or briefcase. Your napkin should go across your lap. Liquids are on the right, and dry foods are served on your left such as; breads. Use your utensils beginning from the outside (farthest from you) working your way to the inside. When you are finished eating put your silverware crossed in the middle of your plate. Don't blow hot soup in a spoon, you may get it on someone. If there is food lodged in your teeth, remove it with your tongue. Don't pick your teeth in public or with a toothpick. Tipping is expected because most waitresses and waiters make minimum wage and depend on the extra money to boost their wages.

9. Boys Only

Your body is changing, and your puberty is in full swing now. Your parents will be able to help you with some of your puberty issues, but you can also do your own research. Your voice is changing and you will be experiencing hormone changes that will cause you to have hair in places you've never had. You are getting taller, your chest is starting to pop out and you may even be getting a muscle or two. You will start to think girls are friendly territory now. You can research at the library, bookstores and on the Internet to find out sensitive or personal information about your body changes and hygiene. Always be a gentleman, respect women, girls, adults and yourself.

10. Girls Only

Your body is changing, and your puberty is also in full swing now. Ask your parents to help you with some of your puberty issues and personal issues. Your voice changes, hormones cause you to have hair in places you've never had and new things will be popping up. Girls start to get breasts and boys start to stare. You will start to think boys are friendly territory now. You can research at the library, bookstores and on the Internet to find out sensitive or personal information about your body changes and hygiene. Always be a lady, respect all adults and yourself.

11. Safety

Safety is always first, in every area of your life; school and personal. Travel in groups and make sure to stay in well-lit areas. Always keep a few extra dollars in your pocket that you never spend. You never know when you may have an emergency, get stranded or need to make a phone call. Look at your surroundings and be aware of anyone walking close behind you. Don't' ride with friends of friends that you don't know, or be the last one to ride home with a stranger. Do not take unnecessary chances, and always keep your cell phone on when not at home. If your intuition (gut feeling) tells you something is wrong, listen to it.

12. Behavior

Your behavior must be respectful at all times, regardless of where you are, or whom you are talking to. Be respectful of all parents, adults and teachers. Try to eliminate unnecessary name calling, screaming or fighting. When you are attending an event make sure you handle yourself with dignity and maturity. There's a time and place for everything. You can have fun and even be a little silly, but don't act disrespectful in public.

MY JOURNAL ENTRY

List 5 things you learned about your ***Pre-Teen Life***. Discuss them with a parent, teacher, mentor or friends.

____

____

____

____

____

THE LAW

The law is one of those things we usually don't pay attention to until we're personally affected by it. The majority of us do not learn about the law until someone close to us, such as a friend or family member, has contact with the police, lawyers or has to appear in court. Here are a few suggestions that will keep you on the good side of the law, or help to guide you if you get in a bind. This is only a reference guide. If you are in trouble or have questions, talk to your parents, counselor, or a law enforcement professional.

12 THINGS TEENS SHOULD KNOW ABOUT THE LAW AND LEGAL STUFF:

1. In Case Of Emergency
In most major cities *911* is the universal emergency number. This is the first phone call you should make in case of an emergency. Some cities have a non-emergency number that you can call for other city information. For example, Chicago uses 311 for city government information on small business, parking enforcement, health department and streets and sanitation information. Check with your city for more specific information on emergency procedures and phone numbers.

2. Denver Boot & Repossessions
The boot is that bright yellow contraption that fits so neatly around your tire when you have too many parking tickets. It's called the ***Denver Boot*** because it's manufactured in Denver, Colorado… for real. You should pay parking violations as soon as you receive them. Tickets double when you don't pay them in a timely manner and they can quickly add up. Overdue parking notices will be mailed to you as a reminder that you owe the city money. Some cities can now boot your car for two or three parking tickets. Try to avoid the towing costs, storage and excessive ticket penalties by paying tickets when you receive them. If you pay now you will avoid paying the ridiculous fees later. ***Repossession*** of a car can happen if you don't make your payments on time. Usually, it takes missing more than one payment to get your car repossessed back to the dealer. When a car is repossessed, this is more heartache than the couple of payments that you owed. If your car is put on the repo list, they will sometimes take your car at night when you least expect it. You will have to pay all of the current payments, towing fees and storage fees before you can get your car back. Not only is this process aggravating and frustrating, it can cost you thousands of dollars. Many people have walked outside and called the police thinking their car was stolen and it had been repossessed.

3. Child Support
If you have a child that is legally yours, you are responsible for the support and upkeep of that child's needs. If you fail to pay child support or take care of that child, you can be taken to court and ordered to pay. For individuals that are working, your pay can also be garnished (taken from your check as the result of a court order *without* your consent). If you can't afford to worry about child support at this time in your life, abstain from sex. If you are having sex, remember that one slip of the condom can change your life's plans. Sex is an adult activity that comes with real adult responsi-

bilities. If you are having sex, wrap it up so you can try and prevent an unplanned pregnancy, AIDs or STD's.

4. Curfew

Regardless if you are 13 or 17, most teens feel they are too old to have a curfew. It's the law and we must abide by it. Several major cities sound horns when curfew time begins. Drivers under seventeen years of age should know that your driver's license becomes invalid after you break curfew. Help your parents out a little and work with them on your curfew. If you compromise and try, they will be more lenient with your time to come in at night.

5. Paying Restitution

Restitution is what you have to pay if it's determined that you owe money to someone that has sued you in court. If you have the money, restitution can be paid with cash. Some people who don't have the money, have been known to pay restitution by serving time or performing community service. Follow the rules of life, abide by the laws and refrain from hanging with individuals that may get you into trouble or that think breaking the law is fun.

6. Getting Arrested - Record/Jacket

If you get arrested or are put in jail, the police will start a record on you. Getting arrested is not only emotional and costly; it gives you a permanent record that will follow you for life. It may even affect your right to vote or get a job. Some police records may be removed depending on the age and circumstances that occurred when you were arrested. However, in most cases, you are stuck for life with that record. It will follow you when employers perform background checks because you will have to check the box that you have been convicted of a crime. This makes it's very difficult to find a job and this is a mark you don't want on your back. Depending on the type of job you apply for, they can use this information not to hire you. For sensitive jobs and financial jobs they can use your background and your credit to determine your eligibility.

7. Expungement and Record Sealing

Expunging your record is where you get your police record removed or closed to individuals researching your background. I have heard this term thrown around a lot, but the percentage of ex-felons that are actually able to have this done is very small. It's very difficult to get an expungement unless you have very special circumstances. You can get a lawyer or contact the governor of your state to try and get this process started. This process is almost as hard as a Presidential Pardon. It's not impossible, but highly improbable.

8. Bail / Bond

Usually when you go to jail, the court will set a bail amount. Bail is the amount of money you will need to get out of jail. If you have a severe case, they may issue "no bail," this means that you must be remanded to a hearing and you can't pay to get out until you've appeared before a judge. Bond is your security, and what is needed when you are arrested and you want to get out of jail immediately. You may be issued an "I Bond," if this is your first offense. Then, you will be released on your own recognizance, with a promise to come to court when they schedule your appearance. If you are arrested, you have to pay ten percent of your bond to get out. If your bond is set at 10,000 dollars you can get out for one thousand, etc. If you have a bond card and you get stopped by a police officer for a traffic violation, they will take your bond card and you get to keep your drivers license. Motor club organizations usually issue bond cards as a part of their membership package.

9. Eviction & Rental Info

As a young adult, you will eventually look to move out of your parent's house and then live on your own. The process of looking for roommates, apartments or rooms for rent can be a challenging one. First, you should know your rights as a tenant. Then make sure your rent is paid on time to avoid late fees and possible eviction. Read your lease thoroughly, know your landlord's policies and when he will impose late fees. Some landlords will issue you a five day notice after the first day of the month while others wail until the fifth of the month. Make sure you know what has to be done to get your security deposit returned to you such as; repairing holes in the wall, cleaning the floors or repainting the walls white or to its original color. Each state has a landlord/tenants guide that is free and usually can be picked up from the Department of Housing.

10. DUI - Driving Under the Influence

Driving under the influence of alcohol or drugs is illegal. This is an offense that will land you in jail if you are caught. Anyone who watches the news knows that teens are dying in car accidents when the person behind the wheel is drinking and being irresponsible. If you are going to be out with friends who plan on drinking, you must designate a driver before the partying begins. The *"designated driver"* should be the person that does not drink. This person could be the difference between life and death.

11. Traffic Stops / Search and Seizure

When you buy a car, you must do what's required by law to keep it legal. This means getting your car registered, having your license plates, city sticker, valid drivers' license and most importantly, having insurance on your vehicle. If you get stopped by the police you must have everything associated with your car legal and up to date. As soon as you know you have a bulb or turning signal light broken, get it fixed as soon as possible because this minor thing will cause the police to stop you. If a police car puts on their lights and pulls up behind you, you must pull over and stop. You are supposed to pull over to the right and usually the police will pull over directly behind you. After that, do as they say. Be ready to produce your license, insurance card and current registration. Keep these items in the glove box of your car so that it's ready when you need it. ***FYI:*** You have rights that preclude anyone from searching you, your automobile or house without *probable cause.* If they search anyway, it's a violation of your Fourth Amendment rights. This right prevents the police from just showing up at your house or stopping you in the street without cause and harassing you. If they do stop you, they can pat you down for weapons, but cannot go into your pockets.

12. Subpoena / Summons / Court Date

A summons or subpoena is a legal order for you to appear in court. Summons and subpoenas are received by mail or by a sheriff hand delivering it to your door. If you don't have a lawyer who can appear on your behalf, you must go in person. The judge can order a "bench warrant" for your arrest if you or your attorney does not show up in court. Most subpoenas and summons have a phone number on them that you can call to get further information on what you are required to do. If you still aren't sure, go to the court house and ask them the procedure for the notice that you have received.

MY JOURNAL ENTRY

List 5 things you have learned about the ***law*** that you didn't know before reading this chapter. Discuss them with a parent, teacher, mentor or friends.

Chapter Two:
High School Stuff!

SCHOOL

School was devised as a way to keep up with you while your parent's are at work. Smile. School is your transitional passage through life beginning with kindergarten and ending up in college or trade schools. School is where you will gain your first real exposure to life via educational venue. High school is where you start to meet kids from different backgrounds, races and beliefs. You all start to mix and mesh right here in high school. You will meet friends, join new organizations, join sports teams and begin to explore different social and cultural settings. Whether you want to be a corporate executive, lawyer, engineer, teacher, rapper, newscaster, doctor or an entrepreneur, you will need the basic hours of school to help you understand life's contracts and operate in the world. In many of the careers that you will choose, school is a necessary prerequisite. Professional fields such as law and medicine will require higher education (six to eight years after high school). Many teens look at today's world and see downsizing, layoffs and company closings – then question why would we recommend that you go to school. You must go to school because it's mandatory, and it will be the lead into college and careers. Learn to set goals, gain skills and knowledge. *Consider school your first job!*

12 TIPS FOR TEENS ON HOW TO MAKE SCHOOL A POSITIVE EXPERIENCE:

1. Friends
Friends are one of the main reasons we enjoy school. It's great to make friends, but school always comes first. Many kids will find friends in school that are closer than family. The socialization becomes an important part of your school life because you get to do it everyday. We must be sure not to let the peer pressure associated with "school friends" overshadow your educational focus. Have friends, have fun, but keep the goal in sight. Your school friends should be a positive crew that is on the same plane with you. Too much socializing with the wrong crowd can distract you away from the prize.

2. What is your DIPLOMA used for?
This is the prize. First of all it's what us mom's use as another document in the pile that explains why we haven't give you up for adoption. It serves as proof of why we are here in the struggle with you. So keep going and give us that piece of paper. You will need your high school diploma when you apply for colleges, trade schools and jobs. Graduation is that carrot we dangle over your head because four years in high school will fly by quickly. Each year you should talk to your counselor and make sure you are meeting all of your requirements to graduate. If you do not graduate you will have to get a *G.E.D.* Why do it later when you can - **G**et your **ED**ucation **Now**.

3. Clubs and Organizations
Clubs and organizations are a great way to meet other teens that are interested in the same types of hobbies and extracurricular activities. High school provides such clubs as French, Math and Chess. There are arts clubs, school newspapers, music, computer clubs, military units, dance teams, sports teams and much more. You may run for class offices such as Class President, Vice President or Secretary. This gives the hard-

to-fit-in teen, shy teen or teen with special circumstances a selection of places to enjoy. Today's schools have more than enough activities for any type of interest. If you can't find anything to be a part of, it's because you really don't want to.

4. Sports

"I'm a Baller"! School is an excellent place to hone in (practice – zero in) on your sport. Participating in sports teaches leadership, health, camaraderie, team play, character and spirit. Most schools have a variety of activities to choose from; basketball, volleyball, football, golf, swimming, tennis, soccer and wrestling. There's also cheerleading, pom-poms and dance. Some kids are playing a sport for the first time, some are natural athletes, others are multi-talented and play more than one sport. One way students are able to get scholarships to college is through playing a sport. Many coaches can advise you on which sports programs would be beneficial to you, but it's up to you to do your own research. Your education should stay in the forefront, keep your grades up, study without being told and try not to use sports as a crutch. Keep your parents and family in the loop and always have a plan B.

5. I'm in High School Now!

- ***Learn the school rules***; it is wise to know what kind of behavior will get you a detention, written up, suspended or expelled. Read your school handbook, stay in touch with your teachers. Don't do anything you know is wrong such as; drinking or using drugs in school.
- ***Teachers:*** Your teacher is your rock. They are a very important part of your educational endeavor. Although sometimes you may disagree with them, remember they are there for you. Respect them, and show them you mean business. Most teachers are good mentors; you just have to meet them half way. They will provide a golden path for you. Open up your mind and let them in.
- ***Peer Pressure*** can be a trip you don't want to travel. It can be good when you are with a positive crowd doing positive things. You have many hours of influence from your friends and classmates. Listen to the little voice that tells you what's right and what's wrong. Make good decisions as much as possible.
- ***Cutting class and bad behavior is unacceptable.*** School is supposed to be a fun, enjoyable learning experience. You don't get extra credit for bad class conduct or being the class clown. Cutting class will get you suspended. Some schools make this a permanent part of your record that will follow you to other schools.
- ***Career choices*** are difficult for adults. For young people making this decision it's equally as hard. You should explore the passion of your dream. There is no career, job, hobby or business that can't be studied. If you're a musician there's Julliard. Teens have opportunities to be actors, poets, electricians, mechanics, doctors, lawyers or entrepreneurs.
- ***Parties, proms, balls & homecoming dances*** will be given all through high school. Make sure you know who is giving it, especially if it's not your school or it's a private party. Cover all drinks and liquids to prevent anyone from putting some-

thing in your drink. If a fight breaks out, refrain from looking and haul it out of there. Limit your attendance at house parties. Try to use a limo on prom, it's safer and you can defray costs by sharing with others. Don't do anything at a party that you'll regret in the morning. Have fun!

- ***SAT/ACT***(*college entrance tests)* They don't seem to be important until you're taking them. Keep in mind that you will need these scores when applying to colleges. Start preparing for these tests as soon as possible. Get a testing study guide from a book store, take a test prep class or you can get free practice tests online.
- ***Scholarships*** are covered in chapter 3. Scholarships are available for specific areas of study, sports and for academic excellence. Start searching as soon as possible looking for opportunities at colleges or universities. Do not leave any stone unturned, this goes for every store, website, military or school scholarship that may be available.
- ***Working*** while going to school is common among teens. Your study schedule is the main challenge. Exercise time management so that you have enough time to balance your homework, extracurricular activities and work schedule. If your grades start to slide, cut back on work or your social schedule.

6. Report Cards

Report cards are a measure of your educational process. It is anxiously awaited by many a parent and child to see how many A's, B's and C's you have and how much we will pay for those grades. When your hard work pays off, we want the world to see. There have been many MIA (Missing in Action) report cards that have gotten eaten by dogs, intercepted by the mailman (why would they?). I have also heard the teacher was so negligent, she gave them to everyone in your class but you, or you forgot to bring it home. Your report card should be your friend. Your grades determine your GPA (Grade Point Average) and if you have enough credits to graduate. If you don't have enough credits after each semester your counselor should advise you of summer school or night school options.

7. Homework ?

"Have you done your Homework?" is the parents National Anthem. You always say "yes', whether you have done it or not. If you are the consistent victim of a homework nabber, you should seek help. You need to buckle down and get your homework ON. This is the first order of business when you get home from school, not the last. Don't procrastinate when studying for tests. For my daughter, homework is done easier with loud rap music and television as a backdrop, this is *not* studying. If I really want it done quickly, I just need to have her friends waiting outside for her. You aren't learning or comprehending a thing. It's really not your parent's responsibility, your teacher or your friend. Your homework is your responsibility. If you find you are having difficulty, here's a few suggestions to get back on the homework track. *(1)* Get a study buddy, to help keep each other on track. *(2)* Make sure you bring your books home even when you don't have homework and study anyway. *(3)* Become disciplined and do your homework as soon as you get home everyday. *(4)* Read and take notes on every chapter to retain what you've read, you'll remember it better if you write it. *(5)* When you have a test, ask the teacher for notes, or double check what you need to study. Carve out separate time away from homework to study for the test.

8. "Click" You're the Star on Camera!

Cliques (click) are prevalent in every school. From pre-school through high school cliques will follow teens through life. You name it and there's a clique for it; *The Nerd/Lame Clique* – computer, smart crowd. *The Popular Clique* – cute kids, name brand have everything first, cell phone with unlimited minutes trend setters. *The Jocks* – sports club, basketball, football players, cheerleaders, baseball, tennis, soccer and golfers. Then there's the *Artsy* – arts, drama and music crowd. Don't let the clique business consume you or turn into a bad peer situation that you're trying to fit into. You may still find you don't fit into one of these sub-clubs or cliques. There will soon be another one around the corner, if not, then start your own.

9. What Brand Name is in the Tag of That Shirt?

Your t-shirt costs over $50, with matching jeans that cost $100 because it has a rappers name on the label. Who would have thought you would pay over a hundred dollars for a terry cloth sweat suit. These outfits are equivalent to a car payment and two other bills. With this costly tag on your shirt, you must ask yourself why would you pay something you can get for half that price. Here are the reasons; peer pressure, all of your friends have it, you just like really expensive clothes or you're scared of the "Clothes Police" that check tags in your clothes. You must get a job if you have to have this stuff. Soon it will come together for you and you will realize it's all over priced and you've wasted a lot of money. When you start spending your own money, you won't be as quick to spend so unconsciously. Name brand clothes should not get out of control. You can buy a few things, but look for sales and discounts as well. Be a smart savvy shopper, look for sales on the Internet or really cool discount stores. Remember, the *Clothes Police* don't get paid; they are harassing you for free.

10. Let's Get Organized!

Are you chronically late to school, leave your I.D. at home every other day and have to buy them? Are you always known as the person that is late to everything? Is your locker so cluttered you can't find anything and you pick the wrong folders for class? If you answered *"yes"* to any one of these questions, it means you are disorganized and you need a little guidance. Here's a few tips to help you; *(1)* Buy or get a planner/schedule book and write down everything. *(2)* Take time to organize your folders and your homework binders weekly. *(3)* Organize your locker according to your class schedule. Clean or refresh your locker weekly. You have to mentally retrain yourself to get up early, leave early and get to your appointments or obligations earlier. Start taking inventory of your time and organizational skills weekly. Make small changes one step at a time, but stay consistent.

11. Reading is Really Fundamental

Many students read way below their actual grade level. It's very important that you pick up your reading skills as soon as possible. Start by reading a book during the summer and squeeze in a couple of books during the school year. Find some interesting novels or small books to read until you find the kind of books you like. You may start reading for pleasure, knowledge or just to escape. Pick up the newspaper daily and skim the headlines to see what catches your eye or interests you – you *will* gain knowledge. Everyone reads at different levels, but start somewhere.

12. Life Preparation

After high school is when life really begins. This is when your maturity is tested. You are now responsible for your own money, living expenses, study habits and eating. Regardless of what grade you are in, start preparing yourself for life after high school. It's going to come, and these four years will fly by. Everything you do should be in preparation for life on your own. Responsibilities move closer to you with every year you live. Teenagers have jobs, credit cards, cars, cell phones and some even pay rent. This means you have to make changes in your lifestyle. Think. Act. Prepare.

Save your money, spend only what you need. Treat yourself, but don't overdo it. Get a checking or savings account. Discipline yourself and start saving your money for a rainy day. It *will* rain. I think that's a song. Smile. ***Study for your SAT/ACT***, before your test so you don't have to worry at the last minute. ***Be respectful to teachers***, principals and all adults. You never know who you may need. ***Eat healthy***, by eating baked and grilled foods. Limit fried and junk foods. Replace pop and acid drinks with water. Learn how to cook basic healthy meals. ***Always buy necessities*** first. Needs first – Wants last. ***Don't look to get a lot of credit***. One year of going overboard can cost you ten years to fix. ***Start preparing for college*** life, train yourself to have good study habits.

MY JOURNAL ENTRY

List 5 positive things you have learned about ***school*** in this chapter. Discuss them with a parent, teacher, mentor or friends.

____

____

____

____

____

____

____

PEER PRESSURE

After careful research of what "peer pressure" really means - it was still a challenge to pin down a definition. The most relevant definition of peer pressure is the **influence** you encounter from other teens in your same age and/or class group. Peer pressure from friends may make you decide to cut class or exhibit behavior you wouldn't ordinarily do. This chapter will help you understand peer pressure and show you techniques to recognize it and deal with it so you can make the right decisions.

12 TIPS FOR TEENS ON HANDLING PEER PRESSURE:

1. What is Peer Pressure?
Peer pressure is that feeling you get from your friend's influencing you to be like the rest of the crowd. It's that lump in your stomach when your friends say, "but everyone is doing it", "you're a lame", "you won't be cool" or "that's why no one likes you". If you agree to use drugs, have sex or exhibit bad behavior that you know is wrong because someone threatens, you are caving into negative peer pressure. Set your own goals, make good decisions and stand firm with your beliefs and the principles you know are right. Be a leader, not a follower, set strong positive standards for your peers.

2. The 3 P's - Positive Peer Pressure
Peer pressure can be very positive and this is the best kind. In life, one wrong turn can mess ya up! Use your peer time wisely. The recipe for the 3 P's is to stay busy, keep a positive attitude and know when to say "NO". Join organizations, clubs, sports teams, church activities and group events. Add good hearted happy friends that are positive and have your best interest at heart. This means they will not make suggestions or ask you to do things that are against the good principles you were taught. They will respect you when they hear "NO" or "I don't want to."

3. Negative Peer Pressure
Negative peer pressure is one of those things you don't realize you're in until its too late. *Hint*: If you have friends that always call you up to do bad or questionable things (ie. cut class, drinking, etc) and can never find any fun things to do, then they're a negative influence. Negative peer pressure usually begins with conversations like this; "You're not cool if you don't take a puff, what's the worse that can happen? I knew you were scared." *News Flash*: Everybody is *not* doing it. The ones that get caught usually say it was their first time ever doing anything like that, or if they get out of this situation they will never do it again. So, prevent yourself from some of life's unnecessary experiences regardless of how bad your friends want you to be involved. Curiosity killed the cat.

4. Boys will be Boys
That's the way we feel most of the time. We expect that you and your buddies will occasionally throw balls, say a bad word, pull some girls hair or engage in some harmless locker pranks. That's cool, but we have been told that peer pressure among boys goes deeper than that. It affects them in choosing sports, schools, clothes and much

more. Kids tease each other about acne, dancing, and hair. You and your boys will talk with each other about girls, drinking, drugs and sex. This is where things get tricky. It's one thing to talk about sex, but quite another story to indulge. There is nothing wrong with *not having sex*. If your friends encourage you or make you feel left out, then they are not friends. Don't look around for some unwilling young woman and take her virginity to fulfill a promise or bet to "the boys". It can come back to haunt you two times over. Just remember when it's all over those same guys will not be there to help you get out of a jam or help you pay child support if you get someone pregnant. They will be saying "wow – you got caught up huh?" If your actions are going to hurt someone either physically or emotionally - then don't do it. Please be respectful of others. Always remember what your parents have taught you. It's what you do with your knowledge that determines your personal growth and maturity.

5. Girls!

Set your own rules, make your own style. Is everybody really doing it? Kissing, sex, cutting class? And so what if they do? This is about you. How will you handle the pressure that will come your way? There are a few things that come up automatically; sex, kissing, boys, acne, weight or body style. This is the nucleus (center) of self-esteem and what drives many teens to making the wrong decisions. For example; let's take weight for instance, everyone watches television and thinks skinny is in, and all the thick girls are having issues. Next, everyone is starving themselves and disappointed with their bodies. Then a movie star enters stage left, and says *big booties* and *thick girls* are in and skinny is no longer the style. Make your own style. Don't give in to sexual pressure or pound your self-esteem. Be your own phenomenal woman, you're not like everyone else.

6. Style

School peer pressure is the most difficult. I heard through a reliable grapevine (my daughter) that it's the "clothes police" who usually ruin a good time. School peer pressure will cause you to take your lunch money and buy some new gym shoes just to fit in. Now for some parents that may not be such a bad thing. Smile. This is where you must be a leader and take charge. It's not where you buy your clothes but how you wear them. ***Create and make your own style! Be your own brand!*** Take chances with you outfits, shop at different stores from your peers. Your peers will want to be just like you. Don't let anyone pressure you into wearing a certain hairstyle or let anyone make you feel bad because you can't afford brand name clothes. Give your parents a break on the name brands, because in the end, you are making the rich richer. Most designers make the same clothes for specialty stores and department stores.

7. Sex & Peer Pressure

Sex is mom's worst peer pressure nightmare. Whether you are a girl or a boy, this scares the heck out of us. If we are the parent of a young woman we're fearful some putz is going to sweet talk her into sex and accidentally get her pregnant. If we are the parent of a young man we don't want him pregnant either. Smile. Don't let someone else make you have sex out of guilt, or because you are the last virgin in the school - if you are, maybe you'll be famous and have your own reality show. Chances are you're not, and when you realize they're lying it's too late. The word *abstinence* (not having sex) is your best friend. It saves you from the harmful diseases you can catch; it saves you from HIV (deadliest disease), STD's and pregnancy. If you are beyond the abstinence stage when you read this, then at least use condoms-EVERYTIME. Just make sure that whatever decisions you make you can live with the consequences.

8. Drinking – Drugs – Smoking

I'm sure it's cool to listen to the kids that say they have gotten high this weekend. Well, being a drug induced human is not cool. Drugs, nicotine and alcohol are all forms of drugs, very addictive drugs. A mature teen using their own mind will know the difference between peer pressure and the right thing to do. We have covered drinking, drugs and alcohol in detail in Chapter 5. You know that drugs and alcohol will ruin your body and smoking causes cancer and other diseases. Leaders must be good at making decisions and having self confidence. If you don't have confidence and self-esteem, then your peers can make decisions for you and "guilt trip" you into doing things you know are wrong. Once you are hooked and it's out of control its not easy to stop. Not only are these costly habits for adults, they are twice as costly for teenagers. Keep in mind, the tobacco industry is a multi-billion dollar business. It hooks teenagers on their products so they are addicted through adulthood. Use your money for something productive of your own choosing.

9. Music Videos & Hip Hop Music

Listening to some thug and gangsta' rap music can subliminally influence your behavior. This is obvious when we witness young children singing suggestive lyrics and imitating actions that they don't even understand. If we forbid it at home, you get the music or learn about it from peers, friends, older family members or acquaintances. Be responsible when listening to any hard core lyrics, not just rap music. Don't repeat bad language, *"Hoe & Bitch"* are way too derogatory and disrespectful. This is no way to refer to a woman. It has become common language today among many young men and even some young women. As a teen, you have a responsibility to youngsters to lead by example.

10. My Body, Let's Start With Acne

You are not the first or last kid on earth to have a pimple. Acne is part of puberty and life. If someone gives you a hard time or excludes you because of it, then they weren't your friend in the first place. If you have acne and someone teases you, so what. Acne is as common as apple pie. So are glasses, braces and all those other common things that happen around or on your face. It's not a reason for you to stop going out and having fun. Ask your parent to take you to a dermatologist (doctor that specializes in skin). Whether you are a young lady or a guy, don't let anyone violate your body. Making fun of others with acne, weight problems, unattractiveness or disabilities is cruel. God doesn't like ugly – behavior that is.

11. Whispering & Gossiping (psst..psst)

Whispering and gossiping seems harmless, and most times it is. Have you noticed when someone is whispering, you always think it's about you? A gentle whisper between friends soon balloons out of control. So when you whisper, point or exclude someone, keep in mind that the next time it may be about you. ***Gossip*** usually starts with ***"Can you keep a secret?"*** This is an ugly way to spread information and it hurts. So if you have to say "I didn't say that" more than 5x a week – either you are a gossip or someone thinks you are. Stop. Check to see if it's true before you repeat it. If it's a secret it's not meant to be told, or repeated. Respect the privacy and trust that someone put in you. Gossip is always juicy until it's about you.

12. Cheating/Lying/Stealing/Gambling

Here's the scoop! By now you know the difference between right and wrong. Your parents have taught you or you've learned through experience. Your friends will now start to ask you to join them in questionable behavior. Just remember when you do something wrong, cheating, lying or stealing, someone will always tell. One of the partners in the crime always buckles under pressure. ***Stealing*** – *It wasn't me*, but "I was with someone who did it." One of your slick friends will say "it's ok as long as you don't get caught." Have you noticed it's always the good ones that get caught the first time? Mom / Dad raised you right and here you are a victim of "If I get out of this one, I'll never do it again." Ok. You're a teen. You get one "idiot ticket", to make "one" mistake. Most kids do this out of innocent curiosity, or just to see if you'll get caught. Shoplifting, pick pocketing, sneaking on the bus without paying are all forms of theft. ***Lying*** - YES! We gotta go here! No one wants to be lied to, lied on or lied about. Also, no one wants to figure out if someone is lying. Lying hurts. I always say give what you expect to get. Bottom lie is…I mean bottom line is, if it's not necessary for life or death, then don't do it. ***Gambling*** - Teens gamble from street corner and school bathroom craps to online Texas Hold-em. They are becoming addicted and loosing money they don't have. This is also a disease. If you think you have a problem, or are addicted to gambling, contact Gamblers Anonymous at www.gamblersanonymous.org

MY JOURNAL ENTRY

List 5 things you've learned about ***peer pressure***. Discuss them with a parent, teacher, mentor or friends.

____

____

____

____

____

____

RELATIONSHIPS & DATING

The first consideration in teen dating is should you date, and if so, at what age should you start? If you are a preteen, you probably shouldn't be dating yet. Once you are in high school you may want to consider a chaperoned outing with a parent or older sibling. With peer pressure looming above you, most teens want to start dating around age 15. Relationships among teens are mostly limited to school friends, people that live in your neighborhood or family friends. You can take the pressure off of dating by taking group outings and spending a lot of time with friends. Always make sure that outings and dates are done smartly, in good taste and safe. Here are some tips on relationships and dating.

12 TIPS FOR TEENS ON RELATIONSHIPS & DATING:

1. Dating 101

Your friends and peers may be dating, but there's no written rule that says *you* have to date. This is when the peer pressure really takes effect, because everyone around you is doing it and you feel like you should also. You won't grow an extra head or have a sign on your chest that says you haven't been dating. Show your independence, take your time and let it happen or *not* happen naturally.

2. What Do Your Parents Think About Dating?

Ok. We know the idea of talking with your parents about dating makes your stomach nauseous. If you share your dating dilemmas with your parents, maybe they can help by offering a solution or advising you on the proper way to date. When you first start dating, you should get permission or introduce your date to your parents. They may not feel you are ready and it's nice to have their blessing. If you sneak around and they catch you, you will lose their trust. This will make your parents feel confident about the type of individual you are going out with, especially if they will be driving. Parents want to know that whomever you are going out with is safe, sober and actually has a driver's license. The more confident the parent feels about your date, the easier it will be for you to go on the next one. Communication is the key.

3. What Age Should You Start Dating?

Some preteens are allowed to start dating in grammar or middle school. This mainly depends on the maturity of the individuals and the acceptability of the parents. Some parents feel chaperoned dating is ok with preteens, others parents are against it. I recommend for pre-teens especially to find a cool group of friends (boys and girls) that like to hang out and plan group trips to the movies or mall. Older teens 16 and up may be able to date in pairs, something light and not too intense is recommended. If you involve your parents and they trust you, they will advise you on their feelings and opinions. Take your time and don't be in a hurry. Do not do anything you are not comfortable with.

4. You Have Never Had A Date
There is nothing is wrong with *not dating*. It's really ok. Peer pressure from friends may make you feel out of place. You look around and it seems all your friends or peers are dating. In the grand scheme of things, everything will happen when it's time. You can always go out with friends of the opposite sex. Sometimes they make the best friends.

5. Feeling Trapped
Being in a relationship can also make you feel trapped. A person may put pressure on you, and you may just want to be friends. Things may not end up going as you had planned and you may not be happy. You may find the personality traits of the other person have changed from when you first met them, or you may have been dating them for the wrong reasons. Whatever the case, if you are feeling uncomfortable or decide you want to get out of the relationship, do it sooner than later. Your inner voice is usually right.

6. First Date Ideas
First dates are important, especially if you want to make a good impression. Keep it light such as; a movie, lunch or sports outing. Meet in a lighted place where there are plenty of people. Go to an amusement park or special event, the more fun the date is the less serious and less pressure you will feel. At home dates can be interesting; you can rent a movie, play board or computer games, and save money while doing it. I hear what you are saying and *YES*, the downside is that parents or siblings may be near, but that's not the worse thing in the world. It may work in your favor. It will also keep the environment guarded, neutral and easier to deal with.

7. Being "Friends Only" With Someone You've Dated
You don't have to fall out with everyone that you date. You may have one or more dates with someone and decide that you don't want a relationship, but you enjoy his or her friendship. This happens all the time. Just talk to them and let them know. Sometimes relationships are too intense for teens and it's just better to have the opposite sex as friends, maybe even a best friend. Judge each situation as it comes.

8. Gifts
If you want to buy a gift for someone, check with parents or another adult to make sure the gift is appropriate. Many times, teens will buy inappropriate gifts for each other with good intentions. To avoid these types of mistakes, or if you're not sure, you should get an adult, whose opinion you value and ask them before you buy it. For instance; lingerie is not a good choice for a young lady or guy unless you have been in a serious relationship for several years *and are over the age of 18*. Lingerie can be a suggestive gift that parents may not appreciate. If someone has hinted they want a gift from a particular store for a holiday, you can get them a gift certificate/gift card, to that store so they can pick out what they want. This will show class on your part and it's easier to do.

9. What To Wear On A Date / How To Act On A Date
When you go on a date you should dress accordingly. Wear appropriate clothing for the type of event or place you are going to. If you are going out to dinner, you should

wear a nice outfit, something similar to what you would wear to church or a dressy event. If you are going to a casual place, you may want to wear something you would wear to school such as; jeans, t-shirt and gym shoes. Whenever you are invited to any

type of event, always inquire about the attire that is expected. This will prevent you from being surprisingly overdressed, underdressed or embarrassed. Listen to your date and learn what they like to do. Don't interrupt them, look around or seem aloof. Don't look as though you are paying attention to others. Pull out chairs for the females and take their coat to hang up if appropriate. Do not say anything that will make someone feel uncomfortable. Do not discuss personal issues or questions that are inappropriate.

10. When Someone Makes You Feel Uncomfortable/Abuse

If someone makes you feel uncomfortable on a date, find a way to end the date and leave. If you didn't drive, you should always keep money in your pocket for emergency transportation. If someone is abusive or you are scared, immediately try to leave or call someone to come and get you. If things are really out of hand, excuse yourself to the washroom and call your parents or 911. If you are in any type of abusive relationship, talk to someone about it to prevent it from going any further. If you are nervous about meeting someone that is potentially abusive or that you don't know very well – meet in public places where there are plenty of people around. There is no love worth physical or mental abuse.

11. Two Friends Like The Same Person

This causes more teen drama than you can imagine and in the end, you'll both agree it wasn't worth it. If your friend dated them first, ask them if it's ok. If you can't make a decision to suit both of you, the best thing to do is not date that person. Someone always gets hurt in these friendship trios. Don't lose your best friend by dating his/her "ex." There are plenty of fish in the sea and you're still young!

12. Drinking & Drugs On A Date

If your driver or date is drinking, refuse to ride with them. If you have a driver's license, refrain from drinking so that you can be sure to make it home safe. Even if driving is not the issue, it's not wise to drink or use drugs on a date. Beware of leaving drinks unattended at parties or events. You want to prevent someone from tagging your drink with "ruphies" or other date rape drugs.

MY JOURNAL ENTRY

List 5 positive thoughts about ***dating*** that you learned from this chapter. Discuss them with a parent, teacher, mentor or friends.

PROM NIGHT & PROM ETIQUETTE

Going to the prom is one of the most exciting days of your teenage life. It should be an unforgettable day for every high school junior or senior. Proms should be fun, upbeat, energetic and most of all memorable. There's plenty to do in preparation for the prom such as; buying or renting your outfit, getting your hair styled or cut, transportation, tickets, after parties and this is just for starters. Although each person will prepare for prom differently and may participate in different events, you should make a list and let your parents know what your plans are for the night. This chapter will help you prepare for this experience by sharing to save you time and money. Here are a few tips to help ensure that you enjoy your prom night.

12 TIPS FOR TEENS ON PROM NIGHT & PROM ETIQUETTE:

1. Early Planning

The earlier you start planning for your prom, the more organized you will be and the more money you will be able to save. Being prepared will also help prevent stress and last minute DIS-organization. Females should start looking for their dress early if they plan to coordinate their colors with their date's outfit. Sales are more difficult to find at the last minute. Rentals for limousines, hot cars and tuxedos are more expensive the closer you get to prom night. Planning will prevent last minute arrangements on the day of prom that may cost you double.

2. Prom Date & Who Pays

Traditionally you are expected to go to the prom with a date. As tradition changes, some teens do not feel the need to have a prom date. Many teens go to prom in groups to take the pressure off of finding a date. Girls can also ask boys to the prom nowadays and will even drive sometimes. Usually, whoever asks is responsible for paying for the prom tickets. Don't let the *"prom date"* stress you out. If there isn't anyone at your school you'd like to go with, then ask a brother, cousin or friend from another school. You're not marrying your date; you just want to have a fun night.

3. Fees & Costs

Fees associated with prom include; prom tickets, grooming, clothes, accessories; transportation, after party, breakfast events, corsages and boutonnieres. Start to budget some of these costs so that they won't come out of your parents pocket all at one time. Prom outfits can be extremely costly. Custom dresses and suits can cost in the hundreds of dollars. Group events and transportation should be split between friends to economize. There are ***free dresses*** and accessories provided by bridal companies at the Glass Slipper Project, subject to location. Information can be found at www.glassslipperproject.org.

4. Grooming

Grooming for prom has become a much more elaborate process then what it used to be. Some individuals get facials, professionally made up by department store consultants, massages and manicures. This is in addition to the fancy hairdos, haircuts, pedicures and other procedures that are normal for prom. Once you know how you want to primp yourself, start preparing a schedule and your budget so that you don't overdo it at the last minute. All of your grooming should be carefully planned.

5. Girls Responsibility

First you must take care of your personal grooming responsibility. If you are going with a date, it is up to you to get your dress and pick your colors in enough time so that your date can coordinate his outfit. Then you must pay for your ticket, fees and after party costs. If it's not your prom, your date is responsible for the prom ticket. If your date isn't driving, you must budget for your share of the limousine, some couples split this cost. It is your responsibility to buy a boutonnière for your date. Do not wait until the last minute and try to buy one that matches his sash or suit if you can. When your date arrives, you should pin it on his lapel. If your date is driving, he should come to pick you up with plenty of time to get to the prom. Allow enough time for the family and friends to take pictures.

6. Boys Responsibility

First there's your personal grooming responsibility. If you are going with a date, it is up to the girl to get her dress in enough time so that you can coordinate the colors in your outfit. You have to pay for your prom ticket, fees and any after party costs. If it's not your prom, your date is responsible for the prom ticket. If you or your date are not driving, you must budget for your share of the limousine. It is the boys' responsibility to buy a corsage for your date. Start looking a couple of days before prom; it is difficult to find matching colors on prom night or at the last minute. You should put it on her wrist when you pick her up. If you are driving, come to pick up your date with plenty of time to get to the prom. If you are driving don't forget to wash your car the day before. Allow time for family and friends to take pictures.

7. Meeting the Parents

In most cases, the parents of the young lady would like to meet the prom date. Sometimes the gentleman's parents may have the same request. This is not unusual, especially if they've never met the date or he/she is a new driver. Do not be offended; instead use this as a chance to show the parents how responsible, well-mannered and trustworthy you are. Parents just want peace of mind before their child goes off to prom and this will show them you were raised properly. The easiest way to get past this is to schedule a short meeting before the prom so the parents can meet your prom date. They may ask a few questions about how you feel about curfews, drinking or your driving record. Be honest, and don't feel uncomfortable this is normal.

8. Prom Night Champagne Sips

This is not really for you to drink champagne. In the past years, invitations are sent out to friends and families to come to the house before the prom couple leaves and have a "champagne sip" or "send off." This is the last official party you will have as a teenager. The family will take pictures and toast to you on your prom night. If you are going to send out invitations please do so at least two weeks before the prom. If you are having a champagne sip, it would be better to substitute *white grape juice or non-alcoholic champagne.* We don't want to promote drinking and driving.

9. After Parties

Each school may have their own after party or after prom event. Some teens decide to go to a particular special event, some organize their own parties and others have been known to have all night sleepovers and breakfast. Each year, the events get more and more creative. Most teens that are 18 consider themselves to already be adults but, the real deal is that you must be careful and more responsible than ever before. You will have to listen to your parents, keep your curfew, pass up drinking, sex and any other *"prom night only"* events. You don't want to ruin your prom night with something that could have been prevented.

10. Transportation, Drinking & Driving

On prom night, teens usually decide to drive their own vehicle, rent a vehicle or carpool in a limousine. Some schools even rent buses for the entire prom party. Group pooling is recommended because teens are able to save money by splitting the cost as well as everyone gets to ride together. Since no one in your group will be of legal drinking age, no one should be drinking. You should definitely not drink and drive just because it's prom night. You do not want to experience a fatal accident or incident. Drinking is wrong, illegal and dangerous. The earlier you make plans, the more prepared you will be when prom night comes.

11. Prom Etiquette

For some, this may be your first formal event in formal dress and you should act accordingly. Your napkin goes across your lap before you start eating. Since this is a formal event, a suit, matching outfit or nice shirt or blouse/slacks or skirt are all appropriate attire. Males should pull out chairs for females at their table. If there is a coat checkroom, hang your coat up. Liquids are on the right, and dry foods such as bread are served on your left. Use your utensils beginning from the outside (farthest from you) to the inside. When you are finished eating, put your silverware across the middle of your plate. Turn your coffee cup upside down if you don't want coffee. Don't blow hot soup in a spoon; you may splash it on someone. If there is food lodged in your teeth, don't pick at it, try and remove it with your tongue or go to the bathroom. For more on etiquette see Chapter 3.

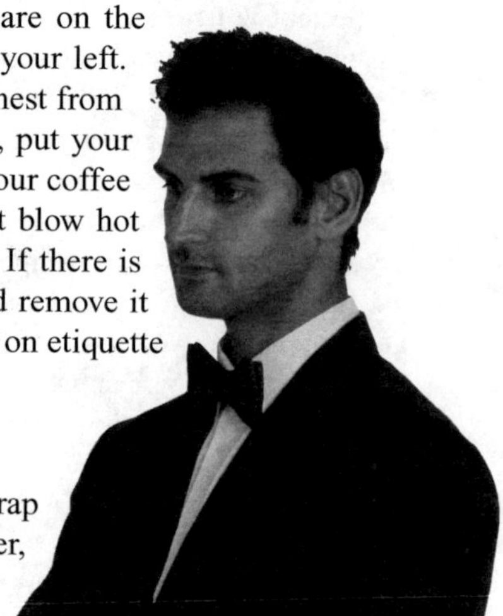

12. "Final Do/Don't List":

<u>Always be on time</u>. ***<u>Ladies</u>:*** Wear a shawl or wrap over a strapless dress, remove gloves during dinner, do not wear rings over gloves, don't forget the boutonniere, it's ok to dance with others at the prom. Don't over-do perfume. ***Gentleman:*** Go to the house to pick up our date, walk her to the door, make sure your date is seated first and stand when a lady stands to leave the table. Don't use too much after shave or cologne.

Prepare the day before by trying on all your clothes in case last minute adjustments need to be made. ***Canceling***: It is irresponsible and immature to change dates or cancel a prom date at the last minute. Always ***thank your prom date***.

MY JOURNAL ENTRY

List 5 things you've learned about ***prom night and prom etiquette***. Discuss them with a parent, teacher, mentor or friends.

GRADUATION

Going to your high school graduation is one of the highlights of your life. It is the significant turning point that says you're now a young adult. It is your first major separation from friends, family and peers, and the beginning of life out on your own. This special day should go as perfect as possible. There are a lot of components to your graduation. Before you graduate you must complete your class requirements, fees and your ancillary graduation events. Graduation and proms should be fun, upbeat, energetic and most of all memorable. There's plenty to do to in preparation for graduation and prom such as; buying or renting your outfit, getting your hair done or cut, transportation, tickets, after parties and this is just for starters. This chapter prepare you for graduation and the related activities you will participate in.

Now that you are graduating – you are going to "the show"! *Translation*: you are entering the real world. Make sure you keep a close watch on your grades the last year. It is important to communicate with your parents and keep them abreast of your grades and progress. You are leaving your parents, your friends, teachers and family. Many of you are going to be on your own for the first time, so don't lose your head. Study hard, save/budget your money and set goals so you will have a plan for your future. Remember, your college life is an important part of your future. It will determine what field of study you pursue and what type of job/career you will have. Take college seriously from the beginning, do the best you can and stay positive.

12 TIPS TO HELP TEENS PREPARE FOR GRADUATION:

1. Graduation Planning

The earlier you start planning for your graduation the better prepared you will be. Your graduation is an important moment in your life. This is the part that mom and dad have been waiting for. It's up to you to make sure you do your part. Your graduation "to do" list should include; your final school requirements, college applications, prom preparation, class ring, graduation trips, clothing for graduation day, cell phones, bank accounts, access to money, personal papers, appliances and items for your dorm room, school supplies and luggage.

2. Graduation Fees & Other Costs

Start to plan and review the list of graduation and event fees that will have to be paid before you graduate. This includes:

cap & gown
prom & graduation tickets

luncheon
class rings
required fees
graduation, prom & luncheon outfit
class trip (which may be out of town and is usually an additional cost)
prom expenses (transportation costs, after party costs, etc)
grooming, (all of these events may require different barber shop and beauty shop trips)
possible manicures and pedicures for some
clothing; rental outfits, specially designed outfits
outstanding fees or debts with the school

I have witnessed students that have neglected to tell their parents they couldn't graduate because of outstanding debts or school requirements that had not been met.

3. Graduation Day

On graduation day you want everything to go smooth. Prepare your clothes along with your cap, gown, tickets, camera and gifts you have for other graduates or friends. If you can't invite all of your family members to the graduation, then it's usually customary to have a party or *"get together"* at your house. You can also rent a space or ask a family member to provide a space for your party, where the rest of the family and friends can celebrate on your big day. You should provide refreshments for your guests.

4. Clothes and Grooming Budget

Years ago, this wouldn't be a concern or hardly need mentioning. Since youth are so clothes conscious and spend a lot of money on clothing, we need to prepare you in advance for your graduation and prom clothing budget. If you are planning to have an outfit made, or buy an expensive prom dress or suit - you may want to include your parents in on that. It's disrespectful to wait two weeks before prom and pout because you decided you want a special outfit and you can't find it, or now it costs three times as much. The stores know when it's prom season, this is their business, they mark up prices during prom season. Plan carefully for grooming needs with your beautician or barber, make a deal in advance for all of your needs, maybe they will give you a discount.

5. Outstanding School Debt

Hmmmm….what is this? This may be a book that you forgot you lost in your Freshmen year that costs $300, and you never paid for it. This is $50 dollars in replacement school I.D. badges. These fees can all easily add up and when you least expect to be paying it back. The moral of this story is to ask at the beginning of the year what fees you may owe. This way you won't be blind sighted (surprised) a few weeks before graduation with exorbitant fees that are due. The school should talk directly with parents if fees need to be paid, especially if it will affect your graduation. After all, they are responsible for paying them. It is recommended that you sit down with your parents and give them the list of fees so that your graduation and all of these events can go smoothly.

6. Ancillary Graduation Events / Trunk Parties / After Parties

Parents sometimes host a party on the day of graduation to celebrate the new graduate moving away and going off to college. At this party you should invite all family, close friends and others who would still love to give the graduate a card, gift or well wish. You also may decide to have a "Trunk Party" which is given before you go away to college, where your close friends and family will bring gifts for the graduate to take to college. This is similar to a "house warming or shower", where you will bring items that a new young adult living on their own will need. Cash is always acceptable. For both parties the host will serve refreshments and send thank you cards afterwards.

7. Rings & Pictures

This is just mentioned to help you and your parent understand the increasing prices in these items since your parents have purchased them. Class rings start at $200 and once you add your birth stone, basketballs, initials or other personalization you can expect to spend about $500 or more. Most schools are now starting to purchase the class ring in the junior year to offset this cost for the senior year. The pictures can be just as expensive, and if you are not careful, you can spend close to a thousand dollars for the pictures and the ring. Do not wait until the last minute to buy these two items, they can be very costly.

8. Prom

We have dedicated an entire chapter to prom etiquette, preparation and prom night. This is just a reminder that youth can spend hundreds of dollars on prom night. From expensive boutique outfits and tuxedo rentals to limousine and car rentals, this evening can calculate up quite a tab. The parties, the breakfast, the hair and other prom related activities also add up. Plan well, and try to stay within your budget.

9. Things to Do Before Leaving Town

When you are preparing to leave the city and in some cases the state, you will need to do the following:

-***Organize all of your important documents*** such as your birth certificate, social security card, diploma, transcripts, driver's license and state identification. Check renewal dates before you leave. Make a copy and leave your originals at home with your parents so you will always have an extra copy. ***Make a list of everyone*** you need to contact. Get phone numbers of friends, teachers, mentors and any emergency numbers of family members you may need to contact while you're gone. Make sure you review the ***college checklist*** in Chapter 7 so that you will have all of your dorm items, school requirements and travel itinerary. If you don't already have a ***cell phone***, try and get one to take with you in case of an emergency.

10. ACT/SAT/GPA

If you are graduating then you have already experienced the application process that goes along with college selection. Partial criteria for specific colleges and scholarships include having a certain ACT or SAT score, (contact them for individual requirements). The average GPA (Grade Point Average) of 2.5, is also required for many colleges and quite a few scholarships accept this as average. However, if your first couple of high school years are rocky, this could be a problem for you later. It's sort of like when you were in grade/middle school and your 7th grade score determined your high school eligibility. If you missed it, you didn't' realize it until it was too late.

When you get to your last year, you may not have the required amount of credits or GPA to apply to specific colleges or scholarships. The key here is not to get discouraged and stay on target, as best you can. The great thing about these tests is that you get to take them over a few more times. Don't depend on this, you may miss an opportunity. For testing preparation most schools will offer pre-test workshops. Practice tests can be obtained online or you can buy the example tests at most major bookstores and study at home.

11. Scholarship & College Preparation

In Chapter 4, there is additional information on scholarships. This is a reminder to make sure you have been relentless and exhausted every scholarship opportunity available. Be prepared to write creative essays and meet other requirements to get a scholarship. Unless you have a guardian angel looking out for you in sports or academics, you will have to go through college by paying in cash, working and using a combination of scholarships, grants and loans. Detailed lists of items you will need for your final college preparation are Chapter 7. You will need to prepare to pack all the items you need for your dorm room. When you talk with the residence hall you plan to live in, you should ask important questions such as; can you take your car, your bicycle and what you will do for storage. Ask how many room mates you will have and as much information as you can gather. Your transition to college should be as smooth as you can make it.

12. Not Going to College – What's the Next Step?

Everyone will not go to college, for one reason or another. Some graduating seniors do not like school, and would like to take a break. Some students will go to junior college and some will attend trade schools. There are some students that are anxious to get jobs and get out into the world. Whichever path you choose, make sure you weigh all of your options, so you can develop a plan. Don't limit yourself and stay focused on your future. Time flies and before you know it you're all grown up.

MY JOURNAL ENTRY

List 5 things you've learned about preparing for ***graduation***. Discuss them with a parent, teacher, mentor or friends.

____

____

____

____

____

____

DRIVING

During high school, most teens are preparing to take drivers education or staring at the new object of their affection – the car of their dreams. In some cases, your parents are as anxious as you are, and want you to drive. They may feel that you still aren't ready yet, or that you need a little more experience. Don't hold that against us. Safety is the main concern when driving a car – the safety of you, your passengers and your car. This is one of the most important responsibilities you will have as a young adult. It's not just your life, it's everyone on the road with you. Here are a few tips to help you become a better driver. If you master these tips, you will be on your way to convincing your parents that you are ready and were born to drive.

12 TIPS FOR THE NEW TEEN DRIVERS!!!

1. Seatbelts and Car Insurance are Mandatory

You may be familiar with the phrase "Click it or Ticket," if you're not familiar with it, you need to not only learn it but live it. Seat belts are essential for your safety and are required by law at all times. Not only should you always wear your seatbelt, if you have passengers in your car, you should make sure they are belted in also. Another state mandate is that all drivers must have auto insurance on any vehicle they are driving. Driving without insurance can change your entire life… if you get into an accident and don't have insurance, you and your parents can be sued for a lot of money. You may also get a $500 ticket if you get stopped without car insurance. Before you hit the road, get insured. If you cannot afford insurance, you cannot afford to drive!

2. Keep your Driver's License, Sticker and Registration Up to Date

Driving is not a right, it is a privilege and you have to be a responsible driver at all times. You must keep your license, registration and license plate sticker up to date. If it's suspended or expired, don't drive. No excuses. Getting stopped by the police without the proper registration for your car can get you fined or put in jail. These renewal fees are costly, but if you get a ticket it will cost you twice as much to replace them after you pay the fine.

3. Rolling Stops

Always come to a complete stop when driving. A "rolling stop" occurs when you come to a stop sign, lightly tap the brakes and keep going. Drivers who use rolling stops sometimes proceed in front of a driver that was there before them, and had the right of way. This is legally considered running a stop sign and is a moving violation that will get you a big fat ticket. Experienced drivers sometime have a habit of doing this and it's a bad habit that new drivers should not copy. It's illegal and can cause a bad accident. Another car already at the stop sign may take their proper turn and you may cause an accident because you failed to come to a complete stop. Exercise caution at stop signs and stop lights.

4. Keep Basic "Emergency" Items In Your Car / Roadside Assistance

You should always keep the following items in your car in case of emergency; a spare tire (in case of a flat), a wrench (to remove lug nuts from the old tire), jumper cables (in case your battery goes dead) and an empty plastic gas can (in case you run out of gas). You should have some type of roadside assistance for emergencies. If it didn't come with the purchase of your car, it may be offered through your cell phone service provider or a company such as "AAA Motor Club." You may have to ask your parents to help you with this one, but it is worth the small expense during an emergency situation.

5. Drive The Speed Limit

Speed limits are not only the law, but posted for a reason. Most of the time the person speeding and passing on the side of you will end up right beside you at the next stoplight. Drive safely, especially in inclement (bad) weather; it may save your life. Rain, slippery roads and snow can impair your driving and you should adjust your speed accordingly. Always drive slowly when near small children and schools. Many drivers speed unnecessarily, if you are driving the speed limit it will help to prevent accidents. Many cities have the capabilities to monitor speed traps from helicopters and they have also installed cameras to take pictures of speeders. How will you know if you've been caught? You will get your picture and your ticket in the mail. Smile.

6. Abide By Your Curfew, Keep Your Promise

Don't use your car as an excuse to stay out later than curfew. Remember, after curfew, you're technically driving without a driver's license. This could mean a ticket, jail or other penalties. If you are the one who has to drive everyone home after an event, leave early enough so that you can make your curfew. Know your city and state curfews, and abide by it, it's not worth taking a chance.

7. Safety First

Always be safe. Don't drive someone home that you don't know or be the last person in the car alone with someone you aren't familiar with. Don't give strangers a ride. Don't have strange friends of friends riding with you. Remember seat belts for everyone at all times. Always ride in pairs when possible and have a friend you trust ride home with you. It won't hurt to call home and let your parents or other family members know that you are on your way and to be on the lookout for you. Always let a friend, co-worker or family member know where you will be traveling. If your car doesn't automatically lock the doors for you when you start the engine, lock your doors as soon as you get into the car. After friends get out of the car, make sure to check that the doors are locked again. Don't leave keys, cell phones, valuables, wallets or purses in view. Keep your eyes open when entering your vehicle, look around for suspicious characters. This will deter someone from attempting to rob you. Always wear a helmet when riding a **motorcycle or mo-ped**.

8. Buying and Maintaining Your Vehicle

If you are in the market for buying a car, make sure you take someone that is knowledgeable about automobiles. If you buy a new vehicle, make sure you ask all the questions you can. If you are buying a used vehicle, make sure you find out all the pertinent information about the history of the car such as the last oil change, mileage, etc. Get a manual for the car so that you will know every aspect of how you must maintain your car. Once you get the manual, read it thoroughly to familiarize yourself with the car. If you purchase a car without one, go to an auto parts store or order the manual off of the internet. Check your fluids, oil, brakes, tires, defrost and windshield wipers on a regular basis. Tune-ups are included in the regular maintenance; some cars get them once a year. Find a good mechanic or family mechanic and make sure the basic "hood checks" are done every couple of months. Keep up the appearance of your car by washing and vacuuming it on a regular basis. This will help keep the paint in good shape and to retain the value of the car in case you want to sell it.

9. Don't Lend Your Car Out And Don't Let Anyone Drive Your Car.
This includes your best friend, best bud or a family member. If they can't afford to buy you a car if they wreck it, they can't afford to drive it. Even if they can afford it, there's no guarantee they (or their parents) will do the right thing. They may have a bad accident, or hurt someone and you'll be liable and responsible. Also, no one takes care of your stuff like you do.

10. Never Run Out of Gas / The GAS Money!
Try and keep at least a half of tank of gas in your car at all times. If you adopt this rule, you will always have gas. Gas is very expensive these days. Some teens don't let you ride without donating some gas money. Others seem to have a hard time asking for it. It's the proper thing for your friends to offer gas money since they would be spending it on public transportation if it wasn't for your chauffeur services. Don't be scared to ask for it. After all, your car is for your own personal enjoyment and transportation. If you are the passenger, offer to feed the tank. You want to prevent running out of gas late at night or on a cold winter morning.

11. A Few More Driving Tips:
You are driving for all 4 corners and the cars in between. Before pulling off at a green light always look one extra time. Right.-Left- Front- Back. Just because the light is green, the car in front of you may not pull off, double check and wait to make sure they pull off before hitting the gas. This extra minute can save your life. Be *alert when sitting at a red light* because there may be a car that is running a light, or a car that is trapped in the intersection while attempting to turn. This may prevent an accident. ***Left Turns***; This is the trickiest part of driving. *The left hand turn.* Pull up to the middle of the intersection, watch for approaching traffic, and go as soon as it's safe so you're not caught in the middle of the street. Watch all areas consistently every moment. ***Stoplight Trapping***; We all have pulled up on the right side of another car while at a red stoplight and sped in front of that car when the light turns green. While I'm not sure if that's illegal, it's certainly risky. Sometimes, the other car, will not let you in which forces you into a tight situation. This can cause an accident if they don't see you or you don't have enough lead room. ***Teen Road Rage*** and cursing adults that cut in front of your car is not necessary. Too many auto accidents and arguments break out because someone cut someone else off or jumped in front of them without a blinker. You pull out a golf club, they'll pull out a gun. A harmless argument can easily turn deadly and it's just not that serious. Let them go, just blow it off!!! The key is to drive safely, and make it home at the end of the day. ***Drag Racing*** is immature, illegal and extremely dangerous. Don't let peer pressure ruin one of the most important responsibilities of being a young adult. ***No Speeding***; This will also get you a big ticket and possibly into an accident. Make sure you allow yourself enough travel time. Leave

early, allow for bad traffic, bad weather or a flat tire. Beware! Some states will revoke the license of teenage drivers if they get two or more moving violations in their first few years of driving.

12. Plan your trip carefully

Trying to find your way around the city as a new driver is quite different than when you were a passenger. Learn to navigate your way around the city safely, or go online to map it out beforehand. Map providers such as Map Quest will be able to give you detailed block by block directions for your trip. Call and ask someone you trust for directions so you aren't driving around lost. Always ask about parking availability, this will save you plenty of time and headaches later. Just to be on the safe side, learn to read a map and keep one in the car. You may travel into a new neighborhood or be forced to make a detour because of an accident or construction. Stay on well lit main streets and bus routes. If you have an emergency you can get help or if necessary ride public transportation.

MY JOURNAL ENTRY

List 5 things about ***driving*** that you learned from this chapter. Discuss them with a parent, teacher, mentor or friends.

____

____

____

____

____

____

____

____

____

____

____

____

____

GANGS, GUNS VIOLENCE AND BULLIES

Violence has increased at an alarming rate among teens. Kids are getting recruited and seduced into gangs at a younger age every year. More and more kids have easy access to guns. You have an important life to live and you should live it safely. Arm yourself with knowledge so that you have the power to make the right life choices. You have a generation following you that needs you to be their role model. It's up to you to stay away from gangs and guns and pass along the message **"stop the violence against teens."**

12 TIPS FOR TEENS ABOUT GANGS, GUN VIOLENCE & BULLIES:

1. Why Do Teens Join Gangs?

Teens join gangs for different reasons; money, friendship, camaraderie, respect, excitement, notoriety, protection and an accelerated lifestyle. None of those reasons include getting killed but unfortunately, it happens frequently. Ask yourself, "Is it worth it?" Gangs have leadership, codes, rules, business operations and recruitment tactics. Many have said if gang activity wasn't illegal, they could make good business people with some of their endeavors – they just need to use the energy for positive ventures. Gangs prey on youth that are having trouble with friends, family or have been shunned by school, peers and society. Environment is also a factor when trying to deter teens from gangs. Some communities make it very difficult for them to stay away from gang members and gang activity.

2. Gang Initiations

Different gangs initiate their members in different ways, none of which are good. Initiation may include fighting, drive-bys, shootings, drugs, robberies, car jacking and killing. These illegal acts can land you in jail or cause retaliation against you and lead to death. You need to realize if you deliver violence it will come back to you. Find something more productive, fun and better to do with your time.

3. Gang Identifiers

Gang identifiers can be a variety of things these days including; clothing, bandanas, tattoos, pro team hats, boots, specific colors, jewelry, khakis, t-shirts, language and hand gestures. Graffiti can also be a gang identifier and it's sometimes used to mark territory. To be safe, you should try not to wear any clothing or colors that are gang affiliated. If you know of any gang members, or gang activity near your home or school, do everything you can to stay away from it.

4. How Do You Avoid Or Prevent Getting Into A Gang?

Communicate regularly, openly and honestly with parents and mentors. Positive alternatives for teens include; joining a church, youth groups or after school programs. When you see problems brewing, talk with parents, counselors or friends right away and try to solve them. Focus your energy and attention on your education and having fun in your teenage life. Do not look for false friendships with gang members or groups that mean harm. It's usually very difficult to get out of a gang once you get in. Occupy you time productively with sports or other group activities. Many communities must pool together to prevent gang activity; this means neighborhood watch groups, providing safe environments and community involvement.

5. Girls, Gangs and Violence

The statistics are in and there are increasing numbers of girls that are recruiting gang members as young as 8 years old. Girls and women are also in gangs and start out as (mules) carrying drugs in some gangs. Girls are viciously fighting each other more than ever before. Knives are their main weapon of choice. Girls fight over boys, argue over staring, their clique, gossip and disrespect. Teen girls that fight regularly usually have problems at home. If you are a teen girl that has gotten with the wrong crowd, talk to your parents or school counselors. Everyone makes mistakes or uses bad judgment, ask for help from someone. Being brave enough to change your behavior is what will set you apart from them.

6. Where Do Teens Get Guns?

The scary reality of this situation is that teens can purchase guns from almost anywhere; the streets, friends, or they can borrow or steal them. Many teens find guns at home that belong to parents or other family members. Gangs and individuals sell illegal guns to anyone that can afford them. Guns are removed from the streets every year just to reappear on another block. It's up to you to say NO. This is the main cause for so many useless murders, homicides and accidental killings. Don't be curious about guns; be smart, you already know what can happen.

7. Teen Suicide & Homicide

More than half of the teens who try and commit suicide use a gun they found at home that belonged to an adult in their house. Guns are the number one way teens commit suicide and almost every teen homicide/assault involves a gun. Individuals involved in gun violence are twice as likely to commit or be involved in gun violence later themselves. There is no "back button" on a gun. Once it's done, it's done and many times, innocent people are the victims or fatalities.

8. How to Eliminate Gun Violence

You can start by not carrying a gun. Remember guns in the hands of minors and teens are illegal. In most states, even adults need to be licensed to carry a gun. Schools will suspend and sometimes expel anyone caught with a real gun, pellet gun or even a look-a-like-weapon. Carrying a gun can increase the harm rate of the person carrying it because it escalates conflicts. Anyone that has a gun should be reported to teachers, adults and the police. Carrying these weapons can get you up to five years in jail. Anyone, including youth, carrying a gun can potentially harm or kill someone including themselves.

9. Boy Bullies

Bullies can be a group of adolescents or one individual that harasses, intimidates and assaults other kids. Bullies tend to have low self-esteem and project their insecurities on someone else. They are sometimes jealous of the person they are bullying and tend to use physical intimidation. They scare, pick fights, and take lunch money or other possessions of the person they are bullying. Sometimes bullies pick on others because of their appearance or because they are alone. Boys also bully sometimes because there is a stigma that they have to be tough and this is the only way they know how.

10. Girl Bullies

Bullies have low self-esteem and tend to project their insecurity onto someone else. They are sometimes jealous of the person they are bullying. Girls tend to bully in groups by isolating one another. They gossip and encourage other girls to do the same. Girls also fight or argue over boys and use jealous tactics to intimidate others. Girls can be vicious; they use mace and fight with weapons.

11. Stop That Bully!

If you want to stop being bullied here are several things you can do to prevent it:

- Report this activity to your teacher, parents or authority figure.
- Talk to an older brother or sister, sometimes they can talk to the bully because teens will listen to older siblings.
- Stay in groups because kids usually pick on kids that are alone.
- Stand up to them; don't let them know you're afraid. Depending on the situation, you may be able to reason with them.
- Worse case scenario, muster up the courage to protect yourself. You will be surprised how many bullies will back down.

12. Breaking the Cycle of Violence

Statistics and research says that exposure to gun violence makes teens twice as likely to be a perpetrator or commit a crime with a gun. It is possible that some of them are prompted to protect themselves after a crime has been committed against them. Teens that witness or experience violence are twice as likely to commit serious violence. This means if you are living with someone that is violent or has violent behavior, you may become immune or numb to bad behavior. To break the cycle, this may mean standing up to family, friends and peers who are doing wrong. Stay away from gangs, bullies, fighting, conflicts, arguments and guns. In the end it will make you feel better about yourself and you will be a better person.

MY JOURNAL ENTRY

List 5 things about ***gangs, gun violence and bullies,*** that you learned from this chapter. Discuss them with a parent, teacher, mentor or friends.

____

____

____

____

____

Notes:

Chapter Three: Money, Jobs and Entrepreneurship

CHECKING AND SAVINGS ACCOUNTS

The money always matters. It is a part of growing up, and learning to manage it will be one of the most important phases of your young adult life. Teens must become more financially literate so they will have money while they are in college and beyond. Your generation must be more financially savvy than the generations before you. Parents may start you off with weekly allowances, which may be your first experience with money. Then we start paying you for additional chores to teach you more responsibility, then the summer jobs come next, after-school jobs and soon the college savings plans. When you get this money you should have somewhere to put it instead of under the mattress or in your pocket. A checking or savings account is where most adults put their earnings. As a teen you are in constant contact with money, if you don't put it in the bank, you will spend it as quick as you get it. This is where the cliché' comes from "money burns a hole in your pocket." Now you must learn to budget, spend wisely and save. You must see money as your friend and not your enemy. You must learn to love having, keeping and saving money. It is a process that will come over time; it must be taught, learned and practiced.

Schools are now providing more financial literacy and financial awareness for pre-teens, teens and young adults. The time between eighth grade and college will fly by and you will start to witness first hand how hard it is to get and save money. You now have more responsibilities than you have money. You can get a job or start your own business, but remember the harder you work, the more you will get from the universe. The more you put in, the more you get out. This chapter does not cover it all, but it will introduce the basic workings of checking accounts, savings accounts and the cycle of money.

12 TIPS FOR TEENS ABOUT CHECKING & SAVINGS ACCOUNTS:

1. Open a Checking Account or Savings Account

Open an account as soon as possible. Ask your parents to help if you are not of age. It will be one of the mature responsible things you must do this year. It will prevent you from carrying money around with you and it will be easier to save your money. As we discussed earlier, you spend unnecessary cash when it's in your hands. Many teens are opening up their own business and will definitely need their own bank account, for this. Some banks will let you open accounts as young as 14. Whether we want to or not, we have to think about saving for college, its right around the corner.

2. Identification

You will need identification in order to open an account. By now you should have state identification or a driver's license. Depending on the state, it can be as inexpensive as $4 - $10 or more depending on the state. You must have two types of identification, so it never hurts to get both state identification and a driver's license. Keep your social security card, school I.D. or work identification cards handy in case you need them.

3. Choosing a bank

Choosing a bank can be easy or a challenge depending on your needs. If you are looking for a bank that is close to where you live or work, this will cut down on the number of banks you will have to choose from. One of the deciding factors may also be how much you need to open the account. Some banks will let you open an account for as little as $100 and others have specials for $50 and offer free services. Take advantage of these services and open up your account as soon as possible.

4. Get Your Own Banker

When you open a bank account, try to find a banker that will work directly with you on your account. When you have a problem you will have a live person that can help you sift through what may be going on with your account. Most banks have private bankers even for the little guy. Establish a rapport with someone at the bank that can help you on a regular basis. If you ever have problems this will be your go-to person.

5. Cash Station Cards / Visa Logo's / Debit Cards

When you open an account, you will get a cash station card so you may have access to your money 24 hours a day. Most banks expect you to use their designated bank for ATM and cash station withdrawals. If you use other banks expect to pay an additional fee for the cash station and your bank in some cases. Certain banks will also issue you debit cards with Visa logos that you can use for purchases. Make sure you check with your bank and know the difference between debit cards, Visa cards and their fees. Most banks do not charge for using the Visa logo (credit), and some have fees for using the debit cards. They each have benefits. It may take several days for these transactions to process, so make sure that you keep up with your balance.

6. Having Your Own Money

Having your own money is King or Queen. You will need your own accounts and your own money in a few short years. Many college students are struggling to survive and wish they had saved more money over the years. Now is the time to learn how to balance and operate accounts. Once you start seeing money in your account you will want to see more. Start making decisions on how you will operate your money now, before you go away to college. You will need money to travel, along with daily operational cash. As the interest on your account increases, you will have additional money growing on top of your deposits.

7. Direct Deposit

Having direct deposit will allow you to automatically have your checks deposited into your account. This saves you from running to the bank or a currency exchange every time you need to cash a check. You won't have to physically deposit your check; it will go directly into the bank by wire transfer. When you cash your check at the currency exchange they charge you fees, which may not seem like a lot initially, but over time it adds up. Most direct deposits are in your account at midnight before the day it's due. You will have access to your money immediately.

8. Fees

There are many type of fees associated with your accounts. The bank will charge you a fee if your account goes into the negative. Avoid a negative balance by not spending more money than you have in your account. Some accounts are restricted and only allow certain ATM machines to be used, and/or a certain amount of checks or transactions per month. Some accounts are charged daily fees when you are overdrawn and this can cause you to rack up a large negative cost in your account. You will want to be educated on the fee structure associated with your account so that you can keep up with which fees are being charged and why.

9. Checks / Check 21 Law

When writing checks your basic accounting techniques should be in order. Just basic addition and subtraction mostly, but the most important factor is remembering to record your transactions in your check register. Occasionally, some accounts may charge you a minimal fee for each check you write. Most new accounts offer *"free checking* and *no fee"* accounts. Having duplicate checks is helpful; this leaves a carbon copy in your checkbook of each check you write. This allows you to keep up with what checks you've written, just in case you forget to notate them when you wrote the checks. It will also prevent you from overdrawing your account (taking it into the negative). A common mistake is forgetting to record cash station and debit card purchases in your check register. ***Check 21*** is a law that was passed in 2004 that will allow banks to process your checks electronically. Local checks may be processed as quickly as 24 hours and non-local checks about three business days. With Check 21, you also may not receive your original cancelled checks.

10. Shared Accounts

Sometimes individuals share accounts with parents, siblings or another person. You must know who you are sharing an account with and what they are doing at all times. Both of you must communicate to each other when you have used the account or spent any money out of it. If two people share check books or cash station cards from the same account, one of you may forget to tell the other what you've spent. This will cause an overdraft in your account. This is a mistake that can be prevented.

11. Interest

Interest is earned on your savings accounts, CD's and money market accounts each month. To determine the amount of interest earned on your account, you must talk with your bank as it will vary. The more money and the longer you leave your money in the bank, the more interest it will gain. Interest is not a huge amount; however you are still getting more than you put in. You will have to leave the money in there for months before you will see a significant dollar increase.

12. Savings Options

Savings Bonds are an inexpensive way to save a little each month that will later mature into more money and their face value may possibly double. It depends on how long you save them before cashing them in. Check with your bank to see what increments of bonds they offer and how long they take to mature. If you are new to saving, you can buy them directly from your bank for as little as twenty five dollars. ***Money Market & CD's*** can be purchased from your bank or a financial planner. You may have to ask your parents unless you are one of those financially savvy teens that know how to go on the internet and trade the market, buying stocks and bonds. CD's are short term savings that you can get for three or six or more months, this way you can take out your money and the interest in a few months if you choose or roll it back over. The money markets are safe ways to save your money. You can research this on the Internet or speak to a financial planner to review your options. Saving money is easier if you have an account that you can't get into very easily. It could be a savings account without a cash station card attached to it. Do whatever you need to do to help yourself save your money or prevent you from miscellaneous spending.

MY JOURNAL ENTRY

List 5 new things that you learned about ***checking & savings*** accounts. Discuss them with a parent, teacher, mentor or friends.

BUDGET & SAVINGS

Making a budget each month may seem like something only adults have to do. I guarantee, you're not too young, and it's not too soon. Many of you are already budgeting on a small scale when your parents give you money at the beginning of the week. You are budgeting your money when you decide how much you have to spend and how much you have to save to make it through the week. Your carfare, transportation, lunch and miscellaneous purchases are all part of your weekly budget. We have included a budget outline you can use to start keeping track of how much money you are really spending. It will shock you, if you are honest. We all spend money we can't account for, we don't even realize it's gone until we're broke and we start remembering we bought candy, gum, CD's, magazines and miscellaneous stuff! Understanding the cycle of money is part of maturity.

12 TIPS FOR TEENS ON BUDGET & SAVINGS:

1. Make a List of All Income & Expenses
Income is your money you receive from paychecks or allowances. An expense is any money you spend for bills, transportation or personal needs. Use the budget outline on the next page to get started. This is very important to do to determine how much extra money, if any, you will have each month. Don't leave anything out, from food to gas and entertainment to clothes.

2. Set Spending and Saving Goals Each Month.
Track your habits and make sure they are on target. If you are spending more than you are making or *broke* right after payday, you must start to set goals to determine how much money you need each month and between paydays. Before you get your money, make a list of everything you have to pay. If you adapt to this system, and make sure you don't buy unnecessary items, you will start to see your money in a different light. Set aside the amount of money that you plan to save each month, and when you get paid, always pay yourself first.

3. Starting A Budget
When starting a budget, be honest about how much you really spend. Write down every pack of gum, bag of chips, gas purchase, carfare, extra milk or pop at lunch. This includes money you lend to your friends or family. Refrain from buying things that can wait such as items from street sellers or convenience stores that will destroy your budget. Be careful to watch out for misleading sales and unnecessary shopping sprees. Impulse purchases put big cramps in your budget, and the money is hard to recover at the end of the month. Other budget snags to watch out for include; spending your emergency money and lending money to others. The important factor is to start using a budget, it takes discipline and a little motivation.

4. Income
Your income is a salary, job paycheck, allowance or income taxes. When working on your budget, you must count all of your income. The two most important rules to remember when discussing income is *(1)* Always pay yourself first, this means take

STUDENT BUDGET

Monthly Income		Monthly Expenses	
Your Pay	$	Rent or Mortgage	$
Other Income	$	Utilities (Phone, gas, electric, cable, etc.)	$
Bonuses	$	Insurance (home, auto, life, health,etc.)	$
Commissions	$	Food (fast food, snacks)	$
Tips	$	Incidental Home (paper products, non-food items, etc.)	$
Interest Received	$	Clothing	$
Investment Earnings	$	Auto (gas, tolls, maintenance, car payment)	$
Tax Refund	$	Debt Payments (auto, credit cards, store cards, etc.)	$
Pension Income	$	Child Care	$
Social Security Income	$	Health (medical, dental, eye, etc./not covered by insurance)	$
Alimony Received	$	Taxes (not taken out of paycheck)	$
Child Support Received	$	Gifts (charities, church, holidays, birthdays, etc.)	$
Other Income	$	Entertainment (movies, vacation, videos, etc.)	$
	$	Personal Allowances	$
	$	Other Expenses	$
	$	Health care	$
	$	Cell Phone, Pagers	$
	$	Savings	$
	$	Misc.(gum, chips)	$
Totals	$	Loans	$

Add up all of your income (+), and then subtract your expenses (-). This is how much money you should have left over after your expenses. In order for this budget to be effective, you must be very honest about the amount of money you spend each month. ** Always save some money for a rainy day.

out your travel, savings, lunch money and anything you need to sustain yourself in between paychecks or allowances. This is money you must put away first, then pay your bills. *(2)* Save something, even it's just a few dollars. When you save money, it should be listed in your expense column (see budget). Your income is important to your budget regardless of how small or large it may be... pennies make dollars.

5. Expenses

Expenses are cell phone bills, gas, car payments, hair, fees, transportation and grooming. Let's explore some of your hidden expenses, spending habits and how to trim them down. When you put gasoline in your car – you'll run out of gas quicker by putting five dollars in at a time rather than filling the tank all the way or at least to half. Don't buy personal items at gas stations, because although you don't realize it, they have to charge more because they don't sell as much. If you go to discount stores, make a list and stick with it. If not, you will spend three times as much in the *dollar store* as you intended. This is just a few spending streams that will cause you to run out of money before your next payday.

6. Cell Phone Bill

A cell phone is a daily use item that is a very important part of your budget. Check your minutes and your plan regularly to make sure you are not running over on your anytime/daytime minutes. When you go over your plan, it is very costly to pay *per minute* on your cell phone bill; this is equivalent to a hold up for some companies. Know what is free on your plan and how many text messages you can send. Download only *free* services and ring tones. You should also notice that when your bill goes up, the taxes also go up and this makes the total bill even higher. This is especially important if you are sharing a plan with others, a mistake on your part can cost others to be without access to their phone. It's difficult to budget your cell phone bill if you are going over your plan.

7. Gas and Transportation

Gas and public transportation costs seem to be going up, which means your budget costs will be increasing each week. When it changes you must adjust your budget and add in additional money for unexpected situations. With the rising cost of gas, try to find the most cost effective way of filling your tank; it may even be wise to use public transportation sometimes. If you are driving friends around, make them pay their share. You are not driving to save them money; you are driving them to make their lives more comfortable and convenient. When buying a car, prepare for additional costs; plates, stickers, parking and auto insurance.

8. Loans

If you have borrowed money from anyone then they should be listed as part of your expenses. Loans are not just personal, this includes; car payments, cell phone bills, insurance or any type of credit that you've established. If it has interest attached to it, it's considered a loan. Loans have to be paid on time or the next bill will have an extra fee attached which will increase your payment. Any loan, credit or bills you have, must be paid on time. Also, regarding personal loans – don't take a loan if you can't afford to pay it back and don't make a loan to a friend unless you don't need the money. Loans to friends have ended many friendships because people never pay you back when you need it the most.

9. Other Expenses: Personal Care Items / Clothing / Food

Your personal care items and clothing must also go into your budget. If you purchase any deodorant, hair care, razors or personal items they are to be listed as part of your budget under *expenses*. Your parents will probably buy a lot of your clothes but you will also buy some on your own. Make sure you include them in your budget so that you can track your spending. Also, when planning your wardrobe, try not to buy a lot of the same item. You want your wardrobe to look like you've spent more money than you actually did. Although eating at home is not part of your budget because your wonderful parents pay for that, you should include the snacks you buy on the run. This also includes lunch money and fast food restaurants you visit throughout the week. *Eating out is very costly, and quickly adds up without you realizing it.*

10. Saving

Saving is a very important part of the money process. The money you save is also part of your expenses. You have to find out which way will work best for you. You can open up a *savings account, checking account* or buy *savings bonds*. If you start saving your money now, you'll have a nice little nest egg once you get to college. You will be in the habit of saving and you will also be able to see your money earn interest. Save for a rainy day or an emergency because you will need it. ***Savings Bonds*** are a safe inexpensive way to save a little money each month. Bonds will mature into more money as they grow over time and their face value may even double depending on how long you wait before cashing them in. Check with your bank to see what increments of bonds they offer and how long they take to mature. You can get savings bonds directly from your bank.

11. Money Market & CD's

You can purchase money markets or CD's from your bank or a financial planner. You may have to ask your parents, unless you are one of those financially savvy teens that know how to go on the Internet and trade the market and buy stocks and bonds. Some money market investments can be purchased for as little as twenty five dollars a month. CD's can be short term or long term savings that you can get for three months, six months or longer. With CD's you take out your money and the interest in a few months if you choose or roll it back over. Money markets are safe ways to save your money. We want teens to become more financially literate so they will have money while they are in college and beyond. You can research this on the internet or speak to a financial planner to review your options.

12. Entertainment

Entertainment costs are sneaky budget killers. If you add up all of the money you spend on entertainment each month you may be surprised. You buy CD's, magazines, DVD's, movie and concert tickets and even pay to go to parties. This also includes; radios, speakers, electronic toys and subscription services that you may purchase along the way. Manufacturers make each gadget flashier than the next, like cell phones and car stereos. Since we live in a gadget society we feel compelled to buy the "next best thing." Curb yourself if you are spending your last dime to get something similar to what you already have because odds are, you'll never be able to keep up with the new technology.

MY JOURNAL ENTRY

List 5 things you've learned about ***budget & savings*** that you didn't know before reading this chapter. Discuss them with a parent, teacher, mentor or friends.

COLLEGE SCHOLARSHIPS/FINANCIAL AID

As we start to think about going to college and we look at the annual cost to further our education, it's kind of scary and overwhelming. The annual cost of college, including tuition, books, room and board, has climbed from $10,000 per year to 20, 30 and over $40,000 for some private, major universities and out of state schools. You can get reduced tuition by attending in-state schools. After being accepted to a school, the first major challenge is weaving through the tangled web of college scholarships, grants and loans. This almost becomes a part-time job. You have to find the right college and then figure out how to pay for it. This chapter previews some of the basics to help you begin to weave through this tangled web. The appendix also has many college scholarships websites. *Before you get started*, find the college (s) of your choice. This is not as easy as it may seem. You may elect to go to the college where your parents or siblings went. Maybe you will get an opportunity to go to a college that has offered you an academic or athletic scholarship.

Many students have found this to be a tedious process. Some schools are on the job and hand hold you all the way. Some individuals and their parents do not have access to everything it takes to fly effortlessly through this college maze. I am currently in the maze and I have 7 pieces of advice. (1) Take practice tests for the ACT/SAT and go to pre-test classes as soon as possible. (2) Rule out important factors such as distance, location, cost and any other reasons you will exclude a college or university. (3) Attempt to decide on your field of study. (4) Work diligently on your scholarships, leaving no stone unturned. (5) Get your counselor involved, *but, if they are lagging, do it yourself. This is your life.* (6) Know which colleges will accept you academically or offer you a scholarship. (7) Make sure your GPA is average or above average each year. You don't want to wait until your senior year to relalize your GPA isn't high enough. This will limit your access to some colleges and scholarships.

12 TIPS FOR TEENS ON COLLEGE SCHOLARSHIPS AND FINANCIAL AID:

1. Types of Colleges

There are many different types of colleges, universities and schools to choose from.

Public Colleges have 4-year programs, are funded by public sources and can charge lower tuition than other colleges. When attending these colleges, you will usually come out with a Bachelors of Art or Sciences degree in a particular field. ***Private and Catholic Colleges*** usually cost more than public colleges, but offer the same program structure. They have a private financial aid structure and come with recommendations from high schools that connect with them. ***Community and Junior Colleges*** are local, usually offer 2-year programs and are less restrictive. The tuition and fees are inexpensive and some students use these colleges to build and increase their GPA while they decide on transferring to a larger or four year college. ***Online and Correspondence*** schools have become extremely popular due to the busy schedule of many students. This allows flexibility in case you need to work or you have other family or personal obligations. ***Trade, Technical and Vocational schools*** focus on a particular field of study such as; computer repair, electrical, mechanical, nursing, medical assistant, plumbing degrees or certificates.

2. Criteria for Financial Aid

In order to receive financial aid, you must be eligible and meet some of the following criteria; you must have a need, be a high school graduate or have a GED and be working toward a specific degree program. You should be a U.S. Citizen and have a valid social security number. You should also be a resident of the state if you are applying for in-state grants. There may be additional criteria set for other programs, you must contact the financial aid office at the school you are applying to.

3. Financial Aid Applications

To receive government financial aid, students must fill out the **FAFSA** (Federal Application for Student Aid) form. This form can be obtained from the school you are applying to or can be filed online at the U.S. Department of Education's *FAFSA Web site*. Students should complete the form even if they haven't yet been accepted at a university. The annual deadline is June 30, but the sooner the form is filed, the quicker students can apply for financial aid. *FinAid.org* is another good place to start. It covers the basics and includes a section about financial aid for students thinking about pursuing careers in the military, as well as veterans and their dependents. Applicants can also file via mail, but completing the form online makes future renewals easier. A new application must be filed each year you seek financial aid.

4. Types of Financial Aid

This is a partial list of scholarships and financial aid that is available. To get a more thorough list, you must check with national websites and the financial aid office at the school or institution you are attending.

The Merit Recognition Program is for students in the top 5% of their class. ***Pell Grants*** are government grants based on need and do not have to be repaid. ***Perkins Loans*** are made through the school and have to be repaid. ***Federal Grants*** include; Work Study Grants, In School Work Study and Monetary Award Program (MAP) grants. ***ITEACH*** are grants for individuals that plan to become teachers in areas where there are shortages. ***Disabled or Physically Challenged*** students are eligible to apply for grants from their state and the school they are applying to. ***Employment and Work-Study Programs*** are financial aid programs that require students to work on campus or in a community related organization that is linked to the school. There are local and Federal work-study programs. You will earn a wage while you are working, and this money is to help subsidize your tuition fees. You can apply for work-study programs in your financial aid office.

5. Grants, Scholarships & Savings Plans

Grants are monetary awards or gifts that do not have to be paid back. Above, we mentioned a partial list of grants that are available at colleges. The Internet is now a major resource for locating grants, loans and colleges scholarships. There are savings plans such as the popular 529 College Savings Plan and the Coverdell Education Savings Account which allows parents to make tax-deferred contributions and tax-free withdrawals for qualified educational expenses. There may be fees, additional expenses and investment risks. Your financial advisor can help you get this started. There are a few restrictions to both savings plans.

6. Loans
A college loan is money that you or your parents can obtain to help you pay for college. All loans have to be paid back. Some times loans will be necessary for assistance with college tuition. If you are attending a school with exorbitant costs you will probably need a combination of grants, loans and scholarships to pay for your college education. This will all be determined by your parent's income and the amount of financial aid they are eligible for. Your parents may have to take out a loan, or you may decide to apply for a student loan. Federal loans have different repayment criteria than personal loans.

7. Financial Aid Office / Financial Award Letter
You are probably wondering what to expect from your school's financial aid office. The financial aid office is located on your college campus. They accept applications, reports and match financial aid packages with student needs. As soon as you can, contact the financial aid office by email or phone to see what requirements you may need to have. The financial aid office has the responsibility of administering financial aid for their respective college. A financial aid award letter will inform you how much it will cost to attend the school of your choice and what financial aid is available. This letter will also include the amount of state and federal aid you may be eligible for. Your financial aid officer will explain in detail what your next step should be.

8. College Entrance Essays
Most colleges now require you to complete an essay to be accepted. There are tons of websites that can help you write your essay. They brag that their expertise may be the difference between acceptance and rejection. Select a good subject, have a beginning, middle and end. You are persuading the admissions department to let you enter their college. If an essay topic isn't provided, consider writing about a major event that had a specific impact on your life or an essay about political or social change. You may want to choose a historical or well known person and show how they impacted you or you may want to write about the college you are attending and why you chose that particular school. The essay should portray that you are a well

rounded young person, if you have done anything significant, it should be written in your essay. This helps the college get a feel for who you really are. If you need to, there are outside sources you can hire to assist you with writing your essay.

9. Getting Into College Is Easier If - You Know The College You Want To Go To

Some teens know from the day they enter high school what college they would like to attend. This makes everything easier and streamlined. You and your parents can start gathering information early, along with researching possible scholarships. This is not the majority, the rest of the high school population is juggling ACT/SAT scores, financial aid and trying to find a major and school that suits them. This does not guarantee that the financial aid process is easier, but it helps to plot the course of money needed. It also helps tremendously, because you aren't looking for financial sources and a college at the same time. Once you narrow down the school, region, field of study, the rest will eventually fall into place. Getting into college will also go a lot easier if you know someone, ***have a hook-up or know family or friends at the school you want to go to***. If you know a professor, student, coach or friend of the family at a college you want to go to, please ring them up. This is where nepotism (family already there) and hook-ups come in handy. Do not be afraid or to proud to call a family friend and ask for a letter of recommendation. Ask them for suggestions or assistance in applying to the school. If you are going to the college your parents went to, see if there's anyone they know. Do your homework, investigate and if you can, call in a favor or two. This is one time in life you really need it. If you know someone that knows someone use every friend, family member, associate or free coupon you can to get to the end result. Email me if you don't know what this means. Smile.

10. Getting Scholarships Are Easier If - You have ACADEMIC EXCELLENCE

Most schools have set aside academic scholarships and grants for students that possess high GPA's, ACT or SAT scores. They have scholarships specifically for kids with high academic standards that placed in the top percentile of their class. Search the schools you are interested in for academic scholarships as well as national scholarships. Research, research, research.

11. Getting Scholarships Are Easier If - You are an ATHLETE (Athletic Scholarships)

If you are an athlete and have been playing sports for your high school team, you may be eligible for an athletic scholarship. If you play more than one sport, your chances are even greater. Most coaches will suggest you contact them by letter with your picture, statistics a highlight tape and all other pertinent information. This letter should also include your major area of study and any references you have. If you know someone at the school or on the team, you can use this person as a reference. You can also have your coach call and put in a good word for you, or write a recommendation letter, this always helps. Take your competitive nature from the court and use it in the competition for scholarships.

12. Getting Into College Is Easier If - You Have Alternative Sources Of Income

Like anything else, you should have a plan "B" and "C." Hopefully, when you and your parents read this chapter you have already pre-planned your college savings or an alternative method of payment. *If you're like the majority*, you may have to consider a college loan combined with state and federal financial aid. However, students are urged to seek out small often overlooked scholarships offered by service clubs, religious associations, unions or their parents' employers. There are also many niche scholarships offered to minorities, women, children of single parents--you name it. Don't overlook field-specific scholarships because they exist in just about every subject: math, chemistry, American literature or art, for example. Most awards are small, but lining up several can amount to some real money.

MY JOURNAL ENTRY

List 5 things you have learned about ***scholarships & financial aid*** after reading this chapter. Discuss them with a parent, teacher, mentor or friends.

CREDIT CARDS & ESTABLISHING CREDIT

Credit is something you must have to function in this world. Not enough credit can be a problem when you begin buying material items such as; cell phones, cars or a home. The tricky part is not to over extend your self or good credit will turn bad very quickly. The number one comment most teens and young adults will say is, "I don't have any credit and no one will give me any." Take your credit very seriously from the beginning and it will happen over time. It is the key to your financial world. Depending on how you treat it – it can be the best or the worst thing that can ever happen to you.

12 TIPS FOR TEENS ON HOW TO OBTAIN AND MANAGE CREDIT:

1. Good Credit
Creditors are people who give you loans or extend credit. They are business owners and finance companies that use the information along with credit scores from the credit bureaus to determine if they are going to give you credit. Good credit is imperative in today's world. To establish good credit, you must pay your bills early or on time. When you pay late, they report your credit pay history to the credit bureau (independent organization that governs credit reports on consumers). Not every company will report to the credit bureau but most will, including utility companies. This is what is used by the next creditor to determine if they are going to give you a new line of credit.

2. No Credit/Bad Credit/Establishing Credit
No credit means you don't have any credit yet. This could be because you have never purchased anything on credit or no one has extended you credit yet. To *establish credit* (get credit) if you don't have any - you should buy something small that you have to make payments on such as; jewelry or an inexpensive car. You may want to get a small credit card or a store credit account. If you have *bad credit*, this means that you have not paid certain bills and they have reported you to the credit bureau. Late fees can build up when you consistently pay bills late. You must get a copy of your credit report from the credit bureaus listed below, and see which companies have reported you so that you may contact them and clear this up.

3. Three Major Credit Bureaus
There are three major organizations that govern the credit reporting industry; Experian (www.experian.com), Equifax (www.equifax.com) and Transunion (www.transunion.com). You can get a copy of your credit report online or by mailing a request to them. Credit scores are used to determine how much credit (loan) they are going to extend to you. If your credit score is low, it is because you haven't established any yet or your credit is not up to their standard. Once you obtain a copy of your credit report, you will know how you are being rated. You will find out when you buy your first cell phone or car if your credit is sufficient or not.

4. Credit Report/Credit Scores
Credit reports and credit scores come from the credit bureaus listed above. If your

credit score is low, it will go against you depending on what you're trying to buy. They may also ask you to put down a deposit. Applying for credit too many times for the same thing such as a car or cell phone, will get you negative points if too many companies check your credit. It will appear as though no one is approving you for credit. Only apply for things you really need or want. Don't give your information to just anyone. Your credit report has information such as your name, address, social security number, and the last job you listed on an application for credit. It also reports what bills you owe (mostly department stores, credit cards, car purchases and cell phones with contracts). It lists how much you owe and how you pay them - if you pay *on time, late or not at all.* Credit scores range from 400 to 800. Below 500 is considered questionable for major purchases, 600+ is ok and 700+ is considered excellent credit. The utility companies are now reporting to credit bureaus as well. This may not affect you now, but you will be going to college soon and starting to pay your own utilities if you live off campus.

5. Paying Cash

Paying with cash is good. It's been said that individuals that pay with cash are buying what they can afford. If you have a credit card, you should pay it off within 30 days so you don't get charged any interest and keep a good credit rating. If you start charging more on your credit cards and only pay off the minimum balance each month, your credit needs an overhaul and you are spending more than you can afford. It will take years to pay the credit off and many times you are just paying off the interest. Cash is always King!

6. Cell Phones

Most teens today have a cell phone; the lucky ones have parents that pay the bill. Everyone else will pay per minute or in advance - also called pre-paid phones. If you want a better rate plan, this requires a contract. In order to get a contract, the cell phone company usually requires a credit check, and they will run a credit report under your name and social security number. Good credit risks will be able to walk out with a "free phone" and a contract, bad credit risks will probably be asked to put down a deposit or they will ask you for a co-signer. See Co-Signer below in #8.

7. Buying a Car

Buying a car on credit is the same principle as a cell phone, but on a much larger scale. If you pay cash for a car, it is not reported to the credit bureau. If you go into a car lot they will check your credit and determine how much you are approved for. This is also when they will look at your credit score and your credit history. Once you get a car, you should make your payments on time; this is a major purchase and will help to boost your credit rating. If your payments are going to be late, just call your car company and tell them when you can pay. Have open communication with them and don't abuse or misuse them, they will work with you. However, if you don't pay your car payment or "car note" as it's called, they will "repossess" it (take your car back). This will also severely ruin your credit. Not to mention, you will be inconvenienced and it will cost a small fortune in fees to retrieve your car back.

8. Co-Signers

When you apply for credit there will be certain occasions when the creditor asks for a co-signer, (someone who has better established credit than you) that will sign under your name in order for you to get certain items such as cars or cell phones. The person that co-signs for you is agreeing in writing to pay your account if you do not pay. For example; if someone co-signs for a car for you and you don't pay, they will go after your co-signer to pay the bill. If they don't pay willingly, it can be deducted from your check, or your co-signer's check. Be careful who you sign for or who you ask to sign for you.

9. Credit Cards

Credit cards are easier to get than they are to pay. Once you get your first one, make sure you make every payment on time or pay it off completely each month. This will eliminate finance charges and keep your monthly bill low so your credit rating will remain good. You must pay off your account before the thirty day billing period. Credit cards are very difficult to payoff once they are charged to the limit. This is a mistake that most adults and new credit card holders always make. Never charge to the limit or go over your limit, the additional fees will increase your payment and reflect negatively on your credit. Once late fees are added to your account, it can sometimes double your payments, so make sure you read the small print.

10. How to Pay-Off Past Due Accounts

If you have an account that is past due, you can always call the creditor directly and strike up a deal that will work with both you and them. This is called a *settlement offer*. They may give you a pay-off amount (an amount to pay in full) or they may make payment arrangements with you. The key is to get a letter or receipt showing that particular account is paid in full and save it for future reference. Please remember, everything must be in writing or it didn't happen.

11. Bankruptcy/Judgments

At a young age, you shouldn't have enough bad credit to file for bankruptcy, however you may have an unpaid bill that turns into a judgment. This is where the creditor decides to write off the bill you owe. You don't get away scott-free because they will report it to the credit bureau and a *Charge Off/Judgment* will lower your credit score significantly. If you have a judgment on your credit report, make an effort to make arrangements to pay it off and clear it up.

12. Identity Theft

Identity theft is the new growing crime. This is a federal crime and individuals will go to jail if they are caught. This is where people steal your identity and use your credit. This wouldn't be so bad if they made it better, but that is usually not the case. They may use your social security number which they have gotten from a misplaced document or the Internet. You would be surprised how many websites have your personal information. When you purchase something, make sure that you use a secure site.

When you try to purchase something and they say you have negative items on your credit report, this usually means someone else has used your credit. You must order a copy of your credit report and write to the company that has reported you negatively and explain what has happened. With identity theft being so prevalent (well known) in this society, they will help you if you can prove that it wasn't you. You should also fill out a police report to show them that you did not have anything to do with these charges. You will be instructed how to clear your name and your credit from the credit bureau.

MY JOURNAL ENTRY

List 5 things you learned about ***credit cards and establishing credit***. Discuss them with a parent, teacher, mentor or friends.

JOB READINESS

Job readiness is an important skill to help prepare teens and young adults weave through the job finding process. Preparing a resume is a crucial part of becoming employed. If you have never written a resumé, please review our appendix for an example. This chapter will give you tips on finding your first job or your next job. You will get a quick overview of everything you need to know so that you will be prepared before your next job interview. We want you to be ready for it all!

12 TIPS FOR TEENS ABOUT JOB READINESS:

1. Job Preparation, Resumes, Research

Be prepared when you start looking for a job. Know what type of job you want, be ready to answer questions about yourself and your work history.

- Have copies of your ***resumé*** with you at all times. As you start applying for jobs, some potential employers will ask you for a resume'. If you haven't written one or know where to begin, you can get a parent or friend to help. There are also software templates that can get you started. As you get more experience under your belt, you can hire a professional to type it. Remember, everything you have done is part of your experience; working at school, volunteer work and summer jobs. Do not leave anything out, regardless of how small it seems. Resumes should be kept to one page if possible.

- ***Research*** the company you are interviewing with. You can do this on the Internet, at the library or by calling them and asking for a brochure or pamphlet. Do not hesitate to talk to the receptionist and ask a few questions about the company. If you find their website, print out the company information and take it with you to the interview. This will help you appear to be familiar with the company if the interviewer asks. This has been known to impress hiring officials because you showed initiative and took an interest in their company.

2. Thank You letters

Whenever you complete an interview, you should always send a thank you letter in a timely manner. It is classy and professional. Once you have completed your interview ask for a business card to make sure you spell the name and title correctly. You can send this via email or by long hand through the mail (which is recommended). This shows your appreciation for their time and regardless of whether you get the job or not, they will have a favorable impression of you. They may decide to call you when the job becomes available - just because you followed up and you were professional.

3. Job Hunting

Job hunting can be done in person, door to door, online, through friends and family or the newspapers. Network, network, network - make sure you let all of your family and friends know that you are looking. Finding a job is hard work, especially if you want to find a good one. It takes tenacity (non stop) and diligence.

4. Interviewing

You can prepare for your interview by first researching the company. Finding out what type of company it is and their mission is a good start. Fill out all applications in as much detail as possible. Be prepared to answer questions about yourself, your skills, school, experience and previous work history. If someone else typed up your resume, make sure you review it in case you are asked a question from it. You don't want to get caught off guard in case your resume' writer added in a few things. Do not chew gum or eat food while interviewing. Always dress accordingly, speak professionally and make eye contact with your interviewer. If you are shy or this is your first interview, you may want to go through a dry run (practice) with family or friends.

5. Grooming

The way you're dressed can make or break you. The first impression can be your last or the only impression you get to make. Your dress code should be business casual. This consists of a shirt with a tie or blouse and slacks or a nice skirt. A suit is always a plus and guarantees a second look. Your grooming should be impeccable (very neat and above inspection). This means hair should be styled neat, nails trimmed and clean, clothes ironed and appropriate. If you have on make-up, perfume, cologne, aftershave or jewelry it should not be loud, gaudy or overdone. If you don't have a lot of interview clothes and all you have is your Sunday's best, pretend it's Sunday.

6. Employment Counseling / Online Resources

There are tons of online websites and resources to help you to get a job. Online resources and newspapers are updated regularly and provide locations where you can post your resume'. This will get dozens of employers exposure to your skills. There are many local agencies such as the YMCA, Urban League and hundreds of non-profit agencies that provide resources and job information. They provide employment counseling services that will allow you to find leads, look at their computer lists and they sometimes have internships and training. In some areas, local community organizations receive grants to run employment programs that provide interview clothing and paid training programs.

7. Job Fairs

Most cities host job fairs that are sponsored by organizations, churches and major corporations. City and state organizations also sponsor job fairs. These fairs have numerous companies that are ready to hire, but, you must be patient because sometimes the person at the table is not the hiring authority. This person usually collects the resumés for human resources. Individuals have gotten hired on the spot at job fairs so be prepared for anything. Always look your best, don't be discouraged, take plenty of résumés and network. The company you have your eyes on may not be the best one for you so keep your options open.

8. Trades and Certificate Programs

There are many opportunities available today in trade and vocational careers. A traditional four year education is not for everyone. Many electricians, truck drivers, mechanics, cosmetologists, barbers and computer technicians go directly into trade schools. The programs are shorter and they specialize in one particular type of career. Some of these schools have job placement and internships. These are also very lucrative career choices that pay very well.

9. Unemployment Office

Employees who lose their job are often eligible to collect unemployment insurance so they still receive some type of pay. There are a few exceptions to this rule such as; going to school or summer jobs. To apply, you must check with the local unemployment office in your community. Most unemployment offices also have employment divisions where they assist you in finding a job. These are free state facilities and you can go there even if you are not applying for benefits. They have computers and resources that you may not have at home to help you find a job.

10. Temporary Employment Agencies

Temporary employment agencies are city and state wide. They are excellent places to work between jobs. When you go to apply you should take a resume' with you. You can apply online, but most temporary agencies prefer that you call for an in-person interview. The good news is that many times the temporary job may turn into a permanent job if the employer likes your work. This is an excellent way to keep the money coming in and gain work experience from different companies.

11. Volunteering

I know you are like "I don't think so," who wants to work for free? Well, *"you do!"* This experience will give you something to put on your resume. Volunteering can include working with schools, teachers, families, churches or community organizations. You should volunteer as much as you can to gain experience in different fields. It will help you be more rounded and learn a craft or skill while giving back to your community. And... you may meet someone that will hire you.

12. Minimum Wage, Overtime/Time and a Half

You can't be paid less than the national minimum wage. When you work over your regular time for a week, which in most cases is either 35 or 40 hours, you may be eligible for overtime. This depends on your job structure. When you work over these hours you usually will get paid what is called time and a half. For example; if you normally make $10 dollars an hour, your time and half pay is $15 per hour. This is your regular pay plus an additional half of your regular pay added together. When you get a job make sure you ask what your pay structure is, when you get paid and if you get paid overtime. * In the past couple of years, many laws have changed regarding wages and pay, please read your company policy and ask questions to be sur

MY JOURNAL ENTRY

List 5 things about ***job readiness*** that you learned after reading this chapter. Discuss them with a parent, teacher, mentor or friends.

KEEPING A JOB

It's been said that it's easier to get a job than to keep one. What this means is once you get your dream job, or any job for that matter, you have to find a way to keep it. There are several reasons why people lose their job. We will cover those reasons and what you can do to keep your job once you have it. With the job market as unpredictable as it is, anything is possible in this shifting job market. After reading this chapter, you will know just what you should do to be the model employee and successful with your job.

12 TIPS FOR TEENS TO KNOW ABOUT KEEPING YOUR JOB:

1. Be on Time and Be Professional
You should always try and be on time, for any job that you have. *If you're early - you're on time and if you're on time - you're late.* It is important to be on time because it shows loyalty, responsibility and dedication. Of course emergencies will come up, and that is expected. Most employers will be lenient and understanding when personal or family situations come up - if you have been a good employee and you communicate honestly with them. *Professionalism is a must in the work place.* It doesn't matter if you are working in a burger joint, delivering pizzas or an administrative assistant. You must be conscientious and careful about what you do. You can only be responsible for Y.O.U. Your professionalism will stand out and you will be noticed. This means regardless of how bad the customer treats you or your co-workers, you must maintain your professionalism. Always be nice, courteous and turn the other cheek when others are acting out. When other positions or promotions become available they will consider you.

2. Promotions
Be realistic with your current job. Make sure you know what's going on at your place of employment. Know your job description and do the very best job you can do. If you want to advance or move up in your organization, make sure you know what the procedures are. There may be specific steps that you have to take in order to advance or apply for other positions at your job. Each company has procedures that you must follow in order to advance within the company. The move may be at a higher position and salary, or it may be lateral (different job, same pay grade). You may have to be an employee for a certain amount of time, or work in certain fields before you can advance. If you want to move up the corporate ladder, know how to climb it in advance.

3. Finding the Perfect Job
Finding the perfect job can be a challenge, but is definitely worth the effort and research. You can research job titles and descriptions via the internet and books on various occupations. There is a book in the library entitled "Occupational Titles" that lists almost every job

description there is. You will also find the descriptions for thousands of other jobs while you are job hunting. Many of the popular websites explain the job descriptions of the positions that they currently have available. You may not find the perfect job, but you can find a job that suits your personality. If you don't like cleaning grills and manual labor, you may not want to work in a hamburger place. This is the same for people that don't like filing and paperwork - they should not apply for office jobs. However, you may need the *"right now I need to pay the bills job"* until you find your dream job. Once you familiarize yourself with job titles, you will know what kind of job you will like or one that you will be good at doing.

4. Exploring Opportunities After High School

If a position becomes available in your company that will get you a raise or move you to a more prestigious job you should take it. For teens, this may mean first moving up to shift leader or supervisor. Weigh the options first of course, but use all of your opportunities to progress. You may want to stay with this company after high school. Many companies have been know to hire teens part-time and kept them as full-time employees into adulthood. Some companies will pay for your college education. If you are at a good company, you may want to talk to your Human Resource Department and see what benefits are available to you. Explore every opportunity for advancement that your company has to offer. You may want to stay longer than you think.

5. Who is The Boss? - Chain of Command

Whether you are in the military or at an everyday job, there is usually a chain of command that you must report through. You have a supervisor or shift leader who reports to his/her manager and they also have a boss to report to. It may be the owner or president of a company. Make a point to know who you report to daily, who is responsible for writing your reviews and who to call for complaints. You don't want to go over your direct supervisor and they find out later. This may reflect badly on you and you could end up with a blemish on your record.

6. Know the Policies

It is up to you to know your company's policies and procedures; some distribute handbooks for you to reference, others may give you verbal instructions. Questions you should ask when you get hired include; procedures for calling off or calling in late, when you should turn in time sheets, when you get paid and how to calculate your vacation or sick days. There is usually an H.R. (Human Resource) Department or Office Manager that handles these types of issues. Some companies have strict policies on calling in, sick time, using leave and/or vacations. Call-in procedures range between companies; some companies allow you to call in and leave a voice mail, punch codes into a computerized phone system, some require talking only with your supervisor or email your request in. When you start with a company, make it a point to know the policies and procedures in order to get a raise or promotion. You will want to know how you are evaluated and how your reviews and performance ratings will be conducted. Each company has their own system they use for ratings and summary reviews. The more you know about how the system works the better you can perform and follow your progress.

7. Quitting Your Job

The first rule of thumb is to never leave your job before getting a new one. There is an old saying that says "it's easier to find a job while you have one." This means that while you have a job, you usually don't have the same pressure as when you are unemployed. It appears to be an easier process, and you don't have to take the first thing that comes along. When you decide to quit your job, make sure it works for you. I have known individuals that quit because someone else encouraged them to do so and then realized they should have waited. Evaluate why you're quitting and prepare yourself by saving money – especially if you have bills or responsibilities.

8. Show Initiative at Your Job

Translation: don't wait to be told to do something if you see it needs to be done, go above and beyond your job description. If you see filing, garbage or general tasks that need to be done, your boss will notice that you took the initiative to complete them. When filing, you may want to ask first in case there are sensitive files or a particular system. When employers use the term "This employee needs little supervision," it means you can do what needs to be done without being told. ***5 Rules to Work By***: *(1)* Always be on time, *(2)* Cooperate with everyone at your job, *(3)* Work hard and diligent, *(4)* Adhere to company policies and *(5)* Stay out of office politics (gossip and stuff). Seems simple, but it's very easy to get caught up. When you start a job, do what's right, talk with your supervisors regularly and check on your progress. Mind your own business, try to get along with your co-workers – remember you are being paid to do a job.

9. Resignation or Leave of Absence

Resignation means you are officially quitting your job. The proper way to resign from a job is to give them a written two week notice. The reason is so that your company has time to find someone to replace you. If you are leaving because of something out of your control; maternity, moving, military or school let your job know. Many times they will leave your name in their files and you will remain in good standing with their company. If you know that you are going to be gone for a specific amount of time, you can request a leave of absence and be able to return.

10. Dress Codes

If your company has a dress code, please adhere (follow) to it. You can be fired / terminated for wearing the improper dress code. Ask questions if you are not sure if you can wear a certain item. Know the difference between casual and business casual. Casual usually refers to jeans or slacks and a shirt or t-shirt if it's very nice. Business casual consists of collared shirts/blouse, slacks/skirt or dress. Business dress is a suit, with or without tie, shirt with tie/slacks, business uniform, pants suit, skirt suit, skirt/blouse or dress. Certain jobs will allow khakis as business casual clothing.

11. Drugs & Alcohol in the Workplace

Drugs and alcohol are totally unacceptable in the workplace. Many companies have specific drug policies in place. If you are using drugs and you know your company prohibits this behavior, you are putting yourself, your family and other employees at risk. If you have a problem, try to address it by entering rehabilitation or talking to someone you can trust. Don't try to get away with cheating on drug tests or working the system. If you have a problem get help, some companies offer assistance and will pay for rehabilitative programs.

12. Complaints

Every company has a procedure for making formal complaints. Complaints range from sexual harassment, verbal harassment to personal complaints against an employee or supervisor. Find out what the proper procedures are and follow them to the letter. This will help you if your complaint needs further attention at a later time. Telling a fellow employee may be good for emotional support, but if you expect proper actions, you must follow the formal company procedures.

MY JOURNAL ENTRY

List 5 things you learned about ***keeping a job***. Discuss them with a parent, teacher, mentor or friends.

___

___

___

___

___

___

___

___

___

___

___

ENTREPRENEURSHIP 101 = THE BASICs

This chapter is for students and young adults that have an interest in starting their own business. Youth entrepreneurship programs can be found almost everywhere from schools and community organizations, to churches and libraries. The job shortage in corporate America and with private companies have led to an increased number of young entrepreneurs in recent years. By starting your own business, you can make hundreds, even thousands of dollars each year. This chapter will walk you through the basic steps of starting a small business. Get your idea, think about how you can make money doing it, create a Mini Business Plan and then get down to business. There are business competitions around the world granting hundreds of dollars to youth entrepreneurs. Teenage business owners are publishing magazines, trading stocks and some are millionaires.

12 TIPS FOR BEGINNING TEEN ENTREPRENEURS:

1. The Idea

Finding an idea is the first step to starting a business. This idea can be a hobby or something you think will be a money maker. You can research similar companies by using the internet or surveying others to see if it's a viable (able to happen) business idea. Just remember, if you do something you love or enjoy you can have fun while the money slowly trickles in. Not all ideas grow money trees, it takes time. If you aren't sure of a business idea yet, you can view our Advanced Entrepreneurship chapter or go the library or bookstore for additional business ideas. Look for books on small business, entrepreneurship or home based business.

2. Your Fan Club / Support System

Your fan club is your support system. Don't be misled. We automatically want this to be our family and close friends. Guess what? In most cases they are not the first to see your vision. You will have to enlist the help of people with minds like yours. This may be other entrepreneurs, teachers, mentors, friends or anyone passionate about your vision. Just remember, it's your vision and they may not see it through your eyes. If you are lucky enough to get your friends or family to work with you, that's wonderful, but don't expect it. Stay focused, determined and on your path. Take the rest as it comes, others will eventually see your bright light.

3. Make Your Business Plan

To start your small business the correct way, you must create your *"Business Plan."* The business plan is the glue that binds your business idea together and turns your dream into a reality on paper. The business plan doesn't have to be intense but it does take time and some thinking of how you "plan" to run your business. You will have to think about; operations, marketing, financial projections, sales and legal structure. This will be your road map to running your business. Once you put it in writing it will be real to you. You will be able to refer to your business plan and make changes to it as often as you like. You can find business plan templates on your computer, in business books, at schools and on the internet.

4. Marketing & Advertising

Marketing and advertising is how you let the world know about your business. They can't buy from you if they don't know who you are. Advertising is where you buy space in print, television, yellow pages or radio mediums and you have an expected degree of return. You want prospective customers to know about your business or service. Marketing is passing out business cards/flyers or creating a website with your company information. Marketing is using different mediums to introduce yourself to the world to let them know that you are in business. If Nike rents a bill board with their new shoe, they are advertising this shoe and hope to drive sales with this ad. If they rent the same billboard with the Nike logo (swoosh symbol), this is an example of marketing, they just want you to think about them, keep Nike at the forefront on your mind, so that when you do buy a sports shoe, you will think about buying a Nike shoe first. In order for your marketing to be effective, you must construct a marketing plan. You will also have to do market research once you decide what business you are going to start. Your research will help you decide if your business idea will sell to others. You can perform market research using surveys, phone research, computer searches and direct comparisons with simular businesses.

5. Sales & Getting the Money

The sale is one of the most important parts of your business. Without the exchange of the dollar between people the sales don't happen. Once you decide which business you are going to be in, how you will market and advertise it, then the next step is how you will make sales. It may take a little practice, but everyone can learn to sell. It's a necessary part of the business process; advertising & marketing gets the customers, the customers are your sales, the sales bring in the money. *Getting the Money*: Now it's time to take your show on the road and reach out to the public – step out of your comfort zone! Many people start businesses and don't make any money. This may mean that the business is still a hobby. In order to make money with your business, you will have to have at least some of the above components in place. You will have to have a clear business idea, know your market and who you want to sell your product or service to. You will also need to know how to make a profit with your business. A profit is the money left over after your initial investment and expenses have been covered. If you are not sure, ask your mentor, teacher or a business professional for some assistance.

6. Resources & Getting Help

Resources for your business are plentiful, once you know where to find them. You can use your teachers, mentors or go out on your own by contacting some of the local entrepreneurship organizations. You can find entrepreneur support organizations (ESO's) at community colleges, universities, community organizations and churches. This is where the Internet and local libraries are helpful. You can also buy books from bookstores on entrepreneurship and small business start ups for youth. Visit our web directory in this book for additional resources.

7. Logos, Letterhead, Business Cards

Your company logo, letterhead, business cards and flyers are all part of your business' marketing. This is your identity and how you will be recognized. When you see certain companies, you automatically know who they are without seeing the name. As a new small business, you can create your own logo by using clip art and design it right from your computer. You can also draw it yourself or find someone that specializes in creating logos. When you start making money, you can hire an artist for a custom design. Business cards are given out to potential business contacts. All of your correspondence must include your letterhead with your special logo. This is all part of your new business identity.

8. Officers and Employees

Officers and employees are all part of your business plan and your business. For most youth and small businesses you will be a sole proprietor. This means you will be wearing all of the hats. You will be the President, Vice President, financial person, marketing person and sales person. You may assign individuals to these positions as your business grows. Ask your mom or dad to be Vice President if you need to, that will be a switch. Smile.

9. Time Management

To be a good business person, you will have to manage your time efficiently. Balancing between work, school, business and family takes planning. This includes any social life you may have and sports or extracurricular activities. Time management is hard for adults; this means it's twice as difficult for teens. Young adult business owners may have to learn how to juggle it all, but you CAN do it. Your challenge will be trying to enjoy time with your friends, and learning to prioritize your responsibilities.

10. Legal

There are several legal entities for your small business. Most small businesses choose *Sole Proprietorships* (you own your business alone) or *Partnerships* (you are in business with a partner). You can have one partner or several partners. The more people you are in partnership with, the more people you have to ask permission from or agree with. When this happens, you must get their permission to make any decisions regarding the business. You must share the profits equally, unless you may have made other arrangements based on the amount of money invested by each partner. You can read up on each one of these types of legal structures, or others not listed here and decide which one will best suit your business and make a decision from there. An attorney can also help you set up the legal structure for your business.

11. Business Licensing & Fees

In order to operate your business, you will need a business license, which you can obtain from your Business Revenue Department. The cost will vary across cities and states. Your business license will validate your business and make it legal. Check with your city small business or revenue department to find out what licenses are needed and what the cost is. They will instruct you on which procedures you should follow to make your business legal.

12. Financials

The financials are the nucleus of your business. You don't have to be a math genius, but you do need to understand basic math because it is important to your business. It's kind of scary at first especially if you're not good with numbers. Someone has to do it and you may be able to purchase a computer program that has a template where you can just insert the numbers.

Business financials include; sales projections, income statements and expenses. Initially, you will have to start small and this is when you should practice on your financial skills. By the time you're making the big bucks you'll have this down to a science. ***Financing Your Business***; Financing is a very important part of your business. You will need to get start-up money to run your business. It may not be as costly as you think. There are several options such as financial gifts from family and friends, self financing, fundraising, investors and loans. If you belong to local entrepreneur programs at school or church, they will help you find resources or funding for your business. Due to the national widespread interest in youth entrepreneurship, there are now more programs than ever to help youth with financing solutions – you just have to find them. ***Operating Costs and Pricing***; You will need operating funds to run your business and you will need to determine how much to charge for your product or service. This is sometimes hard to compute for new businesses. First you must decide if your business is a service or product. A product is a material item that is made or bought and you can sell it; clothes, jewelry, hats, music, instruments, food or other items. A service business is when you provide your skills and charge for them such as; tutoring, fixing items, consulting, singing or speaking. When you have a service business you have to price your time, when you have a product you have to figure how much you purchased the item for and how much you will need to sell it for to turn a profit. Products are usually easier because someone has already done what you are doing and you can use it as a guide. Service businesses are a little more difficult to price. When deciding how much to charge, other factors must be taken into consideration. The cost to operate your business and your wage (paying yourself) will be determined after all of your finances are in place. This is just the beginning. Remember, as a business owner you may not get paid at first, sometimes we get paid last.

MY JOURNAL ENTRY

List 5 things you learned about ***entrepreneurship*** from reading this chapter. Discuss them with a parent, teacher, mentor or friends.

____

____

____

____

____

____

START UP BUSINESS IDEAS

This chapter introduces a partial list of ideas for small start-up businesses. These businesses require little start up costs and can be done with a partner if necessary. Most of these business ideas can be started for under one hundred dollars, money you can get from savings or family loans. There are hundreds of teen business ideas that can be started with a small amount of start-up cash. It takes a little creativity, confidence and nerve to step out and do it. You can also turn a present hobby you have into a business idea. After looking at some of these ideas, you will probably have some of your own. Let's get started.

12 TIPS FOR TEEN START UP BUSINESSES:

1. Babysitting and Pet Sitting

This is a great job for teenagers just starting a small business. There are no up front expenses and you can market through word of mouth or flyers. Benefits include being able to work the business on your own time schedule. A liability includes the fact that you are working at someone else's house. You must also know your limitations. Make sure you can handle any situation in case the kids or pets are disagreeable. If your parents don't mind, you may be able to do this at your own house. You must be trustworthy and dependable. *This business has low start up costs, and your initial marketing consists of friends, family and word of mouth.*

2. Typesetting Services & Tutoring

Typing services are great to market to high school/college students, churches and small business owners. Everyone needs something typed at one time or another. It may be that they don't have time, or maybe their computer went on the blink. All you need to get started is a computer and a printer. The marketing is easier than you think it can be done via word of mouth, flyers and business cards. This can be a lucrative business with college students and small home based businesses. Tutoring is a great small business with hardly any expenses. This is a specialized target market that is easy to pinpoint and identify. Once you decide which level of students you are going to work with, half of your work is already done. You can also connect with a school and work directly with the kids in the school. If you are good, teachers will recommend you to their students. *This business has a low start up cost, and your marketing will spread quickly through word of mouth.*

3. Party and Event Planning

Special parties and events are gaining more popularity which means there are more and more event planners needed. Some event planners are combining party planning with clowning and magic for kids. They are making big money planning small events. Graduation parties are also very popular. If you like events, people and can pay attention to detail, this may be a good business choice for you. This business is not slow-ing down. You can plan birthday parties, graduation parties, meetings, private events or luncheons. The list and the opportunities are endless. *This business has a low start up cost, and your marketing will spread quickly through word of mouth. You will need to be upbeat, work well with people and must be willing to travel.*

4. Hair, Cosmetology and Barber

Hair well, enough said! People spare no expense when it comes to personal grooming. That is why it shouldn't be any different when it's your business. Many teens are doing hair and making the big bucks. Every week teens are in the beauty/barber shop paying to be more beautiful or handsome, whether it can be afforded or not. There are many opportunities to study cosmetology and receive a license to practice. *This business has a low to moderate start up cost, depending on what you are doing with hair and where you start. Barbers will have to purchase clippers and products must be purchased to wash and condition hair. If you are braiding hair some inventory will have to be purchased in advance. Your marketing can be done with business cards, flyers and by word of mouth.*

5. Sports Camps, & Coaching

Every church or community organization has a need for additional sports programs. You can also get paid for coaching or assistant coaching in these programs. If you are experienced you can develop your own camp or program. Spend time around others in the same business, it will make it easier. You may have to enlist the help of an adult or mentor to help put the final pieces in place. *This business has a low start up cost, and your marketing will spread quickly through word of mouth. You will need to be upbeat, work well with people and must be willing to travel.*

6. Entertainment/Music Promotion

There's so much to say about the number of teens performing, producing and writing music. More than ever, teens are making money in the entertainment and electronic game business. If this is your passion, you can make this happen by just talking to someone already in the business. The music business is risky and eats its own young. Translation: Before you get into it, find a professional mentor to point you in the right direction. This business is like professional sports, the odds are stacked up high, however you can climb the ladder, just be realistic about how long it may take to get to the top and do not be scared to ask for help. *This business has varied start up costs depending on what area you decide to go into. If you are a writer, then start up costs are low. If you are going into management, you may need some musical equipment, if you are a recording artist or producer you may need a studio or money to pay for studio time. Your marketing can be industry word of mouth and traditional marketing techniques.*

7. Movers

You can have your own moving business and work it several ways. If you are of age, you can get the truck, pack and move your clients. You will need insurance if you provide the truck. Age requirements and deposits required for trucks may make it a little difficult to rent a truck. Another way to be successful with this business is to provide the labor only and have your customer provide their own transportation. You can meet them at the location, pack their belongings and then unpack them at their final destination. Get as creative as you need to be, just make the money. Everyone will move at least twice in their lifetime. Some people move many more times. *Your marketing can be done with flyers, business cards, word of mouth, television and yellow page advertising. Once you are of age, you may be able to purchase your own truck. Keep in mind, that if you move possessions you may be liable for items that are broken or damaged etc. You can have them sign release forms, and you will need liability insurance.*

8. Cakes, Cookies & Desserts

If you bake sweets, you can make big bucks selling cookies, cakes or any kind of desserts. Teens are also making diabetic products and selling to grocery stores and food chains. You can sell your goods at bake sales, school events or to individuals calling in orders for private parties or events. To save money you can work at home which helps decrease your expenses. Each state has its own requirements for serving and packaging food. Please double check with your local small business department or contact your local health department for regulations. Please check with the Food & Drug Administration (FDA) when producing and selling food to the public. *You will need to buy ingredients when making and selling food items. You will need somewhere to prepare your food. To market this item you will have to get creative. You can sell some to class mates, friends and family. Then you will have to start going to events and shows.*

9. Gift Baskets

Gift baskets can be made from scratch by purchasing the items from wholesale stores. Gift baskets are a great holiday seller. People buy gift baskets for birthdays, major holidays and special events. Some people have lucrative small businesses by designing specialized gift baskets. The more unique, the better. *Gift baskets can be purchased pre-made or you can purchase all of the individual items and customize them to fit a specific holiday or event.*

10. Clothes Design, Fashion & Jewelry

Being creative is a must when working in clothes design and fashion. If you like working with clothes and you love to be creative; this just might be the business for you. Teen businesses have ranged from decorating t-shirts and jeans to designing clothes and shoes. Teens are also airbrushing shirts, pants and gym shoes. *Jewelry* is also a very popular as a business venture. You can buy your jewelry wholesale or make your own jewelry. Handmade jewelry is a great seller and people love personalized products. Whether you buy or design jewelry this is a great business idea. You will need some start up cash to purchase your initial items. There are several places you can set up booths or you can take custom orders. Jewelry is great to sell as an accessory to clothing. These businesses compliment each other. *This business has moderate start up costs; it depends on how much inventory you want to carry. With fashion design you can take specific orders and ask for a deposit up front. Your marketing can also consist of people walking and displaying your work. When selling jewelry, you may have to keep some inventory or equipment.*

11. Silk Screening

Silk screening is also a great business. It can be very competitive so you must be very attentive to your customers needs. This business has very loyal customers if you take care of them. You can get big orders from sports teams, family reunions, and youth groups. You will need some equipment to get into this business, but it can be done. *Some ideas to get started include asking a screen printing company to subcontract with you while you are getting started. Then you can save enough to get your own press machine. You can also print your own screens from a laser printer. The beauty of this business is you can take orders, get a deposit and use their money to buy your inventory.*

12. Artists, Graphic & Web Design

Artists can do graphic design, create logos or paint signs for small businesses. Creativity can go a long way with artists; they can also draw artwork for book covers, cartoons or advertisements. Artists can also be *Web Designers*. This is a great teen business for computer specialists and graphic designers. There are many small businesses that have no idea how to start a website. You can work directly with them, assisting them with their web page and internet decisions or graphic design. *Your initial start up may consist of a computer and specific design software. As you get more clients and start to have more challenging assignments you will need upgraded software and equipment.*

MY JOURNAL ENTRY

List 5 things you have learned about ***Business Start Up Ideas*** after reading this chapter. Discuss them with a parent, teacher, mentor or friends.

___

___

___

___

___

___

___

___

___

___

YOUR SPECIAL TALENTS AND GIFTS

Everyone has a special talent or gift, unique only to them. Your gift may be as an entertainer, athlete, teacher, preacher or entrepreneur. It's that special something that just comes naturally. What's yours? Either you already know or you are desperately trying to find out. You may want to use this talent to work in a job, career or as an entrepreneur. To speed along the process, we'll give you some ideas of talents you may possess and suggestions of how to develop them or take them to the next level.

Your special gift or talent can be a mental or physical skill such as: teaching, writing, mechanical, building, sports, dancing/singing or something in the performing or designing arts. The list is endless. When you recognize yours, you must take the bull by the horns and run with it. You may use this talent as a hobby or a job; some people spend their entire life figuring this out. Get ahead of the game. "Someone once told me that he was more successful than a friend of his that was more talented because *he wanted it more*."

Join school organizations, associations and attend conferences. Join groups outside of school such as youth groups, church groups or community programs. Research the internet for opportunities. Work or volunteer to sharpen your skills and network with others in the same field. Make a demo, compile a resumé, keep statistics and news articles and save any information that you may need later for a portfolio or resumé.

12 THINGS FOR TEENS TO KNOW ABOUT SPECIAL TALENTS & GIFTS AND WHAT TO DO NEXT:

1. Education, Training or Teaching
Can you retain information and facts without trying hard? Do you absolutely love school and can breeze through tests and subjects others often struggle with? You can be a mentor, tutor, and make money doing it. Maybe you will use your talent to be a teacher and help shape the youth of our future. Volunteer your time at your school, church or community organization. Get into some academic decathlons or contests. Make it work for you in every possible way, including scholarships, the works!

2. Business & Entrepreneurship
Some youth have a knack for business ownership or entrepreneurship. Those youth and young adults usually have great people skills and are natural born sales people. They can sell just about anything to anyone, they like excitement and making their own money. Check out the chapter on Entrepreneurship. Ten years ago, teen business owners hardly existed, now they are millionaires. Youth businesses are popping up in schools and organizations across the country. With the Internet you can research and expand your business internationally. If you are naturally organized, self-driven, love selling and have an excellent personality to boot, this may be your special talent.

3. Electronics, Mechanical & Computers
Working with your hands is also a special gift, and not everyone can do it. Can you take apart a computer and put it back together or fix anything with small parts? Can

you fix cars without looking at the manuals? Does your family or friends call you every time a computer or electronic appliance goes awry? You may be a candidate for working with computers, equipment, electronics or mechanics. These jobs can pay very well depending on your specialty. There are tons of certificate programs, as well as four-year degreed programs for auto mechanics, electronics and computer technicians. This is a multi-million dollar business. You can get excellent training and make money doing what you enjoy.

4. Sewing & Clothing Design

If you can sew without a pattern or look at an item and duplicate it, you are a good candidate for a career in sewing, fashion, and alterations. There are many different things you can do as a seamstress or designer such as make and sell gowns for events. You can teach sewing classes and train others. You can also do alterations or go to a design school and learn how to design clothes for stores. Many cities have schools that specialize in clothing related fields such as clothing design, department store buying and alterations.

5. Creative Design & Artists

Today, creative design can be a combination of interior design, graphic design and art. You can go to school for all of this. Artists are often the creative one in the family always doing something with pens and paper from doodling to drawing. You draw people, sports figures, buildings, cars and clothes. Maybe you're on the way to being a renowned artist. It could be that your gift or talent is art or design. As an artist, you can draw and make money at art fairs or draw logos and design letterhead for business owners. Art Design Colleges and schools can be found in most major cities. Get ideas or plans from businesses, art schools, mentors, parents or teachers.

6. Cooking and Catering

Cooking is a wonderful talent and gift. You may have culinary talent if you can make almost any dish, have a knack for seasoning just right, know how to mix dishes, your food always tastes good and everyone always wants you to cook. You can you use your knack in many ways from starting your own small business selling cookies, cakes or dinners, to working or cooking in a restaurant. You may want to go to chef or pastry school with hopes of opening your own business or working in an upscale restaurant one day.

7. Sports

If you have a natural athletic talent and you've been told you are the next Michael Jordan, Venus Williams or Tiger Woods, you need to take your talent seriously. You must document your progress through highlight tapes and start building your resume. Get together with your parents, mentors and coaches so they can help you compile your stats and accomplishments in an organized manner. Start looking at colleges while you are in high school and design a game plan for the next part of your life.

If you are asking, "What do I do with this talent?" here's some friendly advice:

- For starters, respect and listen to your coaches - they usually know someone that can help you get to the next level.
- Find a college that will meet your academic goals.
- Set short and long term sports goals and share them with your parents.
- You must work hard to sharpen your skills and that means practice, practice, practice. Attend camps, clinics and other team affiliations.
- Work with other youth, teaching and mentoring them. This will help build your leadership skills.
- If you are a junior or senior, you should start looking at scholarship opportunities. Start a resume', videotape your games, talk with parents, mentors, coaches and advise them of your intentions.

Do some leg work and put your own elbow grease into the process. You can make it happen if you want it bad enough!

8. Writing

Writing is also a special gift. Can you paint a picture with words? Some people can put words on paper with ease like musicians put lyrics to music. If you have a passion for writing, create a portfolio of your work to show others. You may want to start with poems or short stories. Not only can you write for others, you can try and get your work published. If you have already started writing, make sure to protect your work by copyrighting it before sending it out to publications.

9. Performing Arts

Do you enjoy entertaining your family and friends? Are you the life of the party? If so, you belong in the entertainment industry. There are many facets of this industry such as; playing an instrument, singing/rapping and acting. People who possess these skills are unique because everyone can't get up and perform in front of an audience. If these things are more than a hobby to you, you will need to find a way to perfect your craft. If you are brave enough to take your singing out of the shower, are unstoppable in rap battles or can portray many different characters, you belong on stage in front of an audience. There are also management opportunities within arts and entertainment.

To further your gift, join a choir or group, start singing at functions or events or audition for a play. Take an acting class, music class, singing lessons and find a coach. If you're advanced, start exploring acting opportunities, CD demo's, managers and agents. Network so you can connect yourself with the right group of honest and trustworthy people who are knowledgeable in the business. This industry is tough, so find a way to stay true to yourself and work with others that believe in you and share your vision.

10. Money & Financial

If you like money, enjoy working with numbers and you're excited about how it all fits together; you may become one of the next young persons to work on Wall Street or in the Financial District. Do you take a serious interest in stocks and bonds or follow anything financial? Has math always been a good subject for you, and if you aren't intimidated by formulas, you may want to pursue tutoring. If you have an interest in learning about how to invest money, you may be ready to work in the financial industry. Many teens also run their own financial planning business. The money business may be calling your name.

11. Theological

Are you curious about the bible, God, religions and love spiritually based projects? If you love church and the study of theology this may be what you have been called to do. Many preachers and pastors started at a very young age. Your gift may also be teaching and empowering other youth in some aspect. What should you do next? Study your religion, join a bible study group at your church or volunteer to teach. There are many faith-based colleges that specialize in spiritually based education. Talk to a pastor or mentor at your church and your parents for guidance and most certainly *"pray on it!"*

12. Hair

Is hair styling a talent or gift? It most certainly is. Just look at some hair dressers work and compare it to others. Like any other talent, some people are just natural and others are well trained. If you know how to braid, style and cut hair, you can make extra money while in school. To further your skills, you can take classes in certain high schools and/or go to a college to study beauty, barber training at a full cosmetology school.

MY JOURNAL ENTRY

List 5 ***special talents*** you may have, or are interested in pursuing. Discuss them with a parent, teacher, mentor or friends.

SPORTS CAREERS

So they say sports build character BUT what if you think a hat trick really involves something you put on your head? What if you don't know how to throw down the rock? What if you can't hit the long-ball? What if you've never made it to the end-zone? What if you have no game but the game still has you?

We all know professional athletes represent an elite group; that is why they get paid the big bucks. However, the reality of the wonderful world of sports is that only approximately 4,000 athletes make-up the National Basketball Association (30 teams), Major League Baseball (30 teams), National Hockey League (30 teams) and National Football League (32 teams). In comparison to other professions, the odds of becoming a professional athlete may not be realistic for most. There is hope for those of you who are still avid sports enthusiasts despite your skill level. Ever think about a career in sports off the court, off the playing field, off the ice … behind the scenes? Those of you who have the skills, don't let your talent go to waste. As for the rest, you can still be part of a team – find an exciting job in the front office.

12 OTHER SPORTS CAREERS FOR TEENS TO CONSIDER:

1. Coaches and Scouts

Just because you cannot master a sports skill, does not mean you cannot teach it. If you are knowledgeable in a sport, the sports world can provide numerous opportunities to be a head or assistant coach. You can be a volunteer coach, grammar school coach, high school coach, college level coach or if you master your game, get into the professional ranks. Sports teams also need people who have an eye for talent. These people are scouts and teams employ them to not only get information on the opponents, but to also find new talent that they can add to their roster.

2. Athletic Trainer and Strength/Conditioning Coach

Every athlete needs a good trainer and strength/conditioning coach to perform at their peak. Trainers treat athlete's ailments and minor injuries and help rehab athletes when they get injured during competition so they can play again. Strength coaches prepare athletes with exercise so they can reach their maximum potential. Taking care of their bodies to prevent an injury is what these coaches do. Prevention is what keeps them going so that the team can stay healthy.

3. Dentist and Doctor

If you like a perfect smile then you could be a team dentist. With most sports putting athletes at the risk of contact to the mouth, each team needs to have their own dentist on hand to care for, treat and replace the athlete's teeth. If you have an interest in medicine - you can be a team doctor! Keeping healthy is the main objective of all athletes and they take their well-being very seriously, they need to have a doctor on call at all times to give them medical treatment should they need it. Team doctors and dentists are usually employed by professional sports teams as they are very costly, but hey that's good news for you because you will be the one getting paid.

4. Accountant

All businesses and organizations need to have someone to manage the books. If you are you good at the numbers game, you could be an accountant for a sports team. Use your math skills to keep and analyze financial records – hey someone has to prepare those outrageous checks for the athletes.

5. Announcer

Announcers are a very important part of all sports, they bring the game alive for the fans who are watching it on TV or listening to it on the radio. If you can evaluate a game, you could be a play-by-play announcer or color analyst. Sporting events at all levels also have public address announcers who work courtside to bring the fans in attendance commentary. These people need to have a great voice and outgoing personality. Try a gig at the mic, right in the middle of the action and be the voice of the game as you hype up the crowd.

6. Community and Media Relations

Most professional sports teams take philanthropy (good will toward all people) seriously. If you believe in giving back to your community, you could work in their community relations department and create outreach programs that involve their players giving back to the community they play in. You would assist in organizing outreach events and fundraisers, as well as decide who the charity arm donates money to. Media relations personnel work closely with the community relations department to let the public know about the team's philanthropic efforts. They are also in charge of getting out credentials to all media personnel so they can attend the games and coordinating the distribution of all team relevant information to national and local media regarding the team in the form of press releases, statistics and media guides. They also handle press conferences and interview requests for the team.

7. Corporate Partnerships and Marketing

Work in the corporate sponsorships department and help create revenue while creating partnerships with large corporations. This benefits both the team and corporation by gaining name recognition through your team promotion. The marketing department sends out promotions, gives products away and does whatever it takes to keep fans in the stands and get their team name out there.

8. Game Operations and Promotions

Try working in game-ops and you will be in charge of controlling a sporting event. You will oversee all elements of arena day-of-game activities including contests, player introductions, halftime entertainment and promotions, the national anthem, scoreboard promotions, game performers, music and video presentation. The overall presentation of the game will be in your hands. It is up to you to make sure the fans enjoy themselves by experiencing more than just a game. You can also be a dancer, cheerleader or mascot and perform at the games. Not all fans come to just watch the game. Be a part of the game entertainment and get a chance to strut your stuff in front of a large crowd.

9. Graphic Design & Internet Services

If you are creative and like to design ads, graphics and logos, you could be the person who provides creative direction and design for printed material and promotional vehicles for the sports team. Sports teams produce a lot of things that need to be designed. Without them, game programs would just be a boring compilation of words. If you are creative and computer savvy, you could be a webmaster for a team. This person overseas the electronic communications network that connects computer networks worldwide … aka – the website. The communications department is responsible for keeping the website up to date so that fans can log on and always know what is going on with their favorite sports team.

10. Attorney

The legal department in sports franchises consists of various kinds of attorneys. These people have a huge amount of responsibility. They advise the legal rights and obligations of the team which can include; player contracts, financial reports, salary cap, free agency and other collective bargaining rules. Without them, the team wouldn't stay afloat and may end up getting sued.

11. Reporter

Got what it takes to get the inside scoop? Instead of working for a specific sports team directly, you can also work for a local newspaper or television station and have the opportunity to cover numerous events for their sports section. If you enjoy writing or taking pictures, this would be a great way for you to experience sporting events and be able to express your views of the game to the public.

12. Ticket Sales

Let's be honest, games are more fun when there are fans. Well, someone has to get those butts in the seats. If you are a good salesperson, try working in the ticket department selling tickets to sporting events. By selling season, group and individual tickets, you can work towards a sell-out crowd. You will also have a chance to work on your client skills as you build relationships with the buyers.

Written by: Michelle Ruscitti: Michelle has spent 12 years working in the sports industry including Coordinator of the Chicago Bulls Community Relations Department, Assistant Women's Basketball Coach at Robert Morris College and Coordinator of Marketing and Promotions for the University of Illinois at Chicago (UIC) Athletic Department. While attending UIC she earned a Bachelors Degree in Kinesiotherapy, Masters Degree in Sport Management and a Masters Degree in Urban Youth Development. Unfortunately her passion for basketball did not lead her to the WNBA, but it has lead her to numerous jobs in a basketball setting that allowed her to remain close to the sport she will always love.

MY JOURNAL ENTRY

List 5 ***sports jobs*** you may be interested in. Discuss them with a parent, teacher, mentor or friends.

Notes:

Chapter Four:
Health & Wellness

HEALTHY EATING

It's very important for teens to live a healthy lifestyle which includes eating healthy. We know fast food restaurants are calling your name from every block with their enticing dollar deals, crispy fries and super-sized drinks. This is fine in our fast paced world, but all this greasy food is not good for us. We are constantly trying to see which diet works better. If you plan to diet, seek the advice of a doctor or professional. Your doctor will be able to consult with you regarding any medical conditions that will prevent you from trying a particular diet. Exercise and eating fattening foods in moderation is a good start. Although we know many of the tips listed below, sometimes we need a friendly reminder. Write these tips in your notebook and periodically refer to them when you think you may be overeating or eating emotionally.

12 TIPS FOR TEENS ON HEALTHY EATING HABITS:

1. Make a List of Healthy Menus

This is time consuming but it will help when you are on the run and not able to plan the best meals for yourself. Healthy menus include; salads, low fat lunches and dinners. Make a list at the beginning of the week, of healthy foods you can eat during the week. At least you've attempted to plan. If you can't follow it one hundred percent, the effort will keep your mind thinking in the right direction. Eating normal portions of food along with a few small changes in your daily eating habits will keep you healthy and help to maintain your ideal weight.

2. Emotional Eating

Some people find eating emotionally gratifying. Sometimes we associate food with situations, experiences or events. For example; a hot day may make you think of ice cream. If this is a bad habit for you, then you may want to plan for low fat cool treats such as sherbets and popsicles. A cold day may make you crave hot chocolate or cocoa. When you are at a sporting event where fast foods are convenient, try to get around this by eating popcorn or limiting what you eat. If you notice that you are eating foods that aren't good for you late at night or at a specific time, you may want to change that. ***Shopping when you're hungry*** has been known to cause quite a few of us to overspend at the grocery store. This is a big No-No. You will buy everything off the shelves including junk food. The moral is to never shop on an empty stomach, eat first, bring a list and stick to it.

3. Drink Six To Eight Glasses Of Water Each Day

It will decrease your appetite and replenish your body. Water is a very important nutrient for our body. Our bodies are made up of two-thirds water. Water is essential for us to live. Substitute water for juice and pop when eating meals. We can not survive more than a few days without water because it is expelled through urine, breathing and sweat.

4. One Serving / One Portion

It important when dieting and eating to know what one serving is. There may be times when the word "portion" is used. Familiarize yourself with these terms. A serving is a slice of bread, two or three ounces of meat, poultry or fish. One egg, one cup of vegetables raw or 1/2 cup of cooked vegetables are also examples of a portion or serving. Liquids are 1 cup for one serving. When eating casserole dishes or spaghetti and meatballs, you are probably eating more than one serving.

5. Eating with Peers, Television & Studying

Although this falls into the emotional eating category, peer pressure eating can be big trouble also. If you are with a group that loves to eat out at fast food restaurants every day while you're trying to cut back, this makes it harder for you to stay on your plan. Depending on where you are eating, salads aren't always tasty to teens and may cost more than a full meal. ***Television and Studying***; you should not eat while you are watching television or studying. This happens in almost every household, but this is a habit we must curb. Eating while studying may cause you to snack more and television will also cause you to eat longer and eat more. You probably don't realize it because you are concentrating on your homework or distracted by the television.

6. There Are 6 Factors That May Influence Your Weight

These six factors should be evaluated when you start to plan your diet structure and evaluate your eating habits. *(1) Behavior* affects your weight because for example, we eat emotionally when we're upset. *(2)* Our *health status* may affect how we eat and how we lose weight. If we're physically unable to exercise or eat certain foods. *(3) Family genes* may determine how much weight we lose or gain. *(4)* Our *environment* is a factor because we tend to eat more if we are cold, hot or around friends. *(5) Income* level will determine what kinds of foods you buy. We sometimes eat what is more affordable, which is not always the healthiest meal. *(6) Culture* will sometimes dictate what kind of foods your family eats.

7. About Fiber

Fiber comes from the part of a plant that human enzymes cannot digest. Since we don't digest fiber, we get no calories or energy from it. The good news is that fiber is important to help regulate our bowels, prevent constipation and keep our cholesterol low. Some love and praise the high fiber diets.

8. Curbing Your Daily Fat Intake

You can moderate your fat intake by making a few small changes. Replace whole milk with skim or 2% milk. Take the skin off your chicken and drain all the oils off of it. Substitute mustard for mayonnaise; switch popcorn for chips, a bran muffin instead of a croissant. Eat an apple crisp instead of pie, a boiled or poached egg in place of a fried egg and tuna instead of hamburger. Always broil, bake or barbecue when you can.

9. Fried Foods

Fried foods are the culprit of everyone's diet challenges. Almost everything that's quick and inexpensive is usually from a fast food restaurant and fried. We have to start baking a few days a week and making better choices. Although we can't change overnight, we can make small changes over time. Each change will count somewhere along the path to healthy eating.

10. Eating Out At Restaurants

Eating out is almost impossible to avoid. How do you watch what you're eating while you are in a restaurant? You can order without adding fries or other fatty side orders. Try eating salads, smaller portions, vegetables and diet soda or water. Ask how things are cooked or ask for a vegetarian menu. Due to the increase in vegetarian menus, restaurants are very sensitive to this issue and usually respond very positively.

11. Read The Labels On Your Food

You will be surprised how much sodium is in some of the frozen foods we love. You will also be surprised at how many servings are actually listed in some of the smaller bags or your favorite snacks. You may eat an entire bag of peanuts and find out you've eaten five or six servings. This means that the calorie and fat content are multiplied times five or six. Keep this is mind when reading the labels of the foods that you are eating.

12. Eating Disorders

Many teens suffer from eating disorders. Contact a doctor immediately if you suspect you have an eating disorder. If you're not sure, you may want to discuss it with your parents first. You must get help before it's too late. 5% of the young women in the United States are affected by eating disorders, and at least 15% of them have unhealthy attitudes about food, weight and their body.

> Eating disorders such as ***Anorexia and Bulimia*** (throwing up food and starving yourself) can be life threatening and fatal. ***Depression***, low self-esteem, addictions and obsessive lack of control are all symptoms that lead to overeating and disorders. Signs and symptoms of someone that may be at risk include; eating alone, using excessive laxatives or inducing vomiting. If you or someone you know is doing this, please contact a doctor, school nurse or family member. ***Avoid over indulging*** and unnecessary eating. This means eating because you're bored or have nothing to do. Don't eat just because everyone else is eating or when you're already full. Try not to eat late at night or eat and go directly to sleep.

MY JOURNAL ENTRY

List 5 positive changes to help you start ***eating healthy***. Discuss them with a parent, teacher, mentor or friends.

____

____

____

____

____

HEALTHY TEENS

Teens must do everything within their will power to stay healthy. We can provide you with the information, but you are responsible for you - your personal behavior and your body. With regular exams, proper dieting, exercise and plenty of rest you can live a healthy life. There may be some health concerns that are handed down to you through family genes and are hereditary. Knowing your family history and sharing it with your doctor early can help you catch any medical concerns while you are young. Your body is your temple and you should treat it as such no matter how difficult it may be. This chapter will give you some basic tips on how to stay healthy. *Written by: Dr. Angela Wheeler, Family Practice and Sports Physician.*

12 TIPS FOR TEENS TO STAY HEALTHY:

1. Eating

Physicians recommend a balanced diet that includes *all* food groups. You should eat three meals a day, eliminating fast foods that can be high in sodium and fat. Current recommendations include at least five servings of fruits and vegetables per day. Everyone should start the day with breakfast so the body is properly fueled to begin the day.

2. Rest

Rest is often overlooked, especially with teens. Most people require six to eight hours of sleep each night. Things that may interfere with sleep include: exercising or drinking caffeinated beverages (coffee and pop) in the evening. It's best to get your body on a schedule and go to sleep at approximately the same time every night. Teens tend to sleep more when they are growing, so go ahead and get your beauty sleep!

3. Exercise

Exercise is essential for strength, weight maintenance and good overall health. Regular exercise habits that start while you are young will hopefully continue into your adult life. Exercise improves heart health and helps to delay or prevent high blood pressure, diabetes and heart disease.

4. Immunization

Make sure your immunizations are up to date even after your childhood shots are completed. Your parents will probably take care of this area but you should still be aware of what's going on. A doctor may ask you questions when your parents aren't available. Teens approximately 14-16 years old are usually required to get a tetanus booster shot. Other immunizations recommended include; hepatitis b vaccine and meningitis. Most schools won't let children enroll if they aren't up to date on their immunizations so it is important to consult your physician to make sure you are squared away.

5. Vitamins

Vitamin supplements may be used for teens or adolescents that have poor eating habits or medical conditions that warrant their use. For the most part, vitamin deficiency is relatively uncommon in the United States. Adequate calcium intake is important, particularly in females, to avoid bone density loss that is later associated with osteoporosis (especially in women over 40).

6. Family History

Teens should be aware of medical conditions that run through their family. This type of information will help you make lifestyle choices that may prevent you from developing these same conditions later in life. Conditions to be concerned about include diabetes, high blood pressure, and colon or breast cancer.

7. Food Fads

Food fads are diets people start to lose weight, but they come and go and you can easily gain the weight back. This is a quick fix, and long term results shouldn't be expected. You should discuss food fads with your physician before starting on one. Examples of fad diets include the grapefruit diet and cabbage soup diet.

8. Seat Belts

Buckle up; it's the law for a reason. Put your seat belt on as soon as you get in the car. The most common cause of death in teens is car accidents, and many of them could have been prevented by the use of a seat belt. The nationwide initiative "Click it or Ticket," allows police to give you a ticket and fine for not wearing your seatbelt.

9. Eye Exams & Dental Exams

Eye exams should be done every one to two years. An exam should also be done anytime there is any obvious change in vision. Eye pain and headaches may be indications of a serious visual problem. ***Dental Exams*** are recommended every six months. After a deep cleaning, dental exams look for cavities, plaque build up and tooth alignment. These examinations will determine if you are susceptible to gum disease or if you require orthodontics (braces).

10. Physical Exams

A yearly physical exam is recommended for teens. In general, you probably go to the doctor for injuries, illness and sports physicals. The physical exam gives the physician a chance to review worrisome family history and behaviors that might contribute to the development of chronic disease.

11. Tanning

Tanning is not recommended for teens because it causes cumulative damage to the skin and may lead to skin cancer. Contrary to popular belief, tanning salons are not any better than sun exposure. To protect your skin, you should always use a sun screen with an SPF of 30 or greater.

12. Piercing & Tattoos

Body piercing should be done by a certified professional. When piercings are done, strict adherence to sanitation, and disposal of used needles must be observed. Body piercings are not to be done at home. After a tongue piercing, the studs placed in your tongue can lead to tooth damage. Infection and cheloids (a thickening and scar like change in the skin) are also possible. For more information, see our chapter on body piercings. ***Tattoos*** are considered permanent markings on the skin. Allergies to the dye are possible. Cases of hepatitis and HIV have been reported due to improper sanitation. For more information on tattoos see our chapter on tattoos.

MY JOURNAL ENTRY

List 5 things you've learned about being a ***healthy teen***. Discuss them with a parent, teacher, mentor or friends.

FOR ATHLETES ONLY! AVOIDING SPORTS INJURIES

If you are an athlete, you must avoid injury and stay healthy so you can maximize your performance. You should enjoy the sport you play and play for the love of the game. There are many things that can be done to help you to become a better athlete on and off the court. Most importantly you must be a responsible athlete, which also means paying attention to any requirements you may have from school, coaches or trainers. This chapter will give you tips on how to avoid injury and common mistakes made by athletes. It also includes advice on health, attire and nutrition. *Written by: Dr. Angela Wheeler, Family Practice and Sports Physician.*

12 TIPS FOR TEEN ATHLETES ON HOW TO STAY HEALTHY:

1. Pre-Participation Physicals
Athletes should get physicals a few weeks prior to the first practice. Do it early in case there is a medical concern during your physical, then you will have time to see a doctor and take care of it before the season starts. Medical issues that may be a concern during athletic physicals are: asthma and previous injuries that have not been adequately rehabilitated. Sudden death risk factors include; allergies for athletes who are outdoors and are allergic to bees, insects or outdoor foliage. Physicals are also used to discover any orthopedic or medical problems that will preclude or affect participation in sports.

2. Pre-Season Training
This training should address general fitness and sport specific skill sets. Elite athletes have the opportunity to go to camps for this training. It's not a smart idea to go to the first practice out of shape. Most coaches will inform you of what you should work on during the off season, take heed to these things. Pre-season training should also include getting to your proper weight. Certain sports have strict weight requirement such as; wrestling and boxing.

3. Proper Sport Selection
Athletes should choose sports that they enjoy playing or are good at. Consider physical limitations and endurance when choosing which sport you are going to participate in. Decide whether you'd like to participate in a team, individual sport, sprinting activity, or long distance activity. Sports are broken into three categories; *Contact Collision* – boxing, diving, football, basketball and wrestling. *Limited Contact* – cheerleading, gymnastics, volleyball, ice skating. *Non-contact* – golf, running, swimming, tennis.

4. Hydration
It's important to make sure that you are properly hydrated before practice or a game. Hydrate while you are playing the sport or activity and afterwards. In some cases, athletes lose in excess of 5 – 6 lbs in a game or practice. Athletes that lose that amount

of water should be weighed before and after each session. Athletes who do a lot of sweating will need more than water to rehydrate. Sports drinks are necessary to have on hand or near the practice area. Sodium and potassium need to be replaced and can be done with both foods and beverages.

5. Nutrition & Rest

Carbohydrates are the mainstay nutrient for athletes. Muscles will deplete the carbohydrate supply after an exercise session. It is important to take in a good carbohydrate source within twenty minutes to two hours of your exercise session to replenish the muscle energy supplies. Good sources of carbs are fruits like apples, oranges, pasta and whole grain breads. ***Rest*** allows you to build strength. It is part of your overall fitness and is just as important as the sport itself. Muscles must have time to restore themselves after heavy exercise. *Rest is sometimes "doing absolutely nothing."* Resting between weight lifting or exercise routines means alternating muscle groups on different days. Sometimes rest might involve resting a particular body part for instance; riding a bike versus running would provide rest for ankles, particularly an injured ankle.

6. R.I.C.E. Principal

The RICE Principal involves basic injury management.
R- (Relative) Rest
I - Ice
C - Compression
E - Elevation

Relative rest means resting the injured body part. For specific ways to handle injuries such as; ankles, knees and shoulders see below. The rest would depend on the severity of the injury. When there is an injury, **I**ce is generally applied for twenty minutes to the body part, two to three times a day if possible. **C**ompression helps alleviate accumulation of swelling in an injured body part. Compression can be applied with an ace wrap bandage. **E**levation can be helpful to eliminate swelling in an injured body part. Elevation of an upper body injury can be achieved with a sling or sometimes resting the body part on a pillow. In the lower extremity or leg, elevation is usually achieved with elevating the leg on a pillow.

7. Weight Training

Weight training for teens should be supervised to insure both proper technique and appropriateness of weight lifted. Permanent injuries that may affect growth are of particular concern regarding weight lifting in adolescents. The weight lifting program must be balanced, for example; you must train the biceps and the triceps, abdomen-back, hamstrings-quadriceps. Maximal strength gains will not be achieved by training the same body parts every day. Rest is a must.

8. Sports Related Eating Disorders

Athletes who are required to be a certain weight in order to do their sport (wrestling, boxing), as well as the esthetic sports (gymnastics, ice skating, ballet), are at risk for poor eating habits that can lead into eating disorders. Typically, these athletes restrict their caloric intake and in some cases avoid entire food groups or meat. Eating disorders are also related to poor self esteem and body issues such as; anorexia and bulimia. Individuals with these conditions will need professional support to manage and improve their eating habits.

9. Performance Enhancing Substances

Overtime many performance enhancing substances have become available to athletes such as; anabolic steroids, Creatine, Amino Acids and Mega Dose Vitamins. Some of the supplements are found to have questionable benefits and some have been associated with permanent medical illness and sometimes death. Many of these substances have been banned or prohibited by the NCAA and other athletic governing bodies. In short, performance enhancing substances are not advised, but if they are needed, they should be used only under the strict supervision of a physician.

10. Equipment/Attire

It's important to have the appropriate attire and equipment for the sport you are participating in. You must wear turf shoes if you are playing football or field hockey on artificial turf and you need cleats when playing on grass. When playing basketball you should not wear running shoes. It would be wise to wear light colored fabrics of mesh or breathable material when practicing or playing in hot humid weather. When playing and practicing in cold weather, layered clothing should be worn to protect you from the cold or to avoid frostbite. Helmets and shoulder pads should be properly fitted for athletes who wear them. Mouth guards are important for teeth when playing collision and contact sports.

11. Knee, Shoulder & Ankle Injuries

Knee injuries are common in sports and may involve anything from a dislocation of the knee cap, torn cartilage, to ligament sprains and ruptures. Swollen knees or knees that feel unstable while walking should be evaluated by a sports medicine professional (physician, athletic trainer or therapist).

Knee Injuries in Female Athletes; For reasons not fully understood, female athletes are at an increased risk for knee injuries, particular ACL (Anterior Crutiate Ligament) injury. We see these injuries commonly in soccer, basketball and dancers. Injury prevention includes proper conditioning and proper technique. ***Ankles;*** Ankle injuries are probably the most common sports injury. It is a common practice to walk it off or tie the shoe strings tighter. Both should be done with caution, as it may set the athlete up for further injury or mask what otherwise may be a more severe injury. For milder injuries the RICE Principal can be applied. ***Shoulder Injuries;*** Swimmers, pitchers and weight lifters are at risk for shoulder injuries. Most often these injuries are due to overuse, made worse by improper technique. Shoulder injuries should be evaluated by a physician and then properly rehabilitated under direction from the physician, athletic trainer and/or physical therapist.

12. Genital protection – Males Athletes

Protect your jewels. Male athletes should wear protective genital cups in sports with projectiles such as hockey and baseball. Self testicle exams should be done monthly in athletes over fifteen. Testicular cancer is a potential problem in young men between the ages of 15-35. Discuss self test testicular exams with your physician.

Dr. Wheeler's Bio

Dr. Angela Wheeler is currently a Family Practice physician in Indiana. She also has an additional specialty in Sports Medicine. Her work with the U.S. Olympic Committee, includes; Jones Cup Women's Basketball Tournament in Taipei Taiwan in 1997. In 1998 Wheeler went to the World Youth Games in Moscow Russia, the Pan Am Games in Winnipeg Canada in 1999, and she was also a Team Physician at the Summer Olympics in Sydney Australia in 2000.

Disclaimer: The information provided in this chapter is general information and not to be used in place of visiting a physician or used in place of seeking proper medical attention. If any teen has problems, concerns, illness or injury we immediately urge you to see your family physician. This chapter is to give preventive suggestions of potential injuries that have happened to previous athletes.

MY JOURNAL ENTRY

List 5 things you've learned about ***being a healthy athlete***. Discuss them with a parent, teacher, mentor or friends.

___

___

___

___

___

___

___

___

___

___

___

STRESS & ANGER MANAGEMENT

When your body reacts to something it's called stress. For the most part, we relate stress to being bad or negative. Actually, you can have good and bad stress. Stress can be a very hard strain on your body, physically and emotionally. The key here is to stay away from drugs and alcohol abuse to relieve stress. Severe stress can cause depression, hospitalization and even lead to suicide if not treated. Some stress can make you angry. If you are angry a lot, mad at the world, constantly getting into fights or altercations, you may have anger issues. This chapter will give you some ways to reduce stress and anger issues.

12 TIPS FOR TEENS ON STRESS CONTROL & ANGER MANAGEMENT:

1. Learn to Identify Your Feelings

You should learn to identify your feelings. This will help you on days when you are really upset and trying to figure out what to do next. If you can identify whether you are angry, sad, confused, hurt or having a temporary emotional moment, it will make a significant difference on how you react. Some of these feelings are similar but not the same. Some of these emotions are short term and others may take longer to shake off. This is the road back to normal and freeing yourself of emotional baggage. Hopefully, this subject doesn't sound too grown up, because it is what teens are experiencing in real life. We want you to understand your body, your feelings and your emotions.

2. Signs and Symptoms of Stress

Signs and symptoms include; headaches, bad eating habits, substance abuse, illness and anxiety. This is a partial list of many ways your body can tell you that you are under stress. You may be tired all the time, don't want to get out the bed, excessive crying or not wanting to be around your friends, family or talk to anyone. These are also signs of depression.

3. Healthy Ways To Deal With Stress

Exercise, relaxation and deep breathing are healthy ways to cope with stress. One way to keep your stress level down is by keeping things (*your life*) under control. This means when you notice that things in your life are getting hard to control, stop, get a plan together and follow it. Ask friends and family to help when you notice that you are struggling with an issue. Watch each stress factor closely to determine which one is the worse for you, and which technique works best to combat it. You may want to keep a journal to help you on this journey.

4. Recognizing Different Types of Stress

Abuse; If you have stress at home, you know where it's coming from. It can be from a series of different areas; sexual abuse, physical abuse, family expectations, siblings or parental disagreement. If you have an abusive situation at home, or are dealing with parental abuse you can report it to an authority figure or find a way to leave home. If your parents are the problem, you may have to seek assistance outside the home from a school nurse, counselor or a close trusted family member. They can help you get to the next step. While you are in the home, try to diffuse (stay level headed) the situation. ***Home / Parental Stress;*** If your parents are just getting on your nerves or you have regular personality clashes with your parents, this is probably stressing you out. If you are arguing and disagreeing with everything they say, you are going to have to start having serious sit down talks to get to the bottom of the problem. Problems start to happen when you ignore the problem and it escalates. Do not go in your room, slam the door, scream or disrespect your parent. Ask your mom or dad for some quality time to discuss the specific problem, and then start talking it out. Parents will usually talk it out. ***Relationship & Dating Stress;*** Teen dating causes intense peer pressure on such young minds. Girls and boys are having sex and complicating the relationship before it's time. As a teen, there are sometimes challenges that come with dating. It's should not be a source of stress. If your relationship is not going well, or everyone seems to have a girl/boyfriend but you, time will take care of everything. Be patient, your time will come. ***School Stress;*** Your grades are important so, you must learn to balance school, work, extra curricular activities and homework. You have to deal with teachers, friends and your responsibilities. If you are graduating you have those additional events, ACT/SAT scores, fees and college applications. School can be stressful, but it is your responsibility to juggle it all. When you need help, ask for it from parents, teachers or friends. Do not wait until you are overwhelmed or it's too late. ***Work Stress;*** If you are a teenager with a stressful job, you really don't need it. If your stress is due to you trying to arrange your schedule to keep your job, you should evaluate the job. If you have the type of job that's too demanding, then you must quit. Your job should provide you with extra cash to allow you to buy the things you want to make your life easier. Find a job that's less demanding, that will allow you to do your homework, study, get a sufficient amount of rest and slide a little "fun" in there too. ***Time Stress;*** Time management is very important. Use a palm pilot or planner to keep up with your appointments and responsibilities. Time is very important because you can't turn it back and there are only so many hours in the day. You can't buy more time, so this means you have to organize your time wisely and effectively. You don't want to get to the end of the week and realize you are out of time for your real work "school." ***Peer Stress;*** Peer related stress means your friends are causing you stress. This means your friends are doing something such as; ignoring you, pressuring, talking or gossiping about you. They can create stress for you by isolating you from an event that you usually attend with them. Classmates and peers may cause you stress by betraying you or talking about your clothes, hair or body. If you are suffering from peer related stress, review the source of the stress, then deal with it from there.

5. Positive Stress Reducers / Stress Management Techniques

There are several things that you can do to relieve stress. You can use exercise and relaxation techniques. Here are some simple ways individuals have been know to cope with stress:

- *Sleep and Rest - Listening to music – Laughing - Talking with family or friends - Taking a warm bath or shower - Reading a book, writing, painting or drawing –*

Exercising - Deep breathing techniques or meditation. Vacation, Yoga, Lighten Your Workload, Herbal Tea.

6. Negative Stress Responses

- *Eating too much, binge eating, or starving yourself - Drinking alcohol - or smoking - Using drugs - Getting upset or flying off the handle at people - Avoiding social contact - Driving fast or putting yourself in a dangerous situation - Picking a fight or argument, hitting a wall - Criticizing yourself - Chewing your fingernails - Sucking your thumb.*

7. Identifying Anger Problems

How can you tell if you have an anger problem? Are you mad all the time? Do you get mad for no reason? Are you looking for an argument to break out? Are you on the edge and can snap at the slightest little thing? If you feel like you are mad at the world and don't know why, or you just can't shake something off your back, you probably have an anger problem. Constantly getting into altercations or fights at school also indicates you may have an anger problem.

8. Solving Anger Issues

Once you have figured out that you may have anger issues, you have to find out how to get rid of that nasty bug. Anger issues can cause you to get into unnecessary situations that could have been prevented. When you are stressed out about life's issues, you will let anger take control.

__Stay away from other teens that are__ angry all the time. Two angry people together will not have a good outcome. You can __meditate__ or use yoga to relieve stress or anger. __Join positive groups__, organizations or programs to take your mind off of what may be upsetting you. __Join a church, youth group__ or faith based organization that may also provide counseling, therapy or support groups. Start spending more time around __positive people__ and friends that are engaged in positive actions. __Join a sports team__, dance group or something that's fun and energetic, it will keep your mind occupied and sharp. Take a walk, fresh air will help you think, calm you down and help you feel better. You will not be as stressed. __Count to ten__ when you feel anger taking over. During this time, it will give you time to think about why you are angry, and think of a smarter, calmer less intensive way to handle the situation. __Talk to parents__, friends, family or counselors about what or who has made you angry and see what solutions they have to help you get back on track. Sometimes just talking out problems with others can give you a different outlook on the situation. In some not-so-serious cases, you may want to __talk with the person that made your angry__ and you work the problem out between you, apologize and add in a few hugs. This really works with friends that are having a problem and they want to solve it. You must decide how to channel your anger and turn it into a positive. Seek the help of a __psychiatrist, physician__ or support group that specializes in stress problems.

9. Severe Stress

Many individuals have severe anxiety problems coupled together with phobias. Once identified, this can also be a form of stress. Phobias can cause anxiety, depression and other physical and emotional problems. If you or someone you know is having anxiety or phobia problems, advise them to seek medical attention as soon as possible.

Depression; Many teens suffer from depression and they don't even know it. Depression can lead to stress, which can also lead to suicide. If you cry a lot, are sad a lot of the time and everything in your world looks dark or like it can't be fixed, you may be in a depression. Depression is anger turned inward; find a way to get it out. ***Suicide;*** If you have ever contemplated suicide or taking your life, you must seek professional help immediately. You can contact your school nurse, parent, family friend, church pastor or doctor where you seek medical treatment. Doctors have specialized medication, therapy and counseling for depression. Things are never as bad as they seem.

Anxiety; Is a feeling of helplessness and fear. Anxiety can easily stretch into severe stress mode. ***Panic Disorder***; Fear and having attacks, shortness of breath, faintness, trembling and worries. ***Phobias;*** A Phobia is something you are severely scared of and your life is disabled by this phobia. It could be something you're scared of such as animals or maybe you are Claustrophobic and you can not stand to be in small or congested areas. Some Claustrophobic people are scared of elevators, basements and closets. People that are afraid to go outside are called Agoraphobic. There are many different kinds of phobias, you just need figure out what it will take for you to overcome yours. You may have to seek the help of a professional to get cured.

10. It's Ok To Be Happy

When talking about emotional protection, it's important to know that it's ok to be happy. There is so much negativity in young lives, you must cherish every happy moment you can. Do you know people that refuse to be happy? We all know that person who loves drama; they are never happy and are not satisfied unless everyone's upset. They are the one that will gossip and make everyone mad including themselves. The moral is; "it's ok to be happy."

11. Let It Go

Learn to let some things go and choose your battles carefully. This means, if you are having problems with parents, teachers, adults or friends you may be able to come to a reasonable solution to your problem. Try working things out before you get upset, because sometimes situations look worse than they are. It's best to think and plan your actions. Since you are old enough to say what's on your mind, sometimes you speak before you think and this can get you in trouble. At times, you will feel the need to tell someone how you feel, but choose your words wisely. We can't fix everything. As you get older and more mature, you will learn you have to let some things go and walk away. Don't lose your sanity.

12. Therapists, Support Groups, Counseling

We don't think about going to any of these places willingly. It seems so official, like we are admitting we have a problem. The truth is, if you have a serious problem your friends and family can listen and only help so much. In the long run, a doctor, therapist or trained psychologist is much better equipped to handle your problems. You should let them. The first step in the healing process is admitting you have a problem, it gets easier from there.

MY JOURNAL ENTRY

List 5 things about ***stress and anger management*** that you didn't know before reading this chapter. Discuss them with a parent, teacher, mentor or friends.

SAFETY

People of all ages should be concerned for their safety. Due to the violence escalating in high schools, teens and young adults must be conscientious of their safety on a daily basis. Your safety includes; driving, school, relationships, work, traveling, parties and apartment life. Being safe is important to your health and general well being. When thinking about criminals and bad people, you need to realize that they are sometimes dressed better than you. Unlike years ago, when you could tell by looking at someone - they intend to harm you. Today it's the boy or girl next door you should watch out for. Be safe and alert when getting in cars, buses, working or at home. Get a cell phone for emergencies. Be safe, be smart and most of all be extra careful. Learning how to be safe is another part of maturing as a teen and a young adult.

12 TIPS FOR TEENS TO STAY SAFE AND PROTECT THEMSELVES:

1. School
There is NO such thing as being too careful. Make sure that you close and secure your locker and don't give out your combination. When you are at school late, look behind you while checking for your keys and personal belongings. If you are waiting for a ride, and it's late or dark, wait inside the school or near a crowd. Make sure you read all safety guides and know your school's procedures. Walk, don't run in the halls and watch for items you can trip over or slide on. Be extra careful when participating in extra-curricular activities or sports.

2. Work
Always observe your company's safety rules when working. Work related injuries are very common and reach the thousands every year. Make sure you stay away from hot stoves, pick up items on the floor and be careful not to drop tools or slip and fall. Electrical cords, chemicals and factory machines are all major safety concerns in the work place and should be handled accordingly. It is difficult to be out of work due to a work related injury and not everyone is eligible for workman's compensation or disability. So, do everything you can to prevent even the smallest cut.

3. Personal Safety
Your personal safety is of the utmost importance. Avoid fights, altercations and unnecessary arguments. This includes accidents that could have been prevented such as play fighting, throwing rocks or goofing around by a pool. If there is a fight at school, you should report it to the principal or the police. You should go to class or go home. Many people get hurt by stray weapons or hurt accidentally by being an innocent bystander. Don't play with weapons or shoot pellet (BB) guns. ***If you notice that someone is following*** you after getting off of a bus or in a dark or deserted area, change your path. Look for a well lit area or public place where there are a lot of people. Don't be scared to ask for help, stand in a store or gas station until you feel safe. If you have a cell phone, call someone or pretend to be talking to someone. If someone is following you in a car, change sides of the street and fall back behind them. Don't hesitate to call 911 or the police department. Remember, it's better to be safe

than sorry. Follow your instincts because many people have been kidnapped by slow moving cars, especially women.

4. Travel & Public Transportation

When traveling on public transportation, sit near someone that appears harmless. This is difficult, because criminals and strangers never look the part. Attempt to sit in the front of the bus or near the bus driver. Don't sit at the back of the bus because you think it's cool, or you're expected to. A lot of drama goes on at the back of the bus in the inner city. When using public transportation, try not to stare or look at individuals that may be waiting on trouble. When riding on the train, look for the conductor if you are scared. Take your headphones or a book and mind your own business however; don't be so involved that you are unaware of what's happening around you.

5. Travel by Car

When traveling by car, make sure you exercise caution getting in and out of the vehicle, even when riding with others. While driving, make sure you put your "patience" hat on along with your seatbelt. Let the person trying to pass you go ahead, you'll meet him at the stoplight anyway and you will prevent an accident. Always drive the speed limit and don't take unnecessary chances. When getting in your car, always look around and check the back seat to make sure your car is secure. When riding with people you don't know that well, asked to be dropped off first. Make sure when driving with friends of others - that you feel safe. Don't accept a ride unless someone knows the driver really well, the last thing you want to is to be scared while riding with someone. If you are driving and your car breaks down, put your hood up if you can, then lock yourself in the car until help arrives. This is when a cell phone really comes in handy. Know the emergency phone numbers of parents, friends and an automotive emergency service.

6. Parties, Drinks & Date Rape

When attending parties, be careful and stay observant of people and incidents. Watch your drinks so that no one can spike it or put something in your cup. If you leave your drink for too long, dump it and get a new one. You must watch out for "rhuphies" (rhyphinol) or other date rape drugs. Speaking of date rape, be careful not to be alone with people that you don't know well. Think twice when meeting someone at a party that asks you leave with them. Never leave your group to be with a stranger. Don't give out your home address and telephone number until you get to know the person and you trust them, or a trusted friend vouches for them.

7. Visiting Out of Town

When visiting a new city, always be on the look out for thieves or pick pockets. Watch your wallet, purse and ATM card. Try not to let anyone get too close to you while at a cash machine. When you are in your hotel, sometimes it's best to wait for another elevator if it's just one person on it that looks suspicious. When touring the city in taxis, make sure they are taking safe routes and that you feel comfortable. If they appear to be taking the scenic route or driving a long time, don't be afraid to inquire. You can also check their picture I.D. to ensure that you are riding with the correct driver; this information is usually posted in the cab. The same careful approach should be used when riding public transportation. A nice hotel on the good side of town does not prevent you from foul play or harm. These rules also apply to your hometown; unfortunately, there are bad people everywhere nowadays.

8. Apartment or Home

When in an apartment or house, always check the property to make sure it's safe. When leaving, check the doors, locks, stove and windows. At night, leave a light on, keep your blinds and windows closed and use window guards to limit your window from being raised. When leaving your home, always look around and stay alert, check outside gates and locks. If it's dark, always look behind you when entering your home or apartment and check to see if anything is out of place. If you think something is out of place or someone has entered your home, close the door, leave immediately and call the police. You can never be too safe. When going out of town, use timers to turn lights on and off, and leave on a radio

9. Relationships

Young men and women seem to be getting involved in intense relationships at a much younger age. These same teens find themselves involved in physically abusive relationships. There should be no violence and both individuals should feel safe physically and emotionally. This includes friends, family or someone you are dating. If either of you feel that your safety is threatened, or do not feel secure, it's not worth it. Your safety always comes first. No one should threaten you, hit you, yell at you or make you feel uncomfortable. If you don't feel safe, be smart and get out of the relationship. Your life may depend on it.

10. Carbon Monoxide & Fire

Make sure you have a carbon monoxide detector in your home, apartment or dorm. If you ever have a situation where there is a gas leak in your house, you want to know it. This is just as important as a smoke detector, which you should also have. Even though carbon monoxide is colorless and you cannot see it, it can be even more deadly or fatal than smoke. Check your batteries frequently. ***What do you do if something catches fire in the house?*** Unless it's a small pan fire or very small isolated fire, use your fire extinguisher first. If it looks out of hand, leave and immediately call 911 for the fire department. Remember do not put water on a grease fire. Use flour or sugar or some type of powder. If a person is on fire, "stop, drop and roll." Do everything you can to prevent a fire; double check and triple check all stoves, heaters, candles and potential fire hazards. Keep candles away from walls and curtains. Teach young children not to play with matches.

11. Locked Out?

What will you do if you get locked out of your car or house? First try to retrace your steps so that you can possibly find your keys. If this doesn't work, call someone with a spare set of keys. If you don't have a cell phone (try to get one for next time), then go where there are a lot of people and call someone to come and get you. You can wait in your car if you feel safe, if not, find somewhere that is well lit and populated. Never take chances and always leave a spare set of keys with someone you trust. Again, try to remember where you lost your keys, if a stranger could possibly have them, call police to escort you if you aren't sure - change your locks.

12. Pick Pockets/ Robbers

Watch out for skilled pickpockets that can get your wallet or purse. Skilled pickpockets work in pairs and pass off your items before you realize they are gone. Robbers sometime carry weapons and if you're not careful, you may get injured. Look around at all times when it's dark out and if you feel someone walking behind you, let them pass. In stores or malls, be aware of who's near you and never put your bags down. Be very cautious when it's dark outside, do not walk in alleys or take unnecessary chances.

MY JOURNAL ENTRY

List 5 positive changes about your ***safety*** that you would like to make. Discuss them with a parent, teacher, mentor or friends.

HOMELESS TEENS

Homeless teens are increasing at an alarming rate in America. This group includes teens that are not living or residing permanently with their immediate family. We may not recognize homeless teens because they can blend in with society better than homeless adults. Many of them are hidden among other family members, friends or they live on the street. This is a very scary way to live and hopefully you will seek safe shelter or take advantage of some of the local support systems in your city. If you know a teen that is homeless or that is in a challenging situation, maybe you help them seek support, advice or help.

Homeless teens come from a myriad of different problems such as family crisis that include; divorce, family conflict, school problems, drug use, alcohol use, teen pregnancy, sexual activity and sexual orientation. It is reported in many major cities that the teen homeless rate is as high as 45%.

12 TIPS TO KNOW ABOUT HOMELESS TEENS:

1. Homeless Teens & Shelters

Many homeless teens do not go to shelters because they fear they will have to divulge personal information they wish to keep private. Homeless teens are often afraid of shelters because they have a police record or fear they may be sent back home. This is especially true for underage teens. Shelters were established to provide a safe environment that provides food, sleeping options and other services to the homeless population.

2. Abusive Parents

Parents that have abused their children can possibly go to jail if convicted. The proper authorities or officials must be notified. You can tell a school counselor or doctor, and they are required by law to contact or advise authorities of this illegal behavior. There are also several levels of abuse that range from severe verbal abuse to physical abuse. If you are a teen on the run because of an abusive parent, you can go to a police department and make a report. *Fact:* Teens that leave severely abusive parents sometimes feel safer on the street than at home.

3. Survival on the Street

Homeless teens living on the street have to endure the weather, along with the challenge of finding food, clothing and shelter. This is not their choice, they usually have no choice. They survive by staying in shelters and panhandling. Some teens are fortunate to secure a real job and work while others may turn to prostitution or illegal behavior. If you are a homeless teen try to exhaust all resources find a job and housing before using desperate measures.

4. Sleeping Options

The best and most safe sleeping option of course is with friends and family. If you know a family member that you may be able to stay with, try this before sleeping outside or in a shelter. The next step is a shelter, foster care or other public place.

Homeless teens have been known to sleep in bus stations, park benches, trains, subways, trailer parks, under bridges, in the woods or any type of area that will protect them from inclement weather.

5. Homeless Teen Moms

Homeless teen mothers are too old for foster care which presents additional challenges and limitations on housing placement. Most foster care facilities do not have the capability to house pregnant teens or children. Some community organizations have obtained funding to place homeless teens who are expecting. You can find them through your city crisis hotline or local police department. 53% of homeless teen mothers were daughters of teenage mothers themselves. 41% of homeless teen mothers were placed in foster care as children and 34% were more likely to report witnessing domestic violence in their homes compared to homeless adult mothers.

6. Transitional Living Arrangements

Teens that are too old for the foster care system are able to go to transitional living houses or apartment living. The transitional living facilities house teens while they approach young adulthood. The teens usually reside there from the ages of 16 to 21. They learn the responsibilities and skills needed to transition to adult life and live on their own. They are able to complete school, gain job skills, job placement, and learn about managing their own finances. Most of these programs are state funded and available through children and family service organizations.

7. Disagreements with Parents

If you have a minor disagreement with parents, try your best to work it out before leaving home. Since many of the homeless teens initially leave home because of disagreements with parents and family members, some may be resolved. Therapists and counselors may be able to provide you with some assistance before things escalate or get out of hand. Some arguments can be controlled and redirected into positive conversation and outcomes. It may take work and compromise, but it can happen.

8. Suicide

Suicide is a large problem also plaguing runaways and homeless teens. Once they are out on the streets they sometimes realize it's much more difficult than they ever imagined. If you are contemplating suicide or you know someone that is, please seek the help of a professional, friend, school counselor or family member. This is not only a devastating decision for you, but leaves behind a long trail of guilt and problems for your family. Sometimes families are distraught for years trying to figure out why the decision was made, what could have been done differently and why they couldn't recognize the signs. If you are having problems talk to someone, because many times it is possible that your situation can be helped, and this could have been prevented. Things aren't always as hopeless and as dark as they appear. Light will come in the morning, and many times things start to look up.

9. Alcohol and Drug Abuse

Alcohol and drug abuse are a big part of the homeless lifestyle. One in three homeless individuals are alcoholics. It is also reported that a large percentage of homeless teens deal drugs for money and are users. If you are experiencing substance abuse problems, you may consider a treatment program or attending AA (Alcoholics Anonymous) or NA (Narcotics Anonymous). Most shelters and facilities have information on these free meetings where you can get help. You need to remember that dealing or buying drugs is illegal and if you get caught, you will get arrested and it may go on your permanent police record.

10. Runaway & Homeless Statistics

One out of every seven youth will runaway before their 18th birthday. 46% have encountered some type of physical abuse, 32% have been forced into some type of sexual activity against their will, 47% have left home due to some conflict with a parent or guardian, 17% have dropped out of school and 30% will attempt suicide. Each year, over 5,000 teenagers will die from physical assaults, suicide and illness.

11. Education

It is a myth that homeless teens don't want to go to school. In all actuality, a large amount of homeless teens *do attend school* and *do want to finish their* education. This may be difficult, but it is not impossible. Schools have counselors trained to work with homeless teens that understand their challenges and can help them get an education. There are alternative high schools equipped to handle these types of situations. They can provide alternative educational goals to help personalize plans to help teens through high school and on through college.

12. Resources

Medical Resources; mobile health clinics deal with physical, emotional and physiological problems. They vaccinate the homeless for measles, hepatitis B and tetanus. Medical vans treat foot fungus, pregnancy and dozens of other medical problems. Many homeless teens have not seen a doctor since grade school. The medical vans which operate from donations and non profit efforts only serve a small portion of the homeless teens that are on the street and need medical attention.

Additional Resources for Homeless; needed to assist homeless teens include; mental health, medical assistance, food stamps and food programs, day care, drug abuse assistance, employment counseling and placement, housing, temporary assistance for needy families. Low-Income Home Energy Assistance Program (LIHEAP), Federal Earned Income Tax Credit (for families with children), School Lunch Program, Women, Infants, and Children Nutrition Program (WIC), and Emergency Food. Information is provided in English, Spanish, Russian, and Vietnamese. These services are usually offered through churches, community organizations, city and state funded programs.

The National Runaway Switchboard; reports that homeless youths are very likely to suffer substance abuse problems (one in three are alcoholics), deal drugs for money and engage in unprotected sex. Sometimes, these teenagers will commit crimes because they believe being caught and spending the night in jail would be better than sleeping outside in the cold. The homeless plight for teens is a crisis. If you are a homeless teen, try to make sure you can stay in safe environments. Get all the help you can by networking with hospitals, shelters and community organizations. The phone number is (800) RUNAWAY and the website is www.nrscrisisline.org

MY JOURNAL ENTRY

List 5 things that you have learned about ***homeless teens***. Discuss them with a parent, teacher, mentor or friends.

PIERCING

Piercing is not a new phenomenon, but there are many new places to pierce. Teens are piercing by the millions on almost every part of their body. Piercing used to be limited to the ears. Now you may see a body piercing just about anywhere. Popular places include; lip, eyebrow, navel, tongue, ears, nose and a few unmentionable places. Piercing is less expensive than tattoos, legal for teens, easier and quicker to get. This chapter will hopefully give you a little insight on what to expect when considering body piercing. Piercing is not as permanent as tattoos and can be healed by letting the hole close. You should probably discuss piercing with an adult such as a parent, family member or doctor. There are health risks in any type of medical procedure, regardless of how minor.

12 TIPS TEENS SHOULD KNOW BEFORE BODY PIERCING:

1. How Safe is Piercing?

For the most part, piercing is safe. However, as with any open wound, you always run the risk of developing an infection that may not heal. Bacterial infections can also develop when a piercing is not performed with clean instruments. To prevent this from happening, only let a qualified professional who adheres to safety and cleanliness perform your piercing. This is imperative so that unnecessary mistakes are avoided.

2. Do Piercings Hurt?

Great question! Any time you puncture through skin, and blood is drawn, I'm sure it hurts a little. The different levels of pain may depend on who you ask and where the piercing was done. Ears are probably less painful than tongues and noses are probably more painful than eyebrows. Besides the initial pain when the piercing is done, the area may be sore for a few weeks while it heals.

3. Can You Use Something To Dull The Pain Before Getting A Piercing?

You can get a temporary numbing agent, similar to what you get at a dentist. They can be bought over the counter and are temporary so they only last a few minutes. You will probably have to endure some pain or discomfort; you may want to take a pain reliever or aspirin with you to.

4. Cost of Piercings

The cost of piercing varies and the prices depend on the type of jewelry used. You can get your ears pierced for about $20+ dollars. The more expensive the jewelry, the larger the jewelry and more exotic the piercing - the higher the price will be. Don't let someone on the street corner pierce you just to save a few bucks; it is important you go to a professional who knows what they are doing.

5. How To Care For & Clean Your Piercing

First, always wash your hands thoroughly before touching the area. Never touch your piercing or jewelry with dirty hands. Next, saturate a cotton ball with warm water, and gently wipe away any "crusties" that have gathered around the piercing site.

Throw the cotton ball away. Then, apply a generous amount of liquid soap to your hand, and apply to the piercing site and jewelry. Make sure you get the soap everywhere, but rotating the jewelry is not really necessary unless you notice it trying to "stick" to your skin. Rinse the piercing and jewelry several times with warm water, ensuring that all soap has been removed. Dry your piercing with a clean paper towel, and throw the towel away. You should do this a couple of times a day. Some professionals will give you an antiseptic and anti-bacterial cleaning solution to use.

6. "I Think My Piercing Is Infected. Should I Take The Jewelry Out?"

You should <u>not</u> remove the jewelry before contacting the person that pierced your ears. It could get worse or you could get an abscess if your ear gets infected. There are some cases where you may need to take the jewelry out, you should consult the person that pierced your ears or you family physician. Bacteria or puss can get locked inside if the hole closes up. In some cases, you will need to have the piercing open to allow the infection to drain. Infection can lead to other serious problems, so you should see your piercer or doctor to get recommendations on how to handle it.

7. Is It Ok To Get a Piercing If I'm Sick?

Getting a piercing (or tattoo) when your immune system isn't at 100% - is not a good idea. You're going to need your strength and your white blood cells to heal your piercing. Your body will not function properly if it's battling against a virus and bacteria.

8. Finding The Right Piercing Specialist

Check around until you find someone you're comfortable with, and they meet all of the proper standards of a good studio. This means safe, clean, good prices and referrals or someone you should trust. The studio should have sterilization equipment and gloves visible.

9. The Studio Should Have An Autoclave For Sterilizing

Every studio should have an autoclave (sterilizing unit). All equipment such as needles, forceps should all come out of a clean autoclave bag. If you don't see one, you should ask about it. Your piercing specialist should be wearing gloves and all needles should be sterile and clean and come out of a sterilized bag.

10. Ear, Tongue, Nose, Navel, Eyebrow & Lip Piercings

Ears have several places that can be pierced. The most common being the bottom of the lobe to wear earrings. Ears have also been pierced around the total lobe of the ear. Piercing guns should only be used for piercing on the earlobe. Here are a few more things to know when considering piercing other areas of the body.

> ***<u>Tongue Piercing;</u>*** Tongues can be pierced in different places such as the center of the tongue, under the tongue, or horizontally. Someone inexperienced can pierce under the tongue and cause your teeth to shift. If someone gets pierced under the tongue and the barbell is too long, you can develop small ulcers on the skin. A vein could be accidentally clipped and bleed. ***<u>Nose, Eyebrow & Lip;</u>*** Noses can be pierced in the nostril or through the nasal septum. Eyebrows are pierced through skin above the eyebrow area. Lips are usually pierced on the corner of the mouth. ***<u>Navel Piercing;</u>*** Bellys are usually pierced in the skin above the button.

This area can get infected inside the navel area or in the stomach area. Scar tissue, polyps and Keloids all may form as a result of navel piercings gone bad.

11. Piercing Questions & Answers from a *Professional Piercing Specialist*
Q: Should you get a pierced with a piercing gun? **A:** Most professional piercers say using a gun causes more infection and takes longer to heal. **Q:** Is piercing painful? **A:** It hurts a little, but it's not extremely painful. **Q:** If you get your navel pierced, will it damage your stomach or uterus? **A:** It does not, and you shouldn't be pierced that deep. **Q:** Will half of your face go numb if your eyebrow is pierced incorrectly? **A:** Eyebrow piercing should never be that deep. **Q:** When piercing under the tongue, if you hit a vein will you bleed to death? **A:** If a vein under the tongue is hit, it can usually be healed by going to the emergency room to see a doctor.

12. Tips to Remember
Before doing any type of piercing out of the norm, make sure it's ok with all parties concerned. Translation: Check with parents, coach or your employer to make sure your new piercing won't interfere with any personal, family or religious beliefs, sporting activity or job. You don't want to spend a lot of money on a piercing and then find out it's against your job guidelines or you can't wear it to a certain sporting activity. Consult a doctor before getting piercings or tattoos, especially if you have any family history that makes you concerned.

MY JOURNAL ENTRY
List 5 things you have learned about ***body piercing*** in this chapter. Discuss them with a parent, teacher, mentor or friends.

____

____

____

____

____

____

____

____

____

____

TATTOOS

Tattoos have been a universal art form of expression for many years. Tattoos have always been popular among adults, but have recently become a new phenomenon amongst our teen and young adult population. There are several new reality shows on television featuring tattoo parlors.

This chapter will help you think about why you want a tattoo and some of the issues and topics surrounding this controversial application of skin inking and design. You need to know the process of aftercare and recognize when any problems or medical conditions may occur as a result of your tattoos. We have included different options for tattoo removal. The goal of this chapter is to familiarize you with every aspect of getting a tattoo so that you will make an informed, educated decision. Do it for yourself, not because all of your friends are doing it. This is something you should think about seriously because, it's permanent and will be with you for the rest of your life.

12 TIPS TEENS SHOULD KNOW BEFORE GETTING A TATTOO:

1. What exactly is a tattoo, and how is it put on your body?
A tattoo is a series of tiny puncture wounds that carry dye into the different levels of the skin. When you first get your tattoo, it will scab so it can start the healing process. It may be swollen and there may be some crusting on the surface. This is very normal for a tattoo along with small amounts of blood oozing for up to 24 hours following the application. Your tattoo may also ooze other color fluids that look clear or yellow.

2. Get the right Design
When choosing a design for a tattoo, keep in mind that this is meant to be permanent. Designs on your neck or large designs aren't advised for the first one. Tattoos should have a special meaning, but not someone's name that you may not like in a few years. Smile. Tattoos are difficult to remove and cover. Your first one should be something small and discreet that you can hide with clothing. It should be something that has a personal meaning to you.

3. Choosing the Right Tattoo Studio & Artist
The best way to choose a studio and artist is by recommendations from someone else that has used them. However, sometime people just walk into a studio and pick someone. If you are putting something on your body that will be there for a life time, you should get as many recommendations as you can. Don't rush into this decision.

4. Choosing your Design / Providing I.D.
You must pick out a tattoo design from the studio, unless you've brought one of your own. The tattoo artist will probably ask for identification to check your age, and record your address and phone number in case they need to contact you at a later date for some reason. You will pay at this point; make sure you ask for a receipt in case you have to come back. Tattoos vary in pricing depending on the size and amount of color.

5. Sitting in the Chair

The next step is to sit the tattoo chair. Your professional tattoo artist will review the tattoo you are getting and make sure you are ready before getting started. If you are getting something in a personal or delicate area, and you don't want anyone watching, you may want to mention this to the tattoo artist when you make the appointment. They usually have back rooms or private areas for these types of tattoos procedures.

6. 5 Steps to Your Tattoo

The Shave; once you have confirmed where your tattoo will go, your tattoo artist will start the preparation phase for your tattoo. He/she will then prepare the area with alcohol and then shave it clean. For cleanliness and safety they should use a throw away disposable razor, after it has been used on you. ***Stencil Transfer;*** most studios today use a thermal-fax which prints the stencils out backwards and saves hours of tracing time. Your specific tattoo design gets inserted into the machine, and it transfers it onto a special thermal paper. When your stencil is ready, the next step will be to create the transfer onto your skin. Some artists can draw wonderful free-hand artwork directly onto your skin without the transfer paper; these few are extremely talented and gifted. Artists will use soap and water or deodorant to moisten the skin, this will aid in making the design transfer better and darker onto your skin. Once the paper is pulled away from your skin, it will leave you with a purple-ish and blue likeness of your tattoo design. This will give the artist an outline or blue print to work with. ***Equipment Preparation;*** your tattoo artist should now start preparing their tattoo machine. The inks will be placed in little tiny cups called "ink caps," the needles and tubes will be put into the machine. As with any tattoo equipment, you should make sure you see them remove the items from sterile pouches that hopefully have been in an autoclave (a little square machine that you usually see in dental and medical offices, it sterilizes instruments with heat and saline). Distilled water will be on hand in a cup or holder for cleaning needles during the process while they are changing the colors back and forth. They will also have an ointment sort of like Vaseline to use afterwards. ***Line Work;*** the line work is now done, which is the outline of the artwork. The tattoo artist will trace the line with the appropriate color, and then start to color inside with the color chosen for the tattoo. The ointment/Vaseline will be placed over your transfer design to prevent it from rubbing off, this also aids with the needle sliding along the skin. This may be when you start to realize what is really about to happen, when that first line is done. Go ahead and take that slow deep breath now. ***Shading & Completing;*** once all the line work is done, your artist is a little more confident now that the transfer part is out of the way. Now the shading and color comes, if applicable. Depending on the size of your tattoo, the artist may switch to a different set of needles called magnums (or mags). These needles are specifically designed for coloring and shading. They may put a hot towel over it once it's complete. Once they clean it up, the artist may like your design and want to take a picture of it for his/her portfolio collection. If this is a licensed or private design, or it's in a delicate place, you can ask them *not* to take a picture.

7. Dressing and Bandaging

Your tattoo is finished and clean, but it is still an open wound and it needs to heal.

Ointment will be put over it to protect it. It will be applied to the tattoo to prevent the invasion of airborne bacteria or organisms that cause infection. A bandage, usually a square clear plastic or gauze will be applied to the tattooed area with tape to make sure it won't come off. Your tattoo artist should give you instructions on what to do from this point. Make sure you keep your aftercare instruction handy.

8. Aftercare Instructions

The last part of the tattoo process is time for your aftercare instructions to be given to you by your tattoo artist. They should give them to you verbally and also give you an instruction sheet to take home. It is important to listen to every word and carefully follow the instructions. It is your responsibility to make sure your tattoo is well taken care of. The artist cannot be blamed if you get an infection because you didn't follow their directions. Did we forget to mention that getting a tattoo comes with other potential problems? Read below.

9. Problems that Can Happen As A Result Of Tattoos

Dermatitis; a mild redness of the skin or rash of small red bumps. A more severe reaction can look like swelling with redness and large blisters. ***Allergic reactions*** to tattoo dye are rare but can occur; the different colors in a tattoo are made from different types of materials. For example, the red color comes from mercury, the green from chromium, yellow from cadmium and the blue from cobalt. Allergic reactions to red dyes occur more frequently than allergic reactions to other colors. ***Infectious diseases***, such as; hepatitis B, hepatitis C, tuberculosis, tetanus or HIV can be gotten if a dirty method or equipment is used.

10. A Keloid Scar

A Keloid Scar is a harmless growth of fibrous tissue at the site of a healing scar caused by over production of collagen. Keloids are most common on the breastbone, upper back, shoulders, ears, hands, scalps but they can occur anywhere on the body. Tattoos can turn into Keloids if you are prone to them (already have gotten them from other things such as piercings). If you have ever had a Keloid, you should get an approval from your family doctor prior to getting a tattoo. Some people, especially those with dark skin, are more prone to developing Keloids. Signs and symptoms include; firm, raised hard scars, tenderness, itching, continued growth and claw like projections with color that varies from slightly pink to very dark. Keloids do not require treatment. However, for cosmetic reasons or to relieve Keloid pain or itch, they can be surgically removed or treated with medication. If removed surgically, a Keloid may come back in the surgical scar. Please consult you physician immediately if you think you have a Keloid or desire removal.

11. Removal of Your Tattoo

There will always be a reason where someone will want to remove a tattoo. When people break up with their girlfriend, boyfriend or leave a previous association they may want a tattoo removal. It could have just been a "bad judgment" tattoo, gang tattoo or one you just don't like anymore. There are several ways to remove your tattoo. The *laser technique* is the most effective but also the most expensive because it has to be performed by a doctor. This is the main treatment of choice. The other type of removal is by *surgical excision* where the skin is removed. There are also chemicals that will irritate and remove the skin, which is a form of dermabrasion. A good tattoo artist can possibly *cover up* a tattoo, depending on where it's located, how large it is, the coloring and how detailed it is. If you can't get it covered up with another tattoo, you should consult a physician that can recommend which technique is best for you. A tattoo is a permanent piece of art, think very carefully about the tattoo you decide to get. Get a tattoo that is in good taste and be mindful of using someone's name or an event tattooed on your body.

12. Parents? It's My Body!
Well yes it is. And according to the law, you can do whatever you want to it. However, it won't hurt to run it by the folks, just for the heck of it. You know, just to get their advice. Ask them questions like; have you ever had a tattoo? Did it hurt? Did it fade? If you had the opportunity to do it over again, would you? Ask their opinion on what type of tattoo and where it should go. Hopefully we've provided enough information in this chapter to give you all the information you'll need to present a good case. In some states you have to be 18 to get a tattoo without parental consent. Check your individual state for the legal age limit.

MY JOURNAL ENTRY
List 5 things you learned after reading about ***tattoos*** from this chapter. Discuss them with a parent, teacher, mentor or friends.

ADVANCED ETIQUETTE

The question keeps coming *"why do I need etiquette,* I know how to eat". The answer I keep giving back is, "it's not just about knives and forks". Etiquette comes in handy when you attend luncheons, weddings, formal dinner parties and events. You never know when you will be invited out to a luncheon or dinner, and you don't want to be the only one who doesn't know the basics of why there are 3 forks on the table. This Advanced Etiquette chapter will outline general etiquette tips, restaurant, formal dining, tipping, traveling, how to exit automobiles and elevators.

12 THINGS FOR TEENS TO KNOW ABOUT ADVANCED ETIQUETTE:

1. General Faux Pas (Things that are NO-NO's, and shouldn't be done)
You should never; talk in movies, have on cell phones or ringers once the movie starts. While you're in the movie theatre don't put your feet up or sit in front of someone shorter than you. Do not cut in front of someone or butt the lines. It is improper to ask someone their age, or address them by their first name unless it's a family friend or they introduce themselves this way to you. You should always use their title and last name, (unless it's teen to teen). Do not litter outside, or throw litter outside of cars, you should not wear hats inside of buildings.

2. Restaurant Do's & Don'ts
Don't use your cell phone while eating. Take off your hat and if there is a coat check, put away your hat, umbrella, bulky briefcase or book bag. If you made reservations, attempt to be on time, call or cancel if you won't be able to make it. Don't be too loud or obnoxious, especially if you are in a group. Do not eat with your elbows on the table during the meal. No ashtrays mean "no smoking." Never blow your soup while it's hot. Ask for the check quietly; do not snap your fingers. You should tip if the service is at least marginal. Most waiters and waitresses make very little per hour and rely on tips. If service is poor, feel free to tell a manager.

3. Other Etiquette Tips:
Don't put salt or pepper on food, before your taste it. Hors D'oeuvres are finger foods to eat while mingling at small affairs. They are just there to eat, absorb your alcohol and used for tasters. They are not meant to be a meal. You shouldn't attempt to put them in a doggie bag to take home. Don't pop gum in public or around others. If you are chewing tough piece of meat – remove it gently and put on a saucer or side of your plate.

4. Understanding the Table Setting
(1) ***Dinner plate*** - The center of the place setting. When finished eating, do not push the plate away from you. Instead, place both your fork and knife across the center of the plate, handles to the right. Between bites, your fork and knife are placed on the plate, handles to the right, not touching the table. **(2)** ***Soup bowl*** - May be placed on the dinner plate.

If you need to set your soup spoon down, place it in the bowl. Do not put it on the dish under the bowl until finished. **(3)** ***Bread plate*** - Belongs just above the tip of the fork. Bread should be broken into bite -sized pieces, not cut. Butter only the piece you are preparing to eat. When butter is served, put some on your bread plate and use as needed. **(4)** ***Napkin*** - Placed to the left of the fork with the fold on the left. Sometimes placed under the forks or on the plate. **(5)** ***Salad fork*** - If a salad fork is used, it belongs to the left of the dinner fork. **(6)** ***Dinner fork*** - Placed to the left of the plate. No more than three forks to the left of the plate. If there are three forks, they are usually salad, fish, and meat, in order of use, from outside in. An oyster fork always goes to the right of the soup spoon. **(7)** ***Butter knife*** - Place horizontally on bread plate. **(8)** ***Dessert spoon*** - Above the plate. **(9)** ***Cake fork*** - Above the plate. **(10)** ***Dinner knife*** - To the right of the plate. Sometimes there are multiple knives, perhaps for meat, fish, and salad, in order of use from outside in. **(11)** ***Tea spoon*** - To the right of the dinner knife. **(12)** ***Soup spoon*** - If needed, to the right of the tea spoon. **(13)** ***Water glass*** - Just above the tip of the knife. **(14)** ***Red wine glass*** - To the right of the water glass. - A glass of red wine is held on its stem to preserve the chill. **(15)** ***White wine glass*** - To the right of the red wine glass. **(16)** ***Coffee cup*** and saucer not pictured - If needed, bring at time of coffee service.

5. More About Dining Etiquette

Try not to be intimidated by formal settings. Most formal settings have centerpieces, and plenty of silverware. You will have forks on your left, spoons and knives on your right. Your liquids are all on the right, usually at least 3 to 4 glasses. Your water goblet is farthest to your left, glass for pop or tea, then wine glasses. Start from the outside and work in. The first thing you will probably get is your bread, your soup or salad and then your main course will start. ***Here is an easy tip to help you remember which drink is yours***. Hold both hands in front of you, palms facing each other. Using the tips of your thumb and forefinger, make circles on each hand. The remaining three fingers in each hand point upwards. Your left hand will form a "b" and your right hand will form a "d". Bread (b) is on the left, and drink (d) is on the right. Thank you Martha Stewart for that tip. ***Napkins belong in your lap***. Large napkins can be folded in half or with a quarter folded over the top. They should never be tucked into your shirt like a bib. Wait for the host to unfold his napkin before unfolding yours. In a banquet setting or at a restaurant, simply place your napkin in your lap as soon as you are seated. If you excuse yourself from the table, loosely fold the napkin and place it to the left or right of your plate. Do not hang it over the back of your chair. Do not refold your napkin or wad it up on the table either. ***Food is served from the left.*** Start eating hot food when it is served, do not wait for everyone else to begin. ***For soup, dip the spoon into the soup, from the edge*** of the bowl to the center, moving away from you. Only fill it 3/4 full to avoid spilling. Sip, not slurp, from the edge of the spoon. Do not insert the whole spoon into your mouth. It is proper to tip a soup bowl slightly to get all of the soup. Never turn the glass upside down to decline wine. It is more polite to let the wine be poured and not draw attention to yourself. If you are asked about wine and will not be drinking, quietly decline. ***Do not ask for a doggy bag*** unless it is an informal dining situation. Do not smoke at the table. Do not ask to taste someone else's food. Similarly, do not offer a taste of your food to someone else. Taste your food before seasoning it. ***Do not talk with your mouth full***. Cut only enough food for the next mouthful. Chew with your mouth closed. If soup is too hot to eat, let it cool in bowl. Do not blow on it. Practice good posture. If not eating, place your hand in your lap or rest your wrists on the edge of the table. Remember - do not put your elbows on the table. If hot food is burning your mouth, discretely drink something cool to counteract the food. When dining out, order foods that can be eaten with utensils.

6. Zippers, Wet Spots or Clothing Soils

If you notice someone with an open "zipper or fly" as it sometimes called, you should tell them. Find a nice quiet way to mention it so that the entire room doesn't turn around and say "ooooooo". The same goes if you see someone with a spot or soil in a delicate area on their clothes. The easiest way is always to put yourself in their position.

7. Driving Etiquette

A few things to know about driving; don't park your car at an angle, take someone's parking space intentionally, or take up more than one space. Do not park in handicap spots just because, there's usually someone that really needs it. Don't curse, scream, give "the finger" or cut someone off unnecessarily. If it happens accidentally, give them a nice wave to let them know it was an accident. If you know your signals aren't working or you need to get over in a lane, try to nicely ask the person by hand signals if you can get over, or wait instead of just jumping in front of them.

8. RSVP

Means **Respondez S'il Vous Plait** in French and "RESPOND IF YOU PLEASE" in English. Although people still do not RSVP properly, however - you should if your guests ask you to do so. Becasuse…in some cases they have to order food and pay for it in advance. So, they are not just trying to make your life more difficult, it's just the proper thing to do to confirm that you are coming to an event and how many people are coming with you. This can be very important when the meal plates are $20 plus. This can be very costly at formal events, luncheons and receptions. They usually have to produce a "guaranteed" number of people by a certain date, and they can not get a refund if you don't show up.

9. Tipping

Standard tipping is 15-20% of your total bill, but the final decision is whatever amount you feel comfortable with. Tipping is supposed to be for exceptional service. The other side of the coin is, many restaurants pay servers minimum wage and look for tips to supplement their salary. So, what if the server is having a bad day, or just makes a few accidents? What if you are having a bad day and things just aren't happening according to plan. Most people weigh the service and still tip the server, but not as much as if the service was better. Others that don't like the service, will not tip at all. When traveling in some areas bellmen, desk clerks, waiters and waitresses look for tips.

10. Entering Cars & Elevators

When entering and exiting cars always slide your feet together and lift them up into the car. When entering elevators and cars women should enter first and exit last. If you are with colleagues or business associates, the highest ranking individual should enter the car first and exit last, the same with an elevator.

11. Spitting, Smoking, Chewing Tobacco, Sneezing, Coughing

In the first chapter we mentioned spitting in public. All of the above should be done in private areas. If you smoke, look for designated smoking areas. It is rude to smoke while others are eating or without asking, especially if you don't see ashtrays around. Chewing tobacco is just an interesting and nasty habit - lose it if you can. If you are sick or find yourself sneezing and coughing always cover your mouth or use tissue. Recently someone told me you can sneeze in your elbow to avoid passing germs on your hands. However, if you have a hard sneeze you may end up with mucous on your shirt sleeve. Well uh…..

12. Traveling, Concierge & Hotels

When traveling you will have several concerns such as; reservations, rooms, general travel info, luggage and who to tip. First you have your room reservations, which you should check at least a week before you leave. When you get to your hotel and check in, if the bellman takes your bags to your room, they are usually expecting a tip of a few dollars. Your "Concierge" (pronounced "con-see-er")is used for information, special reservations, restaurants and directions to city events. If you order room service remember it's usually a little higher than actually going to the restaurant. Upper scale hotels have bathrobes, house shoes, snacks and mini bars in your room; these are usually their for your convenience and there is a cost for eating and drinking those items. So, are welcome to use the bathrobe, but if you take it home, you may end up with an additional $50 dollar cost on your credit card bill when you check out or get home. Make sure you find out about any charges before you leave; cots, room service, telephone charges, Internet fees, rental items and additional room charges. Especially if you are on a limited budget.

MY JOURNAL ENTRY

List 5 things that you have learned about ***advanced etiquette***. Discuss them with a parent, teacher, mentor or friends.

____

____

____

____

TEEN PERSONS WITH DISABILITIES

This chapter is designed to educate teens and young adults about school, education, jobs, entrepreneurship and sensitivity issues as it relates to persons with physical challenges or disabilities. As teenagers you must be sensitive to the needs of persons who have physical challenges. Hopefully, after reading this chapter you and your friends will be more educated and help others that are different. Persons that are physically challenged must have access to the world and everything it has to offer. This means including or mainstreaming them to regular high schools, colleges and jobs. These students may have special needs, but in many cases, are fully capable of participating in the same academics, activities and clubs as their peers. They have the same rights to be happy and enjoy living comfortably in their communities and social environment. Their IEP (Individualized Education Plan) will determine how involved and what level they will able to participate. The IEP is a specialized agreement between all aspects and personnel of their lives; parents, teachers, doctors, other medical professionals, the principal and the school board. This main goal of this special team is to ensure the needs and wants of a person who is physically challenged are being met - physically, emotionally, socially and literally. Mainstreaming and the inclusion of physically challenged individuals into regular programs and jobs are common practices in most states.

12 TIPS TO KNOW ABOUT TEEN PERSONS WITH DISABILITIES:

1. ADA Act of 1990

The ADA Act of 1990 guarantees that disabled Americans have the same opportunities and access in the workplace, government programs, public accommodations, transportation and telecommunications that other citizens enjoy. To qualify for ADA protection, an individual must have a physical or mental disability that impairs a "major life activity," such as walking, seeing, hearing or speaking. They must have access to competitive employment and living conditions.

2. Making Friends

It is a difficult enough task for teenagers to make friends. Add being physically challenged to the mix and it's very hard to make new friends especially in high school. If you know a teen person with a disability, and you want to be friends with them, you should do exactly that. Don't be afraid to get to know the person or ask questions. Don't let others dictate who you should be friends with.

3. Sensitivity & Behavior

When you meet a teenager that is disabled; don't pretend that their disability doesn't exist; you should not also automatically assume they need your help. Individuals with disabilities prefer to be called ***"persons with disabilities"***. It is important to be sensitive to someone that is different, it is just human kindness. Most times they are more dependent than you think. If you think they need your help, ask them how you can help. Whether a person is physically challenged or just plain shy, you should treat them as you would want to be treated. Don't make fun of people with disabilities under any circumstances.

4. Going to High School
Teens with disabilities will have to make the adjustment from grade school to high school. They want to fit in and enjoy the experience as well as have the academic opportunities. Make sure that any persons who will be a part of your high school experience be present at your IEP (Individualized Educational Plan) meeting. This includes; your special education department, your contact person, team leader and a friend if possible. Before school starts you should become familiar with the layout of the school and the teacher at your new school. It is also important that the principal in the school knows that you're there and what needs you have.

5. Sports & Exercise
Before entering into an exercise program or activity, a doctor should be consulted. They can also help you decide which program will be best for you to do, and the safest way to participate without furthering an injury. If you are looking for a sports/exercise program or offering a program for teenagers, the following information should be considered; location, what types of games, programs, activities, equipment are offered. Other considerations include; cost of program, dates, times and registration criteria. There are programs and facilities that have adaptive equipment that are specifically targeted to teens and kids with disabilities. These programs can be found on the Internet or through organizations and schools. Teens can benefit from sports and exercise; it helps to keep weight under control, build self-esteem, prevent fatigue, other health problems and make daily tasks easier to perform.

6. Relationships, Dating & Sex
Teens with disabilities are able to have relationships, date and in some cases have sex. This all depends on your emotional and physical limitations but it not impossible. Some teens have physical impairments such as; paralysis, loss of sensations or problems with genital functioning. This may interfere with sexual activity or functioning. This is not unusual for teens with challenges to have emotional barriers that may impair sexual activity. Some sexual problems stem from psychological and social issues. You are able to date and have relationships. It takes patience and understanding on both sides. If there is someone that you like, don't be afraid to let them know. Take it slow and start out as good friends. When there is someone you want to be more than friends with, you must learn how to communicate and experience your confidence level over time.

7. Learning Disabilities
A learning disability affects the way kids of average to above average intelligence receive, process, or express information and lasts throughout life. It impacts the ability to learn the basic skills of reading, writing, or math. The Coordinated Campaign for Learning Disabilities (CCLD), a coalition of national organizations within the learning disabilities community, defines LD as "a neurobiological disorder in which a person's brain works or is structured differently." Learning disabilities fall into two major types, plus another miscellaneous category. Following is a partial list of learning disabilities, and does cover every one. If you suspect that you have a learning disability, see your doctor immediately to determine your next step.

- **Speech and language disorders include:** Difficulty producing speech sounds, difficulty using spoken language to communicate, difficulty with verbal expression, difficulty understanding what other people say. **Academic skills disorders** would cause someone to have problems in the following areas; reading, writing or arithmetic. **Reading** problems are developmental reading disorders. Also called dyslexia, a person cannot identify different word sounds. **Writing** problems, which are developmental writing disorders called dysgraphia. A person with dysgraphia has problems with handwriting or with creating sentences that make sense to others. **Arithmetic** skills problems are developmental arithmetic disorders called dyscalculia. The person has problems with calculations or abstract mathematical concepts.

8. Physical Disabilities

Following is a partial list of physical disabilities; *Cerebral Palsy* - a loss of sensation or loss of ability to control movement, usually frequently caused by trauma at birth, *Spina bifida* – a defective closure of the spinal column with a loss of sensation below the defect, *Cystic fibrosis* – an inherited disease primarily affecting the gastrointestinal and pulmonary systems, *Down's Syndrome* – a congenital birth defect manifesting itself in moderate to severe mental retardation. Other disabilities include; amputations, Asperger Syndrome, Attention Deficit disorder, behavior disorders, burn injuries, cancer, diabetes, Epilepsy, Fetal Alcohol Syndrome, hearing impairments, language problems, mental retardation, Muscular Dystrophy, physical disabilities, speech difficulties and visual impairments.

9. College Preparation & Scholarships

Once you decide to leave high school and prepare to progress to college, you should seek information from your local Vocational Rehabilitation specialist. You can learn about counseling and tutoring services that will help to prepare you for attending college. One way to precede is to narrow your educational and/or employment choices with your IEP team and guidance counselor. Your guidance counselors can help you with interviews, references, applications and can assist you with applying for financial aid. To prepare in advance for college life, visit as many campuses as you can, and for jobs visit as many potential companies as possible. Meet all your deadlines for college admissions, including housing, admissions and registration. You should apply for as many colleges as you can. Research schools that will give you scholarships or have special programs that you can benefit from.

Scholarships; There are scholarships available for college. You can use traditional searches and websites and also take advantage of scholarships that are specifically targeted to persons with disabilities. A. Alvarez is the second Hawaii student in two years to win the Discover Card Tribute Award. In 2003, J. James Eno of Maui also won one of the top national awards. Up to nine are offered. • High school juniors are eligible to apply for the program. Applicants must have a cumulative grade point average for the ninth- and 10th-grade years of at least 2.75 on a 4.0 scale. • Judging is based on outstanding achievements in areas beyond academics. In addition to meeting eligibility qualifications, applicants must describe their future career plans, demonstrate outstanding accomplishments in special talents, leadership and community service and have faced a significant roadblock(s) or challenge(s). More information about the next contest will be posted this fall. For complete eligibility qualifications and more information, visit www.aasa.org/awards_and_scholarships/Discover/index.htm. This is just an example of one of many scholarships available.

10. Finding a Job

When seeking a job, persons with disabilities are eligible for competitive employment. This means they may apply for any job available. When job hunting, it's always best if you look for jobs that compliment your personality, passion, goals and skill set. There are some jobs that you will able to do OJT (on the job training) or OJE (on the job experience), this is always a plus. You will have to decide what job you can do that will not put any additional physical or mental strain on you. Vocational Rehabilitation, organization or state government/ specialist can help you find a job that will be a good match with your specific challenges. Employers are not allowed to ask if there is a disability, once hired the person may ask for accommodations.

11. Entrepreneurship

Entrepreneurship is a great step for a person with physical challenges. Many teenagers are millionaires that have started their own business. If you have a business idea, you may be able work from home and manage your own time and money. There are home based businesses that can be started for very little start up costs. You may want to turn a hobby into a business. There are some organizations such as Junior Achievement and others that help you learn about running a small business. Start your creative thinking as early as possible.

12. Independent Living

Living away from your family can mean moving into your own place. Often, when you first leave home, it can mean living with others, such as roommates in a dormitory, house or apartment. Before making the big move you can work on developing skills to help you make the transition to independent living. *Managing money* – you must learn how to live on a budget, pay your bills and keep up with your finances. *Maintaining your own living space* – you will have to find suitable housing, find resources to clean and maintain your living area. *Personal* - maintaining personal hygiene, clothes and grooming. *Preparing food or eating opportunities* - grocery shopping, cooking or going out to eat. *Clothing* - purchasing clothing items, washing and drying clothes properly. *Transportation* - knowing how to use public transportation and learning how to drive. Independent ***Living Centers*** are nonprofit, community-based agencies that run centers to help people with disabilities achieve and maintain self-sufficient lives within the community. Transitional living facilities are known for helping teens and young adults by providing job training services, money management and life skills training. Services include advocacy, information and referral, independent living skills training and peer counseling. These programs are provided in a residential setting and often offer training in: Life skills, Workplace literacy, Social skills development, vocational and career exploration and training, Time management, banking and budgeting.

MY JOURNAL ENTRY

List 5 things you've learned about ***teen persons with disabilities or physical challenges***. Discuss them with a parent, teacher, mentor or friends.

SELF-ESTEEM & CONFIDENCE

Self-Esteem & Confidence

Self-esteem is one of those vague, unexplainable, hard to define, feelings. It is a complex set of emotions that plague, every teen in America. Self-esteem is high for some teens and low for others. Peer pressure has a large influence in the area of self-esteem, because what teens think about one another is very important. It sometimes determines how one feels about their personal self worth and individual confidence level. We have several suggestions of ways that will boost self-esteem and confidence. Staying involved in activities will help win the esteem and confidence game. Confidence can make a big difference in your presentation, the manner in which you conduct yourself and the way people respond to you.

12 TIPS FOR TEENS ON HOW TO BOOST YOUR SELF-ESTEEM AND BUILD YOUR CONFIDENCE:

1. Exercise

Exercise will help you boost your self-esteem and your confidence level. You can involve yourself in team sports or work out alone or at home. Whatever suits your personality, time and style. Just giving yourself the will power to do it will help you emotionally. You don't have to be an athlete to exercise. Individual ways to exercise include; joining a healthy club, dance class, golf or walking. Exercise is a state of mind not, and *Size* does not matter.

2. Sports

There are plenty of sports teams to join in school, park districts, community organizations and churches. This will boost your self-esteem, while you also learn/perfect a sport and you will get to interact with other kids you may not otherwise have met. They will also become friends or respected teammates. Individuals excel at different things; you may be a good athlete, and it may be your special gift. Receiving trophies and accolades for playing on sports teams, will boost your confidence.

3. Special Clubs, Organizations, Churches & Faith Based Ministries

Schools have academic clubs, decathlons and clubs for almost everyone. There are newspapers, woodshops, auto shops and computer clubs. Regardless, if you're with the smart group, the art group, the jocks or the French club, there is a place for everyone. Get in where you fit in. *Churches* are usually an excellent place to meet other youth and participate in Faith-Based Programs. Some churches and community organizations have as many as 20 youth ministries to include; choirs, sports teams, drill teams, youth ushers and youth ministers just to name a few. These programs start where the school and park districts stop. There are only so many positions in school and park programs. This is where the remaining teens can go to hone in on their skills and get more training.

4. Study & Work hard in School
Every student will not be an "A" student. Do the very best you can and you will be a diligent student. Be responsible for your grades and your work. Study when you have a test and do your homework and school projects without being told. The better your grades and participation in school, the better it will make you feel. Get all of your kudos' and pats on the back wherever you can. Each one is a small pebble on the road to building self-esteem and confidence.

5. Positive Friends and Positive Thoughts
Even as an adult, positive friends surrounding you are important to have. Positive friends help to weigh out the negative things that happen around you. It's good to have those happy, upbeat people around us especially when we are going through trials or tribulations. We're talking about those friends that give us a good belly laugh on a bad day. Your positive friends will see the glass as half full and it will eventually rub off on you. These are the friends that you can call any time of the day or night. If you keep positive friends around, providing positive conversation then you will develop a positive personality style over time. Positive in – Positive out.

6. Grooming & Clothes
Being well groomed is important for your self-esteem and confidence. Every person in the world is not pretty or good looking, but many make up for it by being extremely well groomed and handsome. Make sure that you are well dressed and look good in your clothes. It all makes a biggg difference. How you dress and present yourself will also give you points with the crowd and it will ultimately make you feel good. Try to wear clothes that compliment you, not fads or clothes too trendy. Make sure your hair is taken care of regularly, and that it's washed and trimmed neatly. Take care of your nails and skin regularly. Brush and floss your teeth daily to prevent cavities and plaque build up. Make sure your clothes are ironed when needed then check for stains and lint before leaving the house. Also, if you are into accessories, you may want to take a final look before leaving home to check your ties, belts, necklaces and jewelry to make sure all is matching and you are looking your very best.

7. Health, Eating & Diet
Get regular check ups and pay close attention to your health. This means physical check-ups, getting regular dentist visits and getting your eyes checked every year. Your diet is very important part of taking care of your body. If you have acne, you may feel insecure about it. If you don't feel good you won't project a good image. If you feel that you may have health needs, pain, or need better health, take care of it sooner than later. Teens today are more health conscious than ever, and it is your responsibility to maintain proper exercise, diet and health. If your doctor or trainer alert you to health concerns that may exist with your body, stay ahead of the game. The better you feel physically, the more confident you feel overall. When you are feeling sick or physically not at 100%, you will not have your regular personality or persona. This will also affect the way you act and they way others respond to your actions. You only get one body – do it good. ***Eating & Diet;*** The better you eat, the better you look, the better you feel about yourself, the better others feel about you. Limit your junk food; try to cut back on fried foods, acids and pop. It will help to cut down on your skin breaking out. Some of what you eat will come out or show up in

your skin, weight and other ways. Eat your proper servings of vegetables and water, this will make your hair and skin look healthier. As discussed earlier, when in restaurants, ask for diet or vegetarian menus when trying to cut back. This is very common, and most restaurants or fast food places are glad to comply. In the end, it will make you feel better about yourself. It's a positive circle.

8. Peer Pressure

It is really hard to have high self-esteem and confidence when others are waiting to pounce on you. They have high requirements for you to be a part of their "clique". Then there is pressure from the smart kids, the cute kids, the well-dressed name brand kids, the sports kids and the popular kids. If all this isn't enough then you have the TV. ads, music video and entertainers setting the bar of what you should look like. Here's the *NEW RULE* – work on yourself a little at a time. Do as much as you can, but don't stress yourself out. Don't let others dictate your life, clothes or hairstyle. Be your own brand.

9. Inner Confidence

You must know what YOU want out of life. You must get inner confidence from within. It seems hard, but sometimes when there's no friends, or family around and you are competing in a sport or academic program you have to get your confidence from way down deep within. On one of those days where there's no cheering squad, on one rooting in the stands for you, you must muster up all the courage from your toes and keep going. This comes from knowing who you are, what you want out of life, and not letting anyone stand in your way. This is not what your parents want, what your friends or teachers say is good for you, this is what you want.

10. Body Image & Body Language

Body image is number one in the minds of teenagers. After watching television, teens can feel too fat, too skinny, ugly, too much of this and not enough of that. Teens have confessed to being obsessively concerned about their hair length, type and styles, skin type, color and their weight. You have to work with what you have. The best you can do is stay healthy, have excellent grooming with your hair, nails and clothes. Your body is your temple, take the best care of it that you can. When thinking of your body, imagine that you were made with your characteristics for a reason, do not let anyone tell that a mistake was made. You must be comfortable in your own skins. After all it's yours. Translation: you must love yourself no matter what. *Body Language;* your body language says a lot about you. If you slouch, hold your head down and act like you don't have a care in the world, that's how others will treat you. If you walk straight, stand straight, speak clearly and project yourself, others will follow your lead. Take charge and control of your life and your world. The rest will fall into place.

11. Family Communication & Support

Communicate with your family, especially your parents. I was recently told by my teen daughter that our open communication is a big part of what keeps her grounded and emotionally healthy. She stays busy in pageants, sports tournaments, modeling and singing. I have my own cheering section at every basketball game or event. Some parents have never had the pleasure of watching their children. The busier, the better and the more confidence is gained for you. Your family must not only communicate, but support you. When they do, it makes you feel special. All of this boosts your self-esteem.

12. Public Speaking
Another way to boost your self-esteem and your confidence is to speak publicly. You can start at school, and continue in your community. Take advantage of every opportunity you can to speak in front of a crowd. It will get easier and more comfortable each time, and boost your confidence. If someone asks you at the spur of the moment, to speak or introduce someone, you will do it with ease.

The Self-Esteem Challenge:
The challenge is to find out your self-esteem and confidence level. After you answer the questions, send them to our website or email at info@forteenz.biz, or ForTeenz@aol.com. You will be entered into our monthly "Self-Esteem Challenge" for a drawing. Winners will be posted.

What is self-esteem?
Do you or someone you know have low or high self-esteem? Describe their actions?
What can you do to build your self-esteem?
What is the definition of self confidence?
What are the traits of someone that has low self-esteem or confidence?
What are the traits of someone that has high self-esteem or confidence?
How can you build your confidence?
How do you handle a person who tears down your self-esteem?

List 5 ways to boost your *self-esteem & confidence.* Discuss them with a parent, teacher, mentor or friends.

___

___

___

___

___

___

___

___

___

TEEN PREGNANCY

Teen pregnancy is a very emotional experience for a young person. Your entire life changes once you get pregnant and decide to have a baby. There are choices and hard decisions that will be life altering; it doesn't matter if it's the female or the male, making them. You are both responsible for this situation. Your support system of parents, family and friends will have a lot to do with most of these decisions. In order for you to be successful you must include your parents, and in some cases, the father of the baby. To avoid getting pregnant or contracting STD's, you should abstain from sex or use protection and birth control. Remember, time is one of the things we can't turn back. It's your childhood, have fun and enjoy it to the fullest. You do have options, when you grow up too fast you are taking years away from your life. There are several factors that have to be taken in consideration for young teen moms and dads.

12 TIPS ON TEEN PREGNANCY:

1. It Takes Two to Tango (This is a Dance)
It takes two people to make a baby. A male's sperm and a female's egg are the stars in this movie. So if you are having unprotected sexual intercourse without birth control, there is a chance you may get pregnant. It's that simple. You should be wearing a condom and using birth control. When two people are in the movie it changes the dynamics of it. Translation: This means the person using the condom, could not be using the condom effectively or correctly. The person responsible for taking birth control, forgets or does not take it. One of the parties could tear a hole in the condom, by accident or on purpose. When a condom isn't used at all you are also at risk of contracting HIV or sexually transmitted diseases (STD's). Birth control helps, but abstinence is the only 100% guarantee to keep you from getting pregnant.

2. Mamma's Baby
This is a slang term that parents sometimes use. It means that once you are pregnant, this baby is yours for sure. But, when the father says "he's not sure if it's his baby," you have to then prove it by a DNA test. In most cases, this hurts your feelings and if that's not enough, you now have to worry if he's going to support you emotionally, physically and financially. If you are having sex, you better make sure you are with a responsible person, because if you get pregnant and he says *"I'm not the father,"* it will shake your world. Avoid having sex with multiple partners, you want to be 100% sure who the father of the baby is.

3. Daddy's Maybe
This is another old saying that means the father has to meet the burden of proof. The mother does not have that luxury. If you are having intercourse keep in mind that each encounter with the opposite sex can possibly make a baby. When the female comes up pregnant, you have to be responsible for the part you played in the dance. Don't be hurtful if you know you may be the father. The sooner you deal with the problem, the better the outcome will be for you and the child. If you don't want to be on the other side of the fence, double and triple check your protection. You must buy and

personally put on the "raincoat/jacket/condom." Ask your partner directly about their birth control, but you "wrap it up" regardless.

4. Abstinence

This is the one sure way to avoid pregnancy and prevent catching any sexually transmitted diseases (STD's). Abstinence is choosing not to have any sexual intercourse. Many teens have made the smart decision to abstain from sex until they are in love or married. This is the making of a very strong young person. It's hard to stand up and be different, but smart to follow your own beliefs. There are groups of teens that practice abstinence and travel around the country speaking and motivating other teens. These teens speak at youth groups, churches and youth events to spread their message. They teach pre-teens and teens the benefits of being abstinent. The respect that you will ultimately receive from your partner is that *sex is a part of love.*

5. Signs & Symptoms

Are you pregnant? There are several signs and symptoms that young women may use to determine if they are pregnant.They include; missing your period, frequent urination that's not normal, increased appetite, attitude or mood changes, weight gain, bloating or larger breasts. If you have any of these symptoms listed above you may want to take a pregnancy test. The best advice is to see a doctor as soon as possible, this way you will know how far along you are and what options you have.

6. Pregnancy Tests

If you think you are pregnant, you need to take a pregnancy test. Although you can buy pregnancy tests over the counter, a test from a doctor is recommended to be absolutely sure. Drug stores sell pregnancy tests where a drop of urine is put in a tube and in a few minutes depending on the color it turns, it will let you know if you are pregnant. However, there is a small margin of error where they could be wrong. A doctor has three methods for pregnancy tests; a urine test, blood test and if needed a pelvic exam. The doctor can tell exactly how far along you are and they can tell you if you have any medical conditions that may cause complications.

7. Feelings and Emotions

Depending on the situation you may feel depressed,

uneasy, upset or want to cry. Girls sometimes feel alone and mad at the boy that got them pregnant. You will feel confused about the situation and may even wonder why this happened to you. Despite the stress, you must deal with the difficult decisions you are about to face. When is the right time to tell your parents, friends and family? What will they say or think and more importantly what will you do next? What about the father and how are you going to deal with him? You will have to ask yourself how you feel about pregnancy, abortion, parenthood, babies and adoption. Keep in mind, once this happens your decisions are top priority. What you feel matters most.

8. What to do Next & Other Options

You have been to the doctor or taken your pregnancy test and now it's confirmed that you are pregnant. After you have confirmed that you are pregnant, you must weigh your options individually. First, you must ask yourself *what do you want to do?* If you decide to have the child you must consider the following; **What resources and support systems will you have to assist you? Can you afford to raise a child?** A young baby needs formula, diapers, wipes and food on a daily basis. This is very costly, even with help from parents. The cost of daycare and medical needs must also be factored into raising a child. Will you be raising the child alone or will the father help you? You may decide to have the child and put it up for adoption. There are many adoption agencies that will help you if choose this option. You may decide to terminate your pregnancy and have an abortion. Some individuals have religious beliefs that prevent abortion. Before making a final decision, talk to your doctor, parents, family, the father of the baby, church or family therapist. Talk with anyone that you trust to assist you with weighing your options. Both decisions are emotional and hard to turn back once you've made them.

9. How to Tell Your Parents

How do you tell your parents? This will probably be the hardest thing you've ever done. It's going to be a challenge because you are worried about disappointing them. You feel they are going to be hurt and upset. They will, but its all part of life. Don't wait too late to tell them; pick a time, date and a quiet place to break the news. The number one mistake many teens make is they wait too late to tell their parents or don't tell them at all. This decreases your options. Your parents are always going to be there for you, no matter what. Trust them here. This is part of life, maturity and growing up real fast. There are going to be some hard days trying to climb this mountain and some days when this mountain seems like an anthill.

10. Who Else Do You Tell? Should You Be Ashamed?

This is your life and your business. You are not obligated to tell anyone else if you don't want to. The answer is whatever you think is right. Some teens say they have shared first with friends, church pastor, school counselor, nurse or trusted teacher. I wouldn't tell anyone anything that is not on the "need to know" list. You may decide not to have the baby, and then you've told too many people. The father of the baby has a right to know, some young fathers are very mature, responsible and supportive. Do what you feel is right, it's ultimately up to you. As a parent, I would love to know, so I could help my child with a life-altering decision. I may be disappointed and even upset, but I would want to be there for support. Remember, your parents will always be your parents. ***Should you be ashamed?*** Everyone that is human makes mistakes.

It's how you deal with your mistakes that make you special. You don't have to be ashamed that you are in this predicatament. Only you know how you feel and how many public questions you can handle. If you decide to buy bigger clothes and hide it, then that's your choice. If you are planning to have an abortion or give the baby up for adoption, you may not want to let anyone know so you don't get questioned or judged.

11. School & Life

Many teens decide to finish school even though they have gotten pregnant. This is a very smart decision, because you need your education so you can provide the best life for your child. The school nurse can help in case of an emergency. Your education should not stop unless you are physically unable to go to school. The longer you stay out of school, the harder it is to go back. There will be challenges such as; school, work and life, but you will have to juggle them all. You aren't the first or last person that's had to do it, make it work for you.

12. The Male's Role in the Pregnancy

The male's role in the pregnancy has changed over the years. Many young men are standing up and taking responsibility when a girl or their girlfriend gets pregnant. If she tells you about the pregnancy, you do have a say so. Most of the focus is on the female because, she will have to endure the childbirth, abortion or adoption emotions first and maybe the most. There are costs involved in some of these decisions; she may need financial as well as emotional support. If you are the male in this situation and you want to have some say in what happens with your child, you must step up to the plate and be willing to take the responsibility. Regardless of age, maturity, financial status or what others will say. You must do what you feel, or just do the right thing. This is where your parents can help you make decisions. This has nothing to do with your current relationship with this young woman. Just because you had a one night stand does not mean "you're not the father."

MY JOURNAL ENTRY

List 5 positive things you have learned about ***teen pregnancy*** in this chapter. Discuss them with a parent, teacher, mentor or friends.

____

____

____

____

____

____

Chapter Five: Just The Personal Stuff

SEX/ABSTINENCE/PREVENTION

Sexual intercourse is the act of a male and female engaging in physical contact using their genital body parts. Sex should only happen between consenting, mature individuals. Sex should also be shared with individuals that love each other and are mentally, physically and emotionally prepared for what comes next. Many suggest that this time is when they are married, or responsible for the potential outcomes related to having sex. Abstinence (not having sex) is what many teens and young adults choose as an alternative to having sex. This is a great alternative to prevent STD's and pregnancy. Many teens are proud of their abstinence and their right not to have sex. The peer pressure and curiosity centered around sex is overwhelming. Friends will sometimes put a lot of pressure on you, especially if you act like you haven't participated yet. Remember, adult behavior has adult like circumstances. There are many teen groups around the country that are focusing on abstinence.

Additional resources and information are available from websites, books, friends, parents, family, counselors and trusted adults. This is for teens who need a little more discussion and breakdown on the subject of sex. It's your responsibility to protect and keep your body free from disease. Don't blame others for your mistakes.

12 TIPS FOR TEENS ON SEX, ABSTINENCE & PREVENTION:

1. Abstinence
Abstinence is choosing not to have sex. Abstinence is the only method that can guarantee you won't get pregnant or contract an STD (sexually transmitted disease). You can also contract HIV from having unprotected sex. Abstaining from sex is a great way to enjoy friendships with individuals while learning to respect each other. Don't let anyone pressure you about sex, once it's done, you can't undo it. Abstinence is golden, wait until you're ready.

2. Sexual Intercourse & Safe Sex
Sexual intercourse happens when a male enters a female vaginally. This means that a male inserts his penis into the female's vagina. Sexual intercourse is not all it's cracked up to be by your peers. Some people have sex too early, lose their virginity and never feel the same. Some individuals have gotten pregnant after the first time and others have caught an STD. Before even considering this act, you must read this entire chapter to review and weigh the consequences. **Safe Sex;** you have heard the term "safe sex" used frequently, because your generation needs to be reminded. We used to talk about prevention, now we feel the need to talk more about protection. You must protect yourself from (STD's) sexually transmitted diseases and pregnancy by using condoms, foam, diaphragms, birth control pills and other methods. Protection must happen before engaging in any type of sex.

3. Birth Control
There are several different types of birth control. Birth Control must be used properly in order to be 100% effective.

Condoms are used to cover your genitals and protect sperm from leaving the male and entering the female. The first of course are condoms, which are put on over the genital area. Condoms are made for male and female genitalia, and there are special condoms for oral sex. ***Spermicides*** are chemicals that prevent sperm from traveling to the cervix and tubes where it would meet the egg to start pregnancy. Spermicides come in the form of foams, jelly and creams. ***Birth Control Pills*** are to be taken daily. ***Depo Provera*** shots can be obtained in one month or 3 month intervals. ***Diaphragms*** which are inserted over the cervix to prevent sperm from coming in. They must be measured and prescribed by a doctor. In recent years, a new ***Birth Control Patch*** has hit the market. The patch is put on the body like a band-aid and changed weekly. You can obtain most of the birth control methods listed above from health clinics, over the counter or from your family practice physician.

4. Oral Sex - "It's Not Sex"!!!

Ok kids. We're older, but not naieve. If I hear this one more time, I'm going to throw up. It's sex and although you can't get pregnant from oral sex, it's just as dangerous. You are still transferring seminal fluids, sperm and exchanging bodily fluids to each other that will allow you contract a sexually transmitted disease or HIV. This can make you very sick. The two types of oral sex are Cunnilingus and Fellatio. Cunnilingus is the licking or sucking of a girl's clitoris and/or vagina. Slang terms include; eating, eating out, going down and muff diving. Fellatio is licking or sucking a male's penis. Slang terms include; sucking off, going down, giving head and blow jobs. Male and female condoms should be used when performing oral sex.

5. Sexual Risks

Once you have sex, you may get pregnant, or impregnate someone; you may even contract HIV/AID's or a STD. HIV is a deadly disease still without a cure. Despite all the risks, many teens are still having unprotected sex in record numbers. Some teens also suffer additional physical, emotional and mental problems. They sometimes have regrets and need counseling from therapists or support groups to get them back on the right track. Some teens start going to church or faith-based programs that will help them deal with the emotional aspect. It is possible that you may begin to have medical problems as a result of sexual intercourse or sexual activity. If you are having sex, or contemplating having sex, think of all the risks that come with this grown up activity.

6. Virginity

The word virginity is derived from the word "virtuous" or pure. Virginity infers that a person has *"never"* engaged in sexual activity. Males or females can be virgins. In some cultures, women are required to keep their virginity until they are married. This century would make it difficult for these restrictions to be imposed because of changes that have occurred in sexuality and equality between men and women. We hope that a young woman keeps her virginity to protect herself from unwanted pregnancy and sexually transmitted disease. The social stigma that is associated with (a) being abstinent and (b) boys/girls being a virgin, can sometimes be too much peer pressure for teens. The good news is abstinence is being nationally accepted by more teenagers on television, websites and in schools. This takes away the negative pressure previously associated with it. Then there is additional stigma associated with sex being a "rite of passage for guys," but not for girls. Girl's and boys both have to make informed mature decisions when it comes to keeping their virginity. The longer you keep your virginity, the more you are in control until you are sure you are ready. Trust me, the wait will make the experience all the more worthwhile.

7. Who Do You Discuss Sex With?

It used to be called the "birds and the bees," now it's the real deal. Sex is still a difficult subject to discuss. When you have questions and you want straight answers to personal questions – who do you ask? If you have important concerns, who do you trust? You should start with your parents, close family or possibly a school nurse. If you have friends you can trust you can also discuss private problems with them. However, if you want the best advice start at home. You should be able to ask your parents about anything. I know that some teens have a hard time talking to their parents, but talk to someone. Do research by reading or checking the Internet. There's plenty of teen websites armed with information and resources. It's very sad when you hear teens say they thought they could get pregnant by kissing. Or a young woman saying she accidentally got pregnant because *she didn't think* she could have children. Stay correctly informed and educated.

8. Relationships & Date Rape

At some point in time you will meet someone as a teen or young adult and the subject of sex will come up. The person you are dating may threaten to break up with you if you don't have sex with them. Do what is right, do what you feel or know you should do. Talk to your parents if you can. No one has the right to pressure you about sex. If a person is pressuring you, they are not respecting your feelings. Also, if a person forces themself on you, or you say "no" - this is considered rape. Rape is a very serious offense and should be reported to the police. If your partner is trying to give you an ultimatum, be strong and let them go. It's all about you. Date rape is illegal, if you have reason to believe someone spiked your drink, throw it out, and then – report it immediately.

9. Peer Pressure & Sex

Everyone is doing it. Everyone says they are doing it. They are telling you how great it is, or isn't. They are bragging and now you think you're missing something. They may make you feel like you are not mature. You must prevail (come out on top). Take care of yourself and your body. You will know when you're ready. Don't let friends make that decision for you. Don't let anyone guilt trip you into having sex. If they need to have more notches on their belt, let them get them from a belt maker not from you! If your friends make you feel bad because they seem to be more experienced or know more than you, listen, learn but you don't have to do it. Having sex is one of the most *difficult decisions* you will ever have to make as a teen. Between peer pressure and relationship pressure, the social impact of the subject of sex will always be at the forefront of teenage conversation. Do your research, ask questions, communicate with your parents and family members. Know that these are life-altering decisions, *once you have sex, you can't go to the doctor to get your virginity back.*

10. The difference between Sex and Love:

Sex is the physical behavior that involves the stimulation of the genitals and other parts of the body for mutual pleasure. Making love is about mutual respect, fun and the ultimate desire to share physical pleasure with someone you care about. Love is the feeling you have about someone you want to spend a lot of time with. When you are in love with someone, you care about what happens to them and have genuine concern when you aren't with them. Usually when people get married, they are in love.

11. Same Sex feelings, or Homosexuality

Homosexuality is covered in detail in this chapter. The proper definition is when someone has sexual feelings for another person of the same sex. Although no birth control is needed in same sex relationships, they may still contract sexually transmitted diseases, protection is needed in all sexual relationships.

12. Myths about Sex/Excuses for Not Wearing Protection

- Having sex as a preteen will prevent you from having a baby. *Not true, girls have gotten pregnant as young as nine and ten years old.*
- I thought I couldn't get pregnant, because "I've had sex several times before and it's never happened." *You'll eventually get caught. You must use protection every time.*
- It was a one-night stand so I thought it was ok. *This doesn't prevent you from getting pregnant.*
- Your partner looks clean so they aren't carrying an STD. *You can't tell by looking at someone if they are carrying a sexually transmitted disease. There are no warning signs. No stamp on their forehead.*
- You didn't have the money or the time to buy a condom. *Very bad excuse. A $1 condom now will save you thousands of dollars later.*
- You don't like the feel of a condom, or your partner doesn't like the feel of it. *Again, it's not worth what may possibly happen as a result of not using condoms. Be responsible – not stupid.*
- Your partner said he was going to take care of it and forgot. *Now you are in the middle of the act and it's too late. It's just as much your responsibility; take care of your business.*

MY JOURNAL ENTRY

List 5 things you have learned about ***sex, abstinence & prevention*** after reading this chapter. Discuss them with a parent, teacher, mentor or friends.

DRUGS

Many teens and pre-teens are experimenting with illegal substances at younger ages. This chapter will help you recognize symptoms and learn more about drugs such as; marijuana, LSD crack cocaine, amphetamines, PCP and inhalants. Drugs and alcohol are very easy to obtain. Drug habits may be formed not only by illegal drugs, but legal substances such as caffeine and pain medication. Although this is no excuse, it is the originating cause of some of our chronic drug users. Don't be fooled by experimental drugs and the attraction of pretty colored alcohol. They are addictive and sometimes lead to heavier substance abuse, physical disease and health problems. The drug game is scary and you may never know when your drugs are laced with a chemical additive that can damage your mind and your body permanently. If you are in school and others are drinking, smoking or using marijuana stand up and just say NO.

12 TIPS FOR TEENS ABOUT DRUGS:

1. Drugs are Addictive Substances
If you are using drugs, you may get addicted and have severe emotional and physical problems. Drugs aren't nice to your body and are one of the hardest habits to kick. If you are the child of an addicted parent, you have a higher risk of being addicted to drugs yourself. If you are addicted to drugs, please get help as soon a possible – the longer you wait, the harder the healing process will be. You can speak to a parent, school nurse or trusted family member. To learn more about addictive behavior and drugs you can research the Internet or attend a free session with local Al-Ateen (teen support group).

2. Experimenting With Drugs
Teens have been known to start experimenting with drugs on grammar school, middle school and high school campuses. Schools are trying to combat these problems by checking book bags and periodic locker searches. It is up to you to be responsible, the choices you make today, will affect you tomorrow.

3. Gateway Drugs
Teens that start or experiment with drugs like marijuana will eventually graduate to using heavier substances. Marijuana is called a *"gateway"* drug because it leads to heavier drugs. Most teens think that marijuana (Mary Jane, reefer or blunt) is not addictive and not a big deal. This is not true. You can easily get addicted to marijuana and people often lace it with other drugs. Addicts usually remember smoking a marijuana cigarette first and then getting hooked on harder drugs because the first one is no longer sufficient. Marijuana looks similar to pencil shavings or small leaves that are rolled into cigarette papers and smoked like a cigarette.

4. Peer Pressure & Drugs

Peer Pressure is a significant reason most teens initially experiment with drugs. They are not your friends if they encourage you to do something to hurt yourself. It doesn't really matter if they are friends or family, you know the difference between right and wrong. You must take care of yourself, this is your life, take control and keep a drug free body. *Super Cool Drug* users are the drug users in your school or community that seem to have it all under control. Seems like they are not affected by addiction or the other rumors you have heard about. Here is the part you may not see, they are usually having trouble in school, concentrating or adhering to responsibility. They are experiencing other symptoms such as; depression, self-doubt, self-hatred and many other mental, physical and emotional problems. If your friends call you names, or make you feel uncomfortable for not participating, step up and be a leader and not a follower.

5. Signs of Marijuana Use

Signs that someone that has been using marijuana include; a lazy or lackadaisical attitude, trouble concentrating on studies and at work, sleepy red eyes and losing interest in social activities or school. These drugs can be in your system for up to four weeks and you should know that many employers will now test you for this substance.

6. LSD, PCP

LSD (lysergic acid diethyl amide) is a hallucinogen and one of the most potent mood-changing chemicals. LSD, commonly referred to as "acid," is sold on the street in tablets, capsules and occasionally liquid form. It is odorless, colorless, has a slightly bitter taste and is usually taken by mouth. Often LSD is added to absorbent paper, such as blotter paper, and divided into small decorated squares, with each square representing one dose.

PCP (phencyclidine) is illegally manufactured in laboratories and is sold on the street by such names as *angel dust, ozone, wack*, and *rocket fuel. Killer joints* and *crystal supergrass* are names that refer to PCP combined with marijuana. The variety of street names for PCP reflects its bizarre and volatile effects. PCP is a white crystalline powder that is readily soluble in water or alcohol. It has a distinctive bitter chemical taste. PCP can be mixed easily with dyes and turns up on the illicit drug market in a variety of tablets, capsules, and colored powders. It is normally used in one of three ways: snorted, smoked, or ingested. For smoking, PCP is often applied to a leafy material such as mint, parsley, oregano, or marijuana. Both of these drugs are highly addictive and can land you in the hospital, or lead to an overdose or death.

7. Stimulants

Stimulants such as cocaine and crack stimulate the nervous system. These drugs are sold in small affordable doses, but can quickly become an expensive habit. Crack can be easily found; it's highly addictive and can sometimes be very deadly. Cigarettes and marijuana have been known to be laced with cocaine, and one hit (one pull) has started you on a habit. Most marijuana users start to smoke crack for a more intense high. It is said to be one of the most addictive drugs ever produced. Addiction symptoms include; anxiety, irrational speech, panic attacks and depression.

8. Inhalants

Inhalants are chemicals that produce fumes that are usually sniffed such as; glue, gasoline and nail polish remover. They are called "whippets, poppers or snappers". Teens have been known to sniff other household and daily use items such as; paint thinner, felt markers and cleaning products. The drugs are ingested through the nose and give immediate results. A person that has ingested these drugs resembles a person that is intoxicated by alcohol. If these fumes are being inhaled, it can cause loss of sensation and unconsciousness.

9. Amphetamines

Amphetamines are also called uppers, speed, crank, crystal or tweaks and are similar to cocaine but have longer "high" periods. Users feel panic, confusion and hallucination. Ecstasy, also called "X", is also known to produce a euphoric feeling that induces sexual urges. However, it is also very addictive and causes severe health risks.

10. Driving under the Influence of Drugs – DUI / The Law

Driving under the influence of drugs or alcohol is not only illegal but deadly. You should always have a designated driver. If you are riding with drivers under the influence, you could die along with everyone in the car. Have you noticed the driver never gets hurt in these types of accidents? Driving under the influence will can cause you to loose your license and your car. ***The Law;*** If you get caught buying or selling drugs, you can get a police record and possibly go to jail. If you get caught with alcohol, drugs or cigarettes on a school campus that is an automatic suspension for the first offense and you can risk possible expulsion.

11. Living with Adult Drug Users

If you are living with adult drug users, I'm sure it's extremely hard to resist the temptation to experiment with drugs. There are teens that "get high with their parents," older siblings or family members. To many of us, that's bizarre and ridiculous because it goes against the grain of what the world has taught us. The truth is, it's dysfunctional, but it does happen. Adults participating in this type of illegal behavior should know better. You are now approaching young adulthood and must take responsibility for your own behavior. You know it's wrong, so say "thanks, but no thanks." This is not responsible parenting. It causes a destructive cycle within your family that may be passed down to future generations.

12. Therapy, Resources, Support Groups

Don't be afraid to join a support group or get counseling for problems with alcohol, drugs or smoking. There are several *free* anonymous groups that you can attend to get help with a problem or potential problem. Sometimes it's easier to talk with people that you don't know, but that share the same type of situation or concerns.

MY JOURNAL ENTRY

List 5 things you learned about ***drugs*** as a result of reading this chapter. Discuss them with a parent, teacher, mentor or friends.

DRINKING AND SMOKING

Though millions of Americans smoke cigarettes and drink, these habits are extremely harmful to your health and those around you. It has been proven that second hand smoke can harm others that are nearby. Cigarettes are made with nicotine, one of the most addictive and legal drugs available. Nicotine and Alcohol are two drugs that can cause more substance abuse problems among teens than other drugs. The best way to free your self from this disease, addiction and future medical problems is to abstain from drinking and smoking. This is especially true for teenagers. Life is filled with diseases that cannot be prevented, alcoholism and smoking can be, the choice is yours.

12 TIPS FOR TEENS ABOUT DRINKING AND SMOKING:

1. Smoking is Harmful
Smoking is harmful and hazardous to your health. Hundreds of thousands of people die each year from tobacco related illnesses. You don't want to find out later that you have cancer or an incurable disease that was caused from smoking or second hand smoke. Smoking also turns your teeth colors and sometimes makes them very difficult to clean. Smoking makes your breath, hair and clothes smell. When others are around you, the smoke is picked up in their clothes as well. This is a nasty habit you can do without.

2. Smoking and Tobacco Products are Extremely Addictive
The main ingredient in cigarettes, Nicotine, is an addictive drug and makes smoking a very difficult habit to kick. Smoking is very costly and the prices are continuing to soar even higher. Smoking and nicotine related products have been related to life threatening medical conditions. If you are addicted at a young age, you are getting a jump on ruining your health. Chewing tobacco is also addictive and a nasty little habit that causes you spit constantly. This is something your teen life can do without. Attempting to kick the habit can be done cold turkey (you just decide to stop), you can go to a doctor or purchase an over the counter gum, candy or patch to suppress your cravings. Check with your family physician first before buying or using these items.

3. Smoking & Peer Pressure
Peer pressure is how most pre-teens and teens start smoking. Newsflash: It's not cool and you don't look cool doing it. You don't have to do what everyone else is doing. Find a more productive hobby, one that you won't regret. Real friends will respect your right to say no.

4. Buying Cigarettes is Illegal Until You Are 18
By law, retail stores are required to "card" or request "I.D." prior to selling cigarettes and nicotine products to anyone who looks under 30. Smoking is illegal on high school campuses and is cause for suspension. Your educators don't want to see you doing harm to your body and neither do we. We are aware that this will not stop determined smokers, but hopefully deter some pre-teens and teens from buying cigarettes and smoking.

5. Smoking & Drinking is Harmful to Pregnant Women
Smoking while you are pregnant can cause harm to your unborn fetus. Babies may be born with asthma, allergies or respiratory infections. It is a fact that children who grow up in households with smokers are more likely to experiment or start smoking. *Pregnant women that drink alcohol*; babies that are born to mothers who drink are subject to Fetal Alcohol Syndrome. A pregnant female that smokes and drinks is subjecting her baby to several types of birth defects. If you are pregnant, you should not drink, smoke or use any drugs.

6. Smokers Myths
We have heard many smokers say that smoking helps them to keep their weight down and that's why they can't stop. They say cigarettes help them calm down. For every reason a smoker uses to continue smoking, there's twice as many for them to stop. The most important reason should be so they can live a long healthy life.

7. Alcohol is Illegal
You must be 21 years of age to consume alcohol. Alcohol is illegal on high school campuses and will cause a suspension. If you are drinking or addicted to alcohol, you should talk to someone about it. There are free support groups such as AA (Alcoholics Anonymous) and Al-Ateen (teenage alcoholics) that will help you if you think you are addicted to alcohol. Respect the law, don't drink until you're of age or don't drink at all. Stores and restaurants are not permitted to sell or serve alcohol to you. You aren't missing as much as you think.

8. Alcohol is Very Addictive
For people that have addictive personalities or start drinking regularly, they can easily become addicted to alcohol. Pre-teens and teens are too young to make the judgment whether or not they are able to be a casual drinker. Drinking habits are similar to drug habits, they are easy to start, but hard to quit. You may be an alcoholic if you drink daily, have hangovers regularly, are depressed or upset if you can't have a drink, drink by yourself, desire drinks early in the day or want to stop and cannot find the will power to do so.

9. Alcoholism is an Inherited Disease
Alcoholism has been said to be genetic and you can inherit it from a parent or grandparent. If you have a family history of alcoholism, it is possible that you can also be addicted to alcohol. If this is the case, it is probably wise for you to avoid drinking any type of alcoholic beverages at all. When others are toasting, substitute alcohol with white grape juice, 7-Up or another non-alcoholic beverage.

10. Alcoholic Myths
Some people say that alcohol reduces fears and inhibitions. When under the influence of too much alcohol, people sometime say things they don't mean, or do things they didn't have the nerve to do without the alcohol. Reflexes are slow when drinking, and some use it when they need something to hide behind. Although alcohol does alter your mind and mental status, you are still responsible for your actions and you can't always try to blame the alcohol.

11. Drinking & Peer Pressure

If you go to parties, events or school and someone has liquor, turn it down. You will want to try it because everyone is doing it, but this is how you get into trouble. Underage drinking, drinking at parties and games, drinking while driving or at school are all No-No's. These actions, regardless of how popular and cool you perceive them to be, are all illegal. They can go from an innocent sip to a tragic accident in a matter of moments. Always keep your drinks covered at parties and outings to prevent someone from putting something in your drink.

12. DUI – Driving Under the Influence & Intoxication

Driving under the influence can be deadly. Always have a "designated driver," someone who does not drink or will not drink that night so they can drive everyone home. Make sure your driver is not under the influence of any type of drug and they are sober before you get in the car with them. This could be the difference between life and death. Millions of teens and young adults are killed each year by someone driving under the influence. Alcohol often plays a role in homicides, suicides, arguments, fights and altercations. Alcohol has also been known to negatively influence tense situations. If you are already in a volatile situation and people are upset or mad, do not add alcohol to the mix.

MY JOURNAL ENTRY

List 5 things you've learned about ***drinking and smoking***. Discuss them with a parent, teacher, mentor or friends.

___

___

___

___

___

___

___

___

___

___

___

For Girls Only!

This chapter is for girls only. Every girl and young woman should feel like she is the princess of the universe. She should know her inner "goddess." This means that you are in control of your mind, body, emotions and life. The goal is to encourage girls and young women to respect themselves, each other and demand respect from those who have not yet read this book. This includes the media, friends, boys and the world at large. You will notice after grammar school, your life will start moving really fast. Expectations and responsibilities will all change. Empowerment is the key to growth and knowledge as you mature through your life.

12 TIPS TEEN GIRLS SHOULD KNOW ABOUT TAKING CONTROL:

1. You are the Jewel
You are the Jewel, the Princess. Make sure you are the top priority in your life and respected by all. You can be loved by everyone, but start with yourself. This is to remind you that regardless of what is going on around you, you must stay on top of your game. Sometimes we put others before us and don't pay attention to ourselves. Be confident, self-motivated, and even a little selfish sometimes, but most importantly, have unconditional love for yourself.

2. Relieve Stress – *"Me time"*
You must relieve stress in your life. The best way to do this is to give yourself some "me" time. This means get your hair or nails done, get a massage or go out to your favorite restaurant. You can curl up in the corner and read a book, take a short vacation, enjoy a warm bubble bath, take a walk and get some quiet time to think about your life. Take a nice bubble bath, but just make sure you carve out some personal time just for you. This will cut down on your stress, keep you energized and give you time to clear your brain and think. A few minutes meditating or staring off into the stars can make a big difference.

3. Clean Your Room
You should always pick up your room without being told. Either make up your bed, or at least throw it together, and put away your personal items. Clean your dresser, straighten and organize your closet so it's easy for you to find your clothes. *Keep Your Clothes Clean;* put yourself on a schedule. Wash, fold and iron your clothes once or twice a week. Wash your bed linens once a week, the heavier blankets every other week. Delicate clothes and dry cleaning items should have tags on the inside with specific instructions on how to care for them. Sort your clothes by color and material. For example; if you have cottons you may want to wash them in cold water and fluff dry to keep them from shrinking.

4. Keep Your Body, Hair & Nails Clean
You must take care of your body with regular bathing and showers. Using scented bath oil beads and powders will keep you smelling good. Make a point to keep your hair up, if you can't afford to go to the hair dresser regularly, wash and condition your

hair at home. You may also want to go to a beauty school that gives discounts. You can give yourself a manicure as well with a bowl, soapy water, cuticle remover and a file. You can buy a small kit, but improvise (use whatever you have in the house) in between. Keep personal lotions, creams, deodorants and a favorite perfume on hand at all times.

5. Grooming and Dress

Grooming and dress is very important. You don't have to be beautiful, but you can be well groomed and look beautiful. Before leaving the house each morning, do a grooming checklist. Check your hair, your nails and your clothes. Check the little things you don't like to forget like earrings, a necklace or make-up. Check your shoes to make sure they aren't scratched up or the heel isn't run over. Iron your clothes when you see they need it, or at the beginning of the week. You can be well put together and turn heads by paying a little extra attention to yourself.

6. Be a Lady at All Times

Pay attention to the lady-like actions and etiquette you should practice on a daily basis.

If you are sitting in a skirt – cross your legs at the ankles. If you have a short skirt on – stoop straight down to pick up something you've dropped, do not bend over. ***Watch the way you walk***, because everyone behind you… is watching. Not hard switching – but a confident walk that says you're in control. Don't spit on the ground, use a tissue or go the bathroom. When eating make sure you have a napkin to protect light colored clothes. ***Speak clearly at all times***. This doesn't mean you're trying to be something you're not; you are just speaking proper Queen's English. This is how you will get in the doors of places. This will come in handy when you are trying to get a job or have an important interview. Eliminate "yall, yo yo and fittin to" from your vocabulary. ***R.E.S.P.E.C.T***., This is not just a well known song. Respect yourself and demand that everyone else does the same. Respect must be earned; you have to give it to get it. There has been much said about the media and it's exploitation of girls and women. Know who you are from within and have inner confidence. You aren't a "H" or a "B", or any other derogatory term that has been used to describe women. Read number 1. You don't have to dress provocative or let someone degrade you to get attention. Some people think negative attention is better than none at all – that isn't true. It tells everyone that you have low self esteem. Next they will be calling you names and gossiping. You'll want to take it all back and start over. So earn yourself respect in the beginning. If you don't know how to act around people, take the time to get to know them first. It will all come together when it's supposed to.

7. Exercise, Activities & Sports

It is a statistical fact that girls who participate in sports are less likely to get pregnant; they care more about their health and have higher self-esteem. Participating in sports and activities gives girls a sense of empowerment. Being involved with sports, after school programs, groups and clubs can help with team building skills. This will motivate you to do better in school and at home. Join a youth group or community program that you have interest in. You'll feel a sense of belonging and camaraderie being part of a team or group.

8. Personal Body Stuff

We talked earlier about body cleansing and personal healthy living. Here's a few tips on taking care of the private areas of your body.

Brush your teeth and clean your tongue. Use dental floss to remove all the plaque between your teeth. ***Clean carefully behind your ears*** where buildup comes from gels, hair oils and sprays. Don't forget to clean your ears thoroughly inside and outside around the edges, you can use a Q-Tip, but be careful as you can damage your eardrum. ***You must also clean under your nails*** and inside your belly button. When ***washing your body*** you must pay attention to all the personal areas that carry hidden odors. You must clean inside your vagina and the vaginal walls along with your buttocks. Don't forget to clean your feet and between your toes. You must also take extra care when you are on your ***menstrual cycle*** to stay clean and avoid odor. No one should know you are on your period. Always wrap your pad or tampon in a plastic wrapper and use the disposal boxes provided in the washroom. Never put them in the toilet, it will stop up the toilet system. Use products that deodorizers and smell fresh.

9. Health & Diet

You must keep up with your health. This means working out and watching what you eat. Join a dance class or exercise class at a local park.

You don't have to be an athlete to work out. You can workout at home, go to your school gym or do a small workout routine to stay fit. Walking a little bit each day will help you lose enough inches to make you look good in your clothes. You can walk around your school football field or a park in your neighborhood. You can join a sports team or other activity. ***You must also watch what you eat***, cut down on the junk food, drink water and change a few eating habits to fruit snacks instead of candy and potato chips. The less sugar you eat the better off your teeth will be. You also need to have ***regular medical and dental*** check ups. If you haven't had one, you may want to mention it to your mom or dad. You should have a dental check up and physical at least once a year. Dental visits will whiten your teeth and get the old plaque off. Make sure you get a sport physical if you are an athlete.

10. Birth Control & Sex

You must use or take birth control if you are having sex. You can get birth control from the health department clinics or from your family physician. But, personally being the parent of a teenager, we would like to be included in the process. The following types of birth control are available to you; condoms, birth control pills that can be taken once a day or diaphragms that are inserted into your vagina. Diaphragms must be ordered from doctor in order to obtain the correct fitting. New medical products includes; Depo-Provera shots that are given every 3 months and there is the birth control patch (similar to a band-aid) that you can change once a week.

11. Why Etiquette?

We have discussed etiquette and behavior in other chapters. So by now you know we're not letting up. Teenagers and some adults need etiquette training. Why? You will be attending proms, weddings, formal luncheons and dinners. You will be getting invited to lunches at upscale restaurants where you are expected to sit, eat and conduct yourself in a proper manner. It's never pleasant to be the only one not to have a clue what's going on. This basically means eating with the proper knife, fork, glass or knowing how to signal the waiter properly. Snapping your fingers is inappropriate. Etiquette is the art of learning proper manners to eat and interact with others. It's called exposing yourself and expanding your horizons. Remember, day to day etiquette and manners are equally important.

12. Have a Relationship with Mom, Grandmom or Female Mentor

You only get one real mom or mother figure. It doesn't matter if it's your adopted mother, grandmother, aunt or surrogate godmother. It is a proven fact that girls who have healthy relationships with their mother are better adjusted. There will be experiences in your life where a female bond or connection will be helpful when you need to solve personals issues or problems. So, the moral of the story is to keep a trusted relationship near at all times, you'll never know when you need one. ***Have a Relationship with Dad, Granddad or Male Mentor;*** The same can be said of a dad. Girl's need their dads. Fathers can provide help with friendships, relationships, a feeling of protection and life experience. A father figure does not always have to be the natural paternal father. It may be a grandfather, uncle or big brother. They always come in handy when you need to buy a car, need someone to go with you when you feel unsafe or just provide advice from a male's perspective. Sometimes just having dad or granddad around makes you feel more secure. If you don't live with your father, you can still keep a healthy relationship with him. It may take work, scheduling and understanding, but don't throw away a good potential relationship because you don't live together.

MY JOURNAL ENTRY

List 5 positive new things you learned after reading this chapter. Discuss them with a parent, teacher, mentor or friends.

FOR BOYS ONLY!

This chapter is for boys only. Every boy and young man should feel like he is the king of the jungle and his universe. You should be experiencing full control of your mind, body, emotions and life. The goal here is to encourage boys and young men to respect themselves, each other and demand respect from those who have not yet read this book. This includes friends, family, the media and world at large. You will notice after grammar school, your life will start moving really fast. Expectations and responsibilities will all change. Empowerment is the key to growth and knowledge as you mature through your life.

12 TIPS BOYS SHOULD KNOW ABOUT TAKING CONTROL:

1. You are the King

You are the king of the jungle! Ruler of your universe! Make sure you are the top priority in your life and respected by all. You can be loved by everyone, but start with yourself. This is to remind you that regardless of what is going on around you, you must stay on top of your game. Sometimes we put others before us and don't pay attention to ourselves. Be confident, self-motivated and even a little selfish sometimes but most importantly, give yourself unconditional love. Kings and princes must lead by example, if they don't, the will lose their place. Stand up, respect women, be mature, lead and follow when necessary.

2. Relieve Stress – *"Me time"*

You must relieve stress in your life. The best way to do this is to give yourself some "me" time. This means get your hair cut, a manicure, play basketball with friends or just chill. Take yourself out to your favorite restaurant. Maybe there's a book you've wanted to read, or you just want to take some quiet time to think about your life. Taking personal time just for you. This will cut down on your stress, keep you energized and give you time to clear your brain and think. Meditating for a few minutes or staring off into the stars will make a big difference.

3. Clean Your Room

You should always pick up your room without being told. Either take the time to make your bed, or at least throw it together and put away your personal items. Clean your dresser, straighten and organize your closet so it's easy for you to find your clothes. *Keep Your Clothes Clean;* put yourself on a schedule. Wash, fold and iron your clothes once or twice a week. Wash your bed linens once a week, the heavier blankets every other week. Delicate clothes and dry cleaning items should have tags on the inside with specific instructions on how to care for them. Sort your clothes by color and material. For example; if you have cottons you may want to wash them in cold water and fluff dry to keep them from shrinking.

4. Keep Your Body, Hair & Nails Clean

You must take care of your body with regular bathing and showers. Use scented after shave if you can, it will keep you smelling good. Make a point to keep your hair neat.

If you can't afford to go to the barber regularly, wash and condition your hair at home. You can also go to a barber-beauty school that gives discounts. You can give yourself a manicure as well with a bowl, soapy water, cuticle remover and a file. You can buy a small kit, but improvise (use whatever you have in the house) in between. Keep personal lotions, creams, deodorants and a favorite cologne on hand at all times.

5. Grooming and Dress

Grooming and dress is very important. You don't have to be the most handsome in the bunch, but being well groomed can make a big difference. Before leaving the house each morning, do a grooming checklist. Check your hair, your nails and your clothes. Iron your clothes when you see they need it, or at the beginning of the week. Check your shoes to make sure they aren't scratched up or the heel isn't run over. You can be well put together and turn heads by paying a little attention to the small grooming tips. There are many guys that aren't that good looking, but with well grooming – you can look extremely handsome. .

6. Be a Gentleman at All Times

We call it "home training." A few extra *yes ma'ams* and *no sir's* can't hurt. Open the doors for women and girls and let them walk through the door first. You must give respect to everyone so that you will gain it in return. You don't have to be the life of the party if it means embarrassing someone else. Speaking clearly and properly does not make you phony, it means you are speaking proper Queen's English. This is how you will get in the doors of places. This will come in handy when you are trying to get a job or have an important interview. Eliminate "ya'll, yo yo and fittin to" from your vocabulary. *R.E.S.P.E.C.T.* This is not just a well known song. Respect yourself and demand that everyone else does the same. Respect must be earned. You must know who you are from within - inner confidence. Don't let people call you out of your name. Some people think negative attention is better than none at all – that's' not true, it just tells everyone that you have low self esteem.

7. Exercise & Sports

It is a statistical fact that boys who participate in sports have less of a chance of getting into gangs; they care about their health and have higher self esteem. It will give you a sense of empowerment. Being involved with sports, after school programs, groups or clubs helps with team building skills. This will motivate you to do better in school and at home. Join a youth group or community program that you have interest in. You'll feel a sense of belonging and camaraderie being part of a team or group.

8. Personal Body Stuff

We talked earlier about body cleansing and personal healthy living.

Brush your teeth after every meal. Clean your tongue. Use dental floss to remove all the plaque between your teeth. ***Clean carefully behind your ears***

where buildup comes from gels, hair oils and sprays. Do not forget to clean your ears thoroughly inside, outside and around the edges. Use a Q-Tip, but be careful as you can damage your eardrum. You must also clean under your nails and inside your belly button. ***When washing your body*** you must pay attention to all the personal areas that carry hidden odors. You must clean carefully around your penis, scrotum, genital area and your buttocks. Don't forget to clean your feet and between your toes.

9. Health & Check Ups

You must keep up with your health. This means working out and watching what you eat. You don't have to be an athlete to work out. You can work out at home; go to your school gym to do a small workout routine to stay fit. You can walk a few laps a day; join a gym or sports team. You must also watch what you eat so that you can look good in your clothes. Cut down on the junk food, drink more water, change a few of those bad eating habits to fruit snacks instead of candy and potato chips. The less sugar you eat, the healthier and stronger your teeth will be. All teenagers should have regular medical and dental check ups at least once a year. You should have your teeth cleaned once a year, this will whiten them and get the old plaque off of your teeth. If you haven't had one, you may want to mention it to your mom or dad. Make sure you get a sport physical if you are an athlete.

10. Birth Control & Sex

It seems as though there's a new trend of teenage men of dating older women. We are not talking a couple of years, but several years older. Just keep in mind that although this seems like an enjoyable curiosity, everything comes with a price. If a 25-30 year old woman wants a 16 year old, what does say about her. Take your time to grow up, you will be grown soon enough. Don't let anyone steal your childhood youth; once it's gone, it's gone. You must make sure your partner is taking birth control if you are having sex. If you are not sure, or even if you are sure, you must take control and wear a condom. FYI: Birth control can be obtained from the health department clinics or family physicians. But, personally being the parent of a teenager, we would like to be included in the process. The following types of birth control are available; condoms, birth control pills that can be taken once a day or diaphragms that are inserted into your vagina. Diaphragms must be ordered from doctor in order to obtain the correct fitting. They have Depo-Provera shots that are given every 3 months or the new patches that must be replaced weekly. Although much of this birth control is for girls, you must be educated on what your partner should be doing. In the end you will both be responsible.

11. Why Etiquette?

We have discussed etiquette and behavior in other chapters. So by now you know we're not letting up. Teenagers and some adults need etiquette training. Why? You will be attending proms, weddings, formal luncheons and dinners. You will be getting invited to lunches at upscale restaurants where you are expected to sit, eat and conduct yourself in a proper manner. It's not a pleasant feeling to be the only one who doesn't know how to act. This basically means eating with the proper knife, fork, glass or knowing how to signal the waiter properly. Snapping your fingers is inappropriate. Etiquette is the art of learning proper manners to eat and interact with others. It's called exposing yourself and expanding your horizons.

12. Bonding Relationships & Mentors

Have a Relationship with Mom, Grand mom or Female Mentor:
You only get one real mom or mother figure. It doesn't matter if it's your adopted mother, grandmother, aunt or surrogate godmother. It is a proven fact that boys need loving healthy relationships with their mother. This is just to remind you that it's ok to embrace mom even though she may not have a good jump shot. Mom will be tenacious (stop at nothing) when she needs to protect her cub. So, the moral of the story is to keep a trusted relationship near at all times, you'll never know when you need one. ***Have a Relationship with Dad, Granddad or Male Mentor;*** The same can be said of a dad. Son's need there fathers. If your paternal father is not available, get a substitute to spend some quality time with. This doesn't have to be a hard job, once a week you may want to get with an uncle, grandfather or big brother and shoot some hoops, go hang out or do something positive. Fathers can provide help with friendships, relationships, a sense of protection, some guy talk and life experiences. They always come in handy when you need to buy a car or need a male's perspective. If you don't live with your father, you can still keep a healthy relationship with him. It may take work, scheduling and understanding, but don't throw away a good potential relationship because you don't live together.

MY JOURNAL ENTRY

List 5 things that you have learned or changes you will make as a result of reading this chapter. Discuss them with a parent, teacher, mentor or friends.

SEXUALLY TRANSMITTED DISEASES

The most important thing to know about having sex is that "if" you have unprotected sex, you may potentially catch a sexually transmitted disease (STD). This chapter will give you descriptions of STDs and ways to prevent yourself from catching a STD. We will also discuss symptoms of STDs to watch out for and suggested treatments for the different types of STDs. Types of STD's include; Bacterial Vaginosis, Chlamydia, Genital Warts, Gonorrhea, Hepatitis B, Genital Herpes, HIV/AIDS, Syphilis and Trichomoniasis.

STDs are a result of having unprotected sex with an infected person. Although some STDs are treatable, some of them like HIV/AIDs can be fatal; the treatment methods are sometimes painful and not as effective as you would like them to be. Pay strict attention to prevention and treatments. The National STD hotline is (800) 227-8922.

Abstain from sex, use condoms and birth control. If you don't have condoms, ask your partner or go out and buy some. No excuses. Your life may depend on it. Don't be afraid to ask them. Take control of your body and your health.

12 TIPS FOR TEENS ON STD'S:

1. Sexually Transmitted Diseases - STDs
Sexually transmitted diseases are commonly known as STDs. They are contracted by having sex with someone else who has a STD. This includes all sexual activity that involves the mouth, anus (behind), penis or vagina. STDs are a serious illness that requires medical treatment if you contract them. Also, certain STDs such as AIDS are incurable and could be deadly.

Prevention of STDs; the most effective methods is to remain abstinent (not have sex), or limit the number of partners you have sex with. Don't have sex with a person you suspect or have heard may have a STD. Know as much as possible about your partners and make sure you educate yourself about STDs. The next recommendation is to have a monogamous (one-on-one) relationship with one dedicated partner. Have them get tested to see if they are clean and ask them to bring you the results. You must use a latex condom each time you have sexual relations. ***Untreated STDs;*** if your STDs go untreated, you may risk a serious infection or permanent injuries to yourself. Women can have complications when they try to get pregnant or give irreparable damage to their fetus that include; blindness or pneumonia. This is a vicious cycle and if you let your STD go untreated, you will be passing it on to everyone you come into sexual contact with. You should seek the advice of a doctor as soon as you suspect you may have an STD.

2. Condoms & Birth Control
You must use latex condoms and spermicide to protect you and your partner from contracting any STDs and unwanted pregnancy. Condoms are not 100% effective and should be used in conjunction with other forms of birth control. Other types of birth control include; pills, patches and IUDs. They should be used for all types of inter-

course; oral, vaginal or anal sex. All condoms can be purchased over the counter; male condoms, female condoms and dental dams that are used for oral sex.

3. General Symptoms of STDs:

If you think you may have a STD, the best advice is to seek medical attention as soon as possible. The following are common symptoms related to STDs. If you have any of them, you should make an appointment with your doctor.

- Severe itching in the genital area; near the vagina or penis
- Aches, pains, fever or chills
- Painful urination
- Skin rashes
- Yellowing of the skin
- Swelling or redness near or around the penis or vagina
- Bumps or sores near the mouth, penis, vagina or anus (behind)

4. Bacterial Vaginosis (BV)

BV is a condition in women where the normal balance of bacteria in the vagina is disrupted and replaced by an overgrowth of certain bacteria. It is sometimes accompanied by discharge, odor, pain, itching or burning. This is the most common vaginal infection in women of childbearing age. 16% of pregnant women have BV. Any woman can contract BV, but certain behaviors can upset the normal balance of bacteria in the vagina and put women at increased risk including; having new or multiple sex partners, douching and using an IUD for contraception. *Symptoms include;* abnormal discharge with a strong fish-like odor, especially after intercourse. *Complications;* having BV can increase a woman's susceptibility to HIV infection if she is exposed to the HIV virus, having BV increases PID (pelvic inflammatory disease) and a woman who is pregnant will have increased complications and susceptibility to other STD's. *Treatment includes;* BV is treatable using antibiotics, and pregnant women are at the most risk and should be checked and treated immediately. *Prevention;* abstinence, limiting sex partners and do not douche.

5. Chlamydia

Another common STD is Chlamydia. People between the ages of 18 and 30 contract this most often. *Symptoms in women include;* smelly vaginal discharge, bleeding or pain in between periods, painful sex or urination and itching or burning around the vagina. Women may contract PID, a pelvic inflammatory disease which may also cause problems with pregnancy or make them become infertile. *Symptoms in men include;* clear discharges from the tip of the penis and painful urination or swelling around the testicles. *Treatment includes;* antibiotics prescribed by your doctor.

6. Genital Warts

Warts can appear anywhere on the body including the genital area and are transmitted by sexual contact. *Symptoms for women:* Genital warts look like small pink or red growths near the sex organs. They may resemble cauliflower or clusters, they grow and spread rapidly, they are sometimes painful and may bleed or itch. They may be very small and difficult to see. *Symptoms for men;* genital warts are less common, if they do appear it may be present on the tip or shaft of the penis, or on the scrotum or around the anus. Genital warts may also develop in the mouth or throat of a person if they have oral sex with an infected person. Sometimes warts may take awhile to appear. You must make an appointment with a doctor, so that they may determine the best treatment options. Some treatment includes; laser therapy or removal by freezing.

7. Gonorrhea

Gonorrhea is also called "clap" or "drip" and is a contagious disease that is mostly transmitted through sexual contact with another infected individual. Gonorrhea may also spread though bodily fluids and an expectant mother may pass on an infection to her newborn. Men and women can both contract gonorrhea and it can lead to a bladder infection. For women, it grows in warm places including the cervix, uterus and fallopian tubes. A bacterium also grows in the mouth, throat and anus. *Symptoms in women include;* green or yellow discharge from the vagina, pelvic pain, burning during urination, red itchy eyes, bleeding between periods, burning in the throat or swollen glands. *Symptoms in men include;* the same colored discharge or burning during urination. Symptoms sometimes take up to thirty days to begin. *Treatment: Both partners should be treated by a doctor with an antibiotic.*

8. Hepatitis B

This is a very serious disease that may cause scarring of the liver, liver failure, cancer and maybe death. Hepatitis B is spread through blood and other bodily fluids such as; semen, vaginal secretions, saliva, open sores and breast milk. Hepatitis B is not something you can get rid of easily, if you have been infected for more than six months, you are considered a carrier. You can transmit the disease by sexual intercourse, French kissing and sharing food and drinks. *Symptoms include;* jaundice, fatigue, flu-like symptoms, abdominal pain, nausea and vomiting. You will need your doctor to give you a physical, take blood tests and get necessary immunizations. *Prevention:* Pregnant woman can give Hepatitis to her unborn baby. Make sure you get a vaccination, wear a condom, cover open wounds and don't share razors, toothbrushes, manicuring tools, pierced earrings or needles, etc.

9. Genital Herpes

Herpes are a contagious infectious disease that is usually contracted through intercourse with a person that has infected sores. It can be passed through oral or anal sex. (oral sex is where you use your mouth; anal sex is where someone has sex that includes the buttocks) *Symptoms include;* inflamed, itching, burning skin, blisters or open sores near your genital area. Additional symptoms also include; swollen glands, fever, headache and burning urination. *Treatments* prescribed by doctors include; medications to alleviate pain but there is no cure.

10. HIV/AIDS

Human Immunodeficiency Virus (HIV) is the virus that causes acquired immune deficiency syndrome (AIDS). When this virus attacks a person, it weakens their immune system and ability to fight infections including cancer. One myth is that having HIV means you automatically have AIDS. This is not true. Sometimes it takes many, many years before the AIDs virus is developed. It's just important to know that AIDS cannot be cured. Contrary to popular belief; you can't get HIV from touching, hugging or sharing the bathroom or kitchen utensils. Prevent yourself from getting HIV by;

not having sexual intercourse, not sharing drug needles from an infected person and not receiving a blood transfusion from an infected person. *Symptoms for HIV include;* fevers that won't go away, sweating, tired all the time, flu like symptoms, losing weight and swollen glands. *Symptoms for AIDS include;* tumors and blotches, shortness of breath, difficulty breathing, dementia and chronic diarrhea. We have come a long way with hospitals, clinics, drugs and therapies that are dedicated to providing specialized care and new medications to AIDS patients. You can also get tested at your local city and county clinics. Be sure to ask about the reporting procedures and confidentiality of the test results.

11. Syphilis

This is also a highly contagious disease that, like the others, is spread through sexual activity including oral sex. Occasionally, you can transmit this disease through kissing someone that has also been infected. Syphilis is one of the most threatening of all STDs because it has many additional serious long term health problems such as; blindness, brain damage and arthritis. *Symptoms include;* chancre sores around the mouth or genital areas that resemble bug bites. Pregnant women can also spread this disease to their unborn baby with sometimes fatal results; this depends on the severity of it. You must contact your doctor for tests and treatment. *Treatment usually includes* a dose of penicillin or other antibiotic.

12. Trichomoniasis

Trichomoniasis is a sexually transmitted disease called "trich" or "trick" by most. This is usually carried by women to their partners via sexual intercourse. Most symptoms are more prevalent in women and the men find out they've been infected from their sexual partner. *Symptoms in women;* green/yellowish discharge that has a strong odor, painful urination, vaginal irritation, vaginal itching and painful intercourse. Some *men will have the symptoms* such as; irritation inside the penis, discharge or burning urination. *Treatment;* see your doctor for medication of antibiotic.

MY JOURNAL ENTRY

List 5 things you learned about ***STD's*** that you didn't know before reading this chapter. Discuss them with a parent, teacher, mentor or friends.

____

____

____

____

____

____

HOMOSEXUALITY

This chapter is to educate teens and the public on basic information about homosexuality and same sex relationships. It contains basic definitions, explanations and understanding of terms used to describe gays, lesbians and transgenders.

This is probably one of the most controversial subjects on the planet. However, it is highly likely that in your teenage life you will encounter homosexuals in school, have homosexual friends or family members. They may not let the world know of their status for fear of being ostracized. Gays are sometimes subjected to a vast amount of violence, 80% of which goes unreported for fear of embarrassment. Lesbian, gay and bisexual youth are four times more likely to commit suicide than their straight peers.

If you are having problems dealing with family, friends or school you should seek the help of a counselor or support group. Take care of your life, it's the only one you have. Find your allies with family, friends or someone in school, anywhere you can get them. Carefully ask them to help you chart your path so that you don't miss a step with school, parents, health, living situations and life.

12 THINGS FOR TEENS TO KNOW ABOUT HOMOSEXUALITY:

1. Homosexuality Definition
A person is said to be homosexual if he or she is sexually or romantically attracted to members of the same gender or sex. This doesn't mean that homosexuals are sexually attracted to *all* members of the same gender. It's like saying that every heterosexual person is automatically attracted to every person of the opposite sex. Typically, the words "gay" and "lesbian" are used to refer to homosexual men and women. The term "bisexual" refers to people who are attracted to both men and women.

2. What causes Homosexuality?
No one has been able to explain or knows for sure why some people are homosexual. People who study human sexuality believe that sexuality is a result of genetics, social or individual factors. It maybe one or more of these factors, or a combination. Some say the "born gay" theory is not fully substantiated yet. A misperception or myth is that troubled family life or sexual abuses are causes for teens to become homosexuals. The truth is, there is no scientific data or research that supports this. Some teenagers that are homosexual may have a difficult home environment if their family disagrees with their sexual choices.

3. Is Homosexuality a Disease?
Almost every major mental health organization, including the American Psychological Association has stated that homosexuality is not a mental disorder. Homosexuality is not a disease. However, the uneasiness of life-altering personal decisions and being uncomfortable about those feelings may cause anxiety, stress or physical problems.

4. What is Homophobia?

This term refers to an irrational fear, prejudice or discrimination towards homosexuals. Homophobia comes in many different forms and actions. Homophobic individuals may do something as simple as name calling or teasing, but they have also been known to participate in life threatening events such as assault, beatings, and in some cases murder. 75% of the hate crimes are committed by people between the ages of 18 and 30. Fear and ignorance ignite homophobia which can end in severe tragedy.

5. Can people change back and forth? Bi-Sexuals?

The question is probably *"do people switch back and forth"* and I think the answer is yes. This is where the term "switch hitter" originated from. This is a complicated question and subject. There are countless studies on this subject as to how and why homosexuality exists in people. The one thing that is ultimately true is that all of us our able to control our feelings and our actions. This statement is a true fact regardless of any sexual orientation.

6. What does "Coming Out" mean?

This phrase is used when a person decides to tell people about his or her homosexuality. A person that hasn't "come out" yet is referred to as *"in the closet,"* until the time comes and they decide to tell friends and family. The timing of this is a personal decision and is done when they think it feels right. They may have a fear of losing friends, but true friends will hopefully accept their new lifestyle. Family members may initially be uneasy, but hopefully with open communication they will eventually be understanding and supportive.

7. Support Groups

There are many support groups for teen gays, lesbians and transgenders. Most of them provide information via group meetings, internet sites, books and pamphlets. There are national support groups such as PFLAG (Parents, Families and Friends of Lesbians & Gays) which are made up of individuals that share the same types of concerns. PFLAG helps with life, family issues, legal concerns and gives individuals advice on how to "come out." Support groups can help individuals deal with people and problems regarding employment and other family issues.

8. *Myth & Fact:* Homosexual Parents

Many homosexuals are parents; either they were already parents when they "came out," or they decided to become parents later. Regardless of how the sequence of events happened; research proves that same sex relationships produce heterosexual kids. The children of homosexuals have proven to be well grounded normal children.

9. *Myth & Fact:* Friends

A myth is that homosexuals cannot maintain heterosexual friendships with the same sex. This is NOT true. Most homosexuals maintain lifelong friendships with members of both sexes. Having gay friends does not mean you are gay. This should not prevent you from developing a friendship with a gay or lesbian person.

10. *Myth & Fact:* Name Calling

Myth: It's OK to call gays and lesbians names like "queer, faggot and dyke." To be called "queer, faggot or dyke" is derogatory and insulting. Male homosexuals generally prefer to be called "gays," while female homosexuals generally prefer to be called "lesbians." The term "gay" is acceptable to address both male and female.

11. *Myth & Fact:* AIDS (Acquired Immune Deficiency Syndrome)
Myth: AIDS is only a gay disease. AIDS is caused by a virus. Viruses infect all kinds of people, regardless of their sexual orientation. AIDS is spread through the exchange of bodily fluids, such as blood, semen and breast milk. Many people have contracted AIDS from sharing intravenous needles. Although AIDS has been contracted by a large number of homosexual men, the numbers are continually rising in heterosexual men and women. Just because you associate with gays, use the same silverware or sink does not mean you will get AIDS. For more information contact the National Gay Task Force Hotline (1-800-221-7044).

12. How to deal with your Parents
Make sure that you first understand the feelings they will have as a result of hearing this. They will feel shock, denial, guilt and dis-belief. Some parents have been known to disown their children; you should have resources and information available before you tell them. You may want to find a family friend that supports you and can go with you when you tell them. You must be comfortable with your sexual orientation, and have a plan B in case things don't go according to plan. Examine your life and decide how you will survive if you choose not to remain at home. Consider every aspect of everyone's life that this will affect; moral views, the emotional and psychological aspects. Think of why you are telling them and prepare yourself for the questions they will ask. Think this through before doing it so that hopefully you will get a positive response.

MY JOURNAL ENTRY
List 5 things about ***homosexuality*** that you have learned after reading this chapter. Discuss them with a parent, teacher, mentor or friends.

____

____

____

____

____

____

____

Notes:

Chapter Six: Teen Testimonials

TEEN TESTIMONIALS

What I Wish I Would Have Known About High School

By: Dominique Jones, 16

1. One thing that affected me the most is that - some people are not going to like you no matter how nice of a person you are.
2. Freshman year is very important academically in determining what your GPA is going to be in the rest of years in High School.
3. Having a bad attitude is not going to get you any where.
4. The teachers are stricter than they were in grammar school.
5. You have to take more responsibilities for your actions.
6. Organization is a key factor in maintaining good grades.
7. You have to do a lot more studying THAN YOU THINK.
8. You can't wait to the last minute to do anything such as homework, projects, and studying.
9. Your parents are not going to get up everyday to take and pick you up from school.
10. The boys in high school are not as nice as the boys in grammar school.
11. If you get in just a little argument with someone, it can possibly lead to bigger consequences.
12. Excuses that you use in grammar school for not doing homework and projects will not work in high school.
13. Just because you have more freedom doesn't mean you take advantage of it.
14. The same friends that you have in grammar school might not be your friend in high school cause everyone goes their own separate ways.
15. The teachers are not going to baby sit you as they did in grammar school.

What I Wish I Knew About Boys

By: Demi Lobo, 17

1. Boys make better friends than girls, because they don't gossip as much.
2. When a boy says he is going to call you back, they forget sometimes. Don't let it bother you.
3. Boys don't like to talk on the phone as much as girls.
4. If you want a boy to respect you, don't exploit yourself as promiscuous.
5. Keep them at a distance; make him think you don't like him as much as he likes you…then they'll stick to you like glue. Smile.
6. If he disrespects his mother, he'll disrespect you.
7. Most cute boys already know they are cute. The more you fawn over him and tell him he's cute, the more girls flock to him.
8. Don't go after conceded guys that care more about their clothes and cars than anything else.
9. Boys don't expect for you to get mad if they spend 90% with their male friends.

10. You will have less drama if you date a boy that does not go to your school. Then you don't have the entire school managing your relationship.
11. Times have changed, and now boys are expecting for girls to ask them out. So don't be afraid to ask a boy for their number.
12. You should go on a "Dutch Date", with a boy you just want to have a friendship with. "Dutch" is where you pay your own way. If it's a formal date with a boyfriend or guy asking you out, "he must pay".
13. Girl athletes sometime intimidate guys and they want to label you as a "tomboy," just straighten them out. Tell them you care about your body, you're working out and stand up for what you believe in. You have just as much right to engage in sports, that's why there is a "WNBA".
14. Put yourself, your family and your friends first; if you don't they may not be around later when you need them.
15. Reminder: You are the jewel the precious one. Make sure they treat you well all the time, if they don't – they are not <u>the one</u>. Let them go ruin someone else's world.

What I Wish I Knew About Life

By: April Miller, 16

1. Friends: I wish I would have known that true friends are there for you when you need them, not just when they need you.
2. Friends: I have learned that friends come first, because they will be there when the guy is gone.
3. Boys: Infatuation is not love, just because you really have strong feelings for someone does not mean you are in love with them.
4. Boys: If I would have known that there was a good guy out there, I would not have settled for less. No boy is worth your tears, but the one who won't make your cry.
5. School: I wish I would have known that school can only be hard as you make it – there is plenty of time for fun, but learning comes first.
6. School: School is what will help develop your life, not boys and fashion.
7. Money: I wish I would have known that you don't need money to have fun. A penny saved is a penny earned.
8. Clothes: I have learned that it doesn't have to be designer or name brand to be cute.
9. Clothes: You should have your own style because you can wear your personality.
10. Jobs: I wish I would have known that when you finally get a job, they deduct a lot of taxes.
11. Jobs: Just because you have a job, doesn't make you independent enough to not have to ask your parents for anything.
12. Relationships: Most teenage relationships eventually come to an end, it's just a matter of when, where and how.
13. Relationships: Relationships are only strong if there's trust.
14. Parents: Your parents are your friends too, and they are only there to help you.
15. Parents: You should always respect your parents because you never know how long you have with them.

What Teens Should Know About Challenges & Obstacles

By: Darius Brown, 17 & Tom Sewell, 16

1. Try to always surpass your limitations
2. Obstacles are put in your path to make you stronger.
3. You can overcome any challenge in your life, just stay focused and determined.
4. Obstacles inspire you to make changes and solve problems in your life.
5. When you have an obstacle or challenge that is too hard to fix, don't be afraid to ask your parents for help.
6. Try not to waste time with petty arguments, be mature, take the high road and walk away. Save your positive energy for when you really need it.
7. Obstacles are temporary challenges that make you a better person, they bring out the talents you already have.
8. Time management is important; if you plan better you can prevent unexpected challenges that pop up.
9. Overcoming your obstacles is your hands.
10. Be strong don't wear your feelings on your shoulder, if you are having challenges – you don't have to let it show.
11. Commitment builds loyalty between your peers and your friends.
12. Creativity makes you unique, you'll stand out with your own flavor.
13. If you believe in something stick with it, don't let anyone stand in your way.
14. Always keep a positive attitude, it will help you to avoid negative challenges.
15. This is your life, enjoy it while you can, you'll look around and you'll be 20.

MY JOURNAL ENTRY

List 5 things you learned after reading ***teen testimonials***. Discuss them with a parent, teacher, mentor or friends.

____

____

____

____

____

____

____

____

SPIRITUALITY, RELIGION & FAITH-BASED PROGRAMS

Many teens are involved in their church, community or a faith-based program. Either you practice what your parents practice, or you have the responsibility to choose what you want to do. Once you are educated, you will be able to make your own decisions. Our goal is not to persuade you, but to inform you. Some teenagers follow or practice religion because it is part of their heritage, tribe, ethnicity or family culture. Some never practice anything. One objective of religion for some, is said to give specific groups of people a sense of identity and purpose. For teens who aren't popular, don't have friends or find it hard to cope with others sometimes find comfort in faith-based programs. We interviewed teens that are involved in faith-based programs and they enjoy them and are very involved. Many of the teens say that faith in a higher power is the most important element of their success. Youth are able to join local ministries and programs that allow them to express themselves. Churches and faith-based programs have drill teams, choirs, mentoring, educational tutoring and ministries for the youth. Churches and organizations have food, clothing, shelter and medical referral services. Many youth prefer smaller more intimate programs they can not participate in at school.

12 TIPS FOR TEENS ABOUT SPIRITUALITY & RELIGION & FAITH-BASED PROGRAMS:

1. Religion

There is no simple definition that can describe the many religions in the world. Every society has their own religion they practice. For many people, religion is an organized system of beliefs, rituals and ceremonies, personal practices and worship directed toward a supreme power or deity (God). Some people follow religions that do not worship specific religiosity. There are also many people that practice their own religious beliefs in a personal way, independent of any organized religion. Most people that participate in a particular religion believe that a divine power is at work in the world and can influence their lives in many different ways. Some believe that you should work in positive harmony with the universe. Believers also follow certain religion because they believe it will make their life better now, guarantee them a peaceful afterlife and save them from eternal damnation. The three religions that have been the largest influence are; Judaism, Islam, and Christianity. Others are; Buddhism, Catholicism Confucianism, Hinduism, Shinto and Taoism. There are almost too many religions, beliefs and faiths to list. We just want you to be informed of some of the background behind spirituality and religion, the decision is yours.

2. Spirituality

Spirituality means different things to different people. The definition is described as; having something that in ecclesiastical law belongs to the church or to a cleric, having sensitivity or attachment to religious values. The quality or state of being spiritual or the true and strict definition is directly related to a spiritual being or development of a spiritual being. The highest spiritual achievement ever. *Are you a spiritual person? What does this mean to you?*

3. Faith
The substance of things hoped for - the evidence of the things not seen, or the **idea** that something can be made true, merely by wishing it to be so. The **proposition** that something is true, even if there is no evidence to support it.. The **belief** that something is true, in spite of evidence to the contrary. *Do you have faith? When is having faith important?*

4. Do You Believe That You Get Out Of What You Put Into The Universe?
Many people believe that you get out of the universe what you put in. If you are positive and abide by the basic ***Golden Rules Of Mankind*** it will all come back to you. Golden Rules include; do unto others as they do unto you, treat others as you wish to be treated, be nice, do not lie or steal. Respect your parents, elders, teachers and adults. Study, stay in school, communicate properly, don't curse or exhibit bad behavior in public. Don't smoke, drink or use drugs. Speak kindly and don't criticize or embarrass others. If you listen to music with bad lyrics don't mimic them or degrade others. Use basic good judgment and do what you know is right. Be a good sportsman, eat properly and stay healthy. This just about covers most of it. If you put good into the universe, it will come back to you.

5. *When teens were interviewed;* "Do You Belong to a Faith or Practice Religion?"
Some answered no; they don't believe in anything. Some say they practice Baptist, Catholic and United Church of Christ. Some teens say they don't practice religion, but they are a spiritual person. ***Demi L. 17; High School Senior****, I attend church weekly. I belong to the United Church of Christ and love my church. When asked would I attend church without my parents - absolutely. I enjoy church and would feel very lost. My parents did initially make me go to church, but I don't think I would have the values I do without their intervention. I think my church is very special because we have 80 ministries at Trinity United Church of Christ in Chicago, and over 20 youth ministries. I participate in Drill Team, the Athletes For Christ athletic ministry and I used to belong to the youth choir. It's fun to participate with other peers in the youth church activities.*

6. *When teens were interviewed;* How Do You Practice Your Religion or Faith?
Teens answered; they practice in church, at home or in Mosques. Some engage in regular prayer and worship services. Some teens say they belong to a church, but do not go all the time. Teens that go to Catholic school say they have mandatory Mass they must attend along with classes they are required to take. Christian teens also say they attend bible study classes. Others attend services and religious programs at their church and synagogues. Some religions require individuals to pray several times a day. ***Tim B. 17, High School Senior,*** practices Christianity. He attends church every Sunday and was introduced by his parents. He goes whether they go or not. He has a belief in God, a relationship which he says is very important to him and helps him to make most decisions. He would have a problem dating a young woman that was not a Christian. He may consider going to a Christian college.

7. What Do You Do When You Need To Center Yourself And Your Inner Spirit?
There are times when the world just comes down on you and takes hold. You may be upset, depressed or agitated and you need to get your center back. Some teens may

use illegal substances, but we know that is only temporary, addictive and a bad choice. For the rest of us we must find ways to keep our lives under control and calm down when things get out of control. Teens say they rest their mind and center their spirit by doing the following techniques or exercises; deep breathing, travel, rest, chant, play their favorite sport, listen to music, read books, find quiet time, exercise, yoga, meditation, go to church or pray.

8. *When teens were interviewed;* "I am Atheist, I don't believe in any type of Faith or Religion".

Atheists are classified as disbelievers, non-believers or unbelievers. They deny the existence of God or any higher power or being. Atheists feel that religious institutions profit from you by collecting money from church donations. They feel that you don't have control over your sex life because most states, it's illegal to commit adultery, fornication and sodomy. Relationships are difficult for Atheists because it's hard to find other non-believers or have a relationship with a non-religious person. They feel that religious believers have control or influence over national health issues because in conjunction with politics have forbade fetal tissue research that would help to prevent disease. Lastly, Atheists also feel that believers will not allow the teaching of evolution in science classes, and that education suffers because of this.

9. How are Faith-Based Programs, Community Programs or Church Programs beneficial to teenagers?

Churches, Faith Based and Community Programs have changed the lives of many teens. Some teens say faith-based programs have been a refuge due to their lifestyle or personal family problems. Faith-based programs have helped them to cope. They believe the people working within these programs are more understanding and non-judgmental of their unique problems. Some of the churches and faith-based programs provide counseling for teens in trouble. Youth are able to join local ministries and sports programs that allow them to express themselves.

10. Faith Based Resources & Outreach Programs

Sports Programs; churches, parks and communities are combining resources to provide faith-based sports leagues, such as; basketball, football, baseball, bowling and soccer. Teens and youth enjoy competing in these organized leagues. ***Schools, Colleges & Universities;*** teens like having the option of going to a faith-based high school, college or university. This is especially a perfect match for a teen that wants to leave high school and go to college to study theology or attend seminary. ***Churches and Youth Outreach;*** churches and youth programs provide outreach for teens such as; food, clothing, counseling referrals for health care and programs that keep them safe from the streets. ***Transitional Living Programs;*** the national Transitional Living Program and the Family Youth Service Bureau provide resources for local organizations to assist teens (beginning at age 16) with long term residential services. These faith-based and community organizations provide youth with stable, safe living accommodations that help them develop the skills necessary to move to independent living. ***Job Readiness & Entrepreneurship;*** many faith-based organizations are now providing training programs to teens and young adults in job readiness training, career development and entrepreneurship. ***Drug and Alcohol Programs;*** churches and community organizations provide drug and alcohol programs. There are many faith-based drug and alcohol programs that are structured for youth, designed to cut down on the number of youth that are using drugs and alcohol and provide outreach support for those that are currently in need. ***Shelters & Resources;*** churches, community and faith-based programs help the needy by providing food, clothing and shelter. They also help the homeless with jobs, training, and financial assistance. ***Housing / Building Programs;*** there are faith-based, community housing organizations that provide housing construction/rehabilitation training programs for low-income high school dropouts that teach them how to construct and build houses. This is done with classroom training and on the job training. The teens learn a skill, get paid and obtain housing. ***Medical Resources,*** most churches, local community and faith-based organizations provide free medical programs, health fairs, testing, and other resources. This is highly beneficial for teens and their families that need health screening, referral services, emergency care or physicals. www.fbci.org, faith-based community initiative.org.

11. *When teens were interviewed;* What are your feelings about Prayer?
Many teens believe that prayer does work. People that practice certain religions pray to different higher powers. Depending on the type of religion, these higher powers could be God, Jesus Christ, Confucius or Muhammad. Believers feel that a supreme power (God) watches over them. They request help or protection through prayer or other rituals. Prayer is the "act of praying or asking for a favor". It is an earnest request, a petition or act of addressing supplication to a divinity. Prayer is the offering of adoration, confession and thanksgiving to the Supreme Being. Prayer is also a form of using words, a formula so to speak.

12. Topics for Discussion or Thought
Do you believe in a higher power? Why? What is the purpose of life? What is the final destiny of human beings, animals and the earth? Do you believe that people will go to heaven or hell? What is the different between right and wrong? How does it affect the way you think? Why is there suffering? Why do young or innocent people die? Why are there disasters such as tornadoes, hurricanes and earthquakes? What obligations do we owe to other people and to the world? What makes a person decide on a particular religion or faith?

MY JOURNAL ENTRY
List 5 positive things you have learned about ***Spirituality, Religion & Faith-Based Programs.*** Discuss them with a parent, teacher, mentor or friends.

____

____

____

____

Chapter Seven: Life After Teenagership – Entering The Real World

COLLEGE PLANNING & PREPARATION

Leaving home for the first time can be very difficult. You should be mature and grounded when you depart your home town for a new life and new environment. You won't have Mom and Dad to sit out front and watch when you come home. As I write this book, I am also in the process of helping my daughter find a college. For some it will be easy, for others it's a discouraging process. Hint; the earlier you start, the easier the it will be. It's now time to make good choices on your own.

This chapter will help you to plan for college life. We want to help you bridge the gap between college and going away to new surroundings. This could mean moving in your current city or going away to school. You will be leaving life as you know it - and before you get there, here are a few things you need to know. What to expect from a new environment, new terminology you will hear in college and what you may need to take with you. We've prepared several detailed checklists of items to help you get started; school & study aids, confidential paperwork, personal items, clothing, dorm items, communications, electrical, kitchen and organizational tools. After high school you will have to make the decision to transition to college or another program such as; trade school or directly to a job.

12 TIPS TEENS SHOULD KNOW ABOUT COLLEGE PREPARATION:

1. Tuition & Fees

You have heard this term before because there is usually someone in your family that has paid tuition. College tuition is charged per hour, per credit. If someone takes 1 class that has 3 credit hours and each credit costs $50, then the total class will cost $150 ($50x3). 12 + hours is considered a full-time student. There are additional fees you may have to pay each semester. These could be lab or parking fees. Your fees are usually due at the end of the semester. Make sure you know which fees have to be paid, and keep an account of them. You don't want any surprises when you sign up for the next semester.

2. Semester Hours/Credits/Class Schedules

Semester hours refer to the amount of classes that you register for. In most cases, one credit is equal to one semester hour. When someone takes 12 hours, which also is considered full time, they will get 12 credits for all of their classes. When you are registering for class you will get to pick your schedule. This will determine which days and what times you will take each class. Some classes may be one, two or three days a week depending on what type of class it is, or if it has a lab attached to it. Make sure that you can handle the schedule that you pick. Check with your counselor and make sure you are not over taxing yourself.

3. Books

Books can run you hundreds of dollars. If you receive financial aid, some of it may be used for certain books. You will be able to find out which ones can be purchased using your grants or loans. Students usually sell their old books back to the bookstore, which makes them available to you at a discount. Check your schedule when you register along with book costs. You may be able to complete work study or find other available means to pay for your books.

4. Campus Rules, Safety, Housing & Other Stuff

Once you've selected your college, check to see what rules apply to incoming freshman. The do's and don'ts of the campus; housing, cars and working for starters.

Campus Rules; ask all important questions such as; what to do if you have a car, where to park it etc. Know where you can and can't drive. Check to see how you find roommates, dinner times, location of campus cafeteria and anything else that will affect your life style. Learn about lab times, computer labs, music, dorm life and more. Investigate as much as you can. ***Campus Safety;*** take every precaution to be safe. There's no such thing as being "too safe". Check out the campus safety and security rules, and what is being said about off campus activities. Let your instincts and common sense jump in also. Be aware of everything that's going on around you. Walk with a partner and use the buddy system when it's dark or late outside. Do not ride with strangers or all men if you are a young lady. Choose your new friends carefully. Watch out for drinks at parties etc. Do not ever take unnecessary chances. ***Student Housing / Off Campus Housing;*** if you are going to school out of town, you are probably planning to live on campus in student housing or the dormitory. Freshmen may be required or expected to live on campus. However, there is usually limited housing and you must apply early. This is normally the most inexpensive way to go when getting started. Plan early and when you are applying to a school, make sure to let them know you want on-campus housing. ***Getting a Job on Campus;*** as you prepare for college and your new city it's never too early to start getting information for jobs. There are only so many jobs on campus and in the surrounding areas near campus. A visit to the campus and surrounding area would be suggested.

5. School & Study Aids You May Need

Binders, calculator, calendar, computer, computer disks, brief case, back pack, tape, paper clips, binder clips, envelopes, stamps, phone cord, dictionary , earplugs, folders, highlighter pen, hole punch, loose-leaf paper, markers, notebooks, note cards, organizer or daily planner, pens, pencils and erasers, printer and paper, rubber bands, ruler, scissors, stapler, staples, and staple remover, thesaurus, white-out, writer's guide or grammar book. ***You may not have room for all of these items, choose only what you will need.*

6. Confidential Paperwork & Personal Money

When traveling, moving or in case of an emergency, you will need all of your confidential documents. Make sure you have all of these documents when you go to your new destination. You should have all bus, plane or train schedules handy while traveling. Identification is now required along with boarding passes. You must have all class schedules and school paperwork together. Make copies of your birth certificate, medical insurance card, Social Security card and other identification. Leave copies of your original birth certificate at home with parents for safe keeping.

7. Personal Items You May Need

Nail clippers, fingernail files, nail polish remover, over-the-counter stomach meds, antacids, anti-diarrhea, Pepto-Bismol, decongestants, cough medicine, throat lozenges, pepper spray , pillow, photo album of friends and family, post cards and thank you cards, prescription medications and refills, Q-tips, razors, shaving cream, deodorant, toiletries, rubbing alcohol or peroxide, safety pins, shampoo and conditioner, sheets and pillowcases, shower cap, small tool kit, soap or shower gel, sunscreen, suntan lotion and magazines, thermometer, tissues, toilet paper, band aids, first aid kit, eyeglasses, prescriptions, aspirins, toothbrush and toothpaste, towels and washcloths, tweezers, umbrella, vitamins. ** *You may not have room for all of these items, choose only what you will need.*

8. What Clothing To Pack

Athletic shoes or sneakers, bathing suit, baseball cap, bathrobe for making your way down the hall to the bathroom, boots, coat, dressy shoes to go with your outfit, favorite t-shirts, gloves or mittens, hat, jackets-light for cool weather, heavy for cold, jeans, jewelry, lint brush or tape roller, long underwear, pajamas, pantyhose and/or tights, purses, raincoat, rubber flip flops for shower, sandals, scarf, short, small sewing kit, socks and underwear, slippers or scuffs, suit or sport coat, sunglasses, sweat clothes, sweaters, ties, watch. ***You may not have room for all of these items, choose only what you will need.*

9. What Dorm Items You May Need

Area carpet for your room, blankets or comforters, cork bulletin board, curtains and/or tapestries, glow-in-the-dark ceiling stars, clothes basket or hamper, hammer and nails, tacks, or self-stick adhesive, houseplant, mattress pad, pictures of family and friends, posters and pictures for your walls, push pins or thumbtacks for your bulletin board, room deodorizer, screwdriver, sleeping bags, small bookcase, stuffed bear or other favorite stuffed animal, tape, wipe-away message board and dry erase markers. * **You may not have room for all of these items, choose only what you will need.*

10. Communications, Technology and Electrical Items You May Need

Adapters for phone lines so it can connect two phones into one line, alarm clock, answering machine, batteries, cable cord for cable-ready televisions, camera, cell phone, computer, cordless phone, extension cords, fan, film, flashlight, headphones, humidifier, lamp, personal book light or night visor, personal stereo and favorite CDs, DVDs or tapes, printer and printer ink, sewing machine, space heater, surge protector or power strip, telephone, three-prong adaptors, tv/vcr and movies, wall clock, money, computer, organizer/palm pilot, alarm clock, shower, television, cell phone and fan. Know how much all this costs so that it can be included in your budget. Get what you need, and the save the rest for later. ** *You may not have room for all of these items, choose only what you will need.*

11. Kitchen Items

Aluminum foil, brown paper lunch bags, can opener , coffee cup or mug, coffee maker and coffee packets, cutting board, dishes: a few plates, silverware, cups and glasses, storage containers, dishwashing liquid, favorite soft drink or bottled water, hot-air popcorn popper, hotpot, ice cube trays, microwave, paper towels, napkins, dishcloths, plastic wrap, ramen noodles, salt and pepper shakers, self-sealing plastic bags, small refrigerator if the school doesn't supply them, stockpile of candy, gum, other favorite treats, toaster, water bottle. ***You may not have room for all of these items, choose only what you will need.*

12. Organize Yourself

Organization tools; address book, palm pilot, backpack, baking soda, basket for shower items, bicycle and bicycle, lock, birthday cards, blank CDs , calendar, clothes pins-useful for everything from, keeping the chips closed to hanging clothes, closet organizer, coat hangers, daily planner, desk organizer, drying rack for clothes you don't want to put in the dryer, emergency car kit-that includes a flashlight, emergency tire inflator, and jumper cables, envelopes, extra car key, flashlights, foot locker or storage box, garbage bags, glue and/or superglue, ice scrapers, laundry bag or basket, light bulbs, lock box or money box, magnets for posting things on refrigerator or microwave, makeup holder/case, night stand, padlock or combination lock for the gym or library, plastic crates to store your stuff, small suit case, stationery and stamps, utility knife, tape-the five kinds: duct, electrical, masking, medical, scotch, tape measure, travel guide or map, trunk, wastebasket. * **You may not have room for all of these items, choose only what you will need.*

MY JOURNAL ENTRY

List 5 things you learned after reading ***college preparation***. Discuss them with a parent, teacher, mentor or friends.

____

____

____

____

____

____

____

____

LIFE PREPARATION

What happens after graduation on the way to life!

Now that you've graduated, it's time to enter the real world. Parents are now trying to struggle with letting you go, but when we do - we want to know that you will be a safe, responsible and capable young adult. You must think of every little thing that you have to do while transitioning to the next stage of your life. You are now graduating from high school and the real challenge begins. It's time to decide if you are going to college or explore a job opportunity. If you are a young adult and you are not going to college, then you must be going to work. This chapter will explore the tasks and transitions you must accomplish after graduation.

12 LIFE PREPARATION RESPONSIBILITIES FOR SUCCESSFUL NEW YOUNG ADULTS:

1. After Graduation
Now that you have graduated the real work begins! Make sure you have all of your documents and paperwork needed to go to college from high school. If you are going to school out of state, it will be much more difficult to obtain information once you are out of your home state. This means before leaving the state, make a checklist of everything you will possibly need, no matter how small it seems. Group your lists by subject, then in order of importance such as: school, personal and business documents.

2. I.D. Identification
There are several forms of acceptable identification. You should keep all of these documents handy at all times. The list is as follows; your driver's license is top dog, then a state I.D., Social Security card, birth certificate, insurance cards, passport, military I.D., school, work I.D., voters registration, auto club cards, bond cards, card or library cards. When you go to the driver's license bureau you will need proof of who you are. They will usually accept a utility bill and other current mail. If you need your birth certificate you may obtain it by ordering from the original county/state you were born. You can also order a copy online or from your local currency exchange. There is a charge to replace your identification, birth certificates and other information.

3. College Preparation
Please take a final review of any last minute scholarships that may be available. Check with your school to ensure you have all documents, forms and information that you need before leaving. To get started, here's a reminder list of things that will also need your attention: Use every resource, friend, family member, school, church and community organization for reference letters, referrals and contacts. Once you find a school, then you must prepare for your new college life by organizing your transcripts, fees, school info, books, moving and living costs. If you want, or need, to find a job you should start early. Check and see if there any requirements for the state you are moving to. Get phone numbers, emails and addresses from all of your friends and family before you leave town. You never know when you may need a little support from home.

4. Budgeting & Finances

Your budget and financial status is very important. This entails creating your monthly budget and how you will be spending your money. You can determine if you will have to work, and how much your grants, loans and scholarships will cover. If your parents are going to be giving you a monthly stipend, you need to know how much you are getting, when should you expect it, and how you will get it. You may want to open your own bank account or an account with your parents so they can transfer money to you. You should have your own cash station card and checks. Budget money for food, gas, utilities, phones, clothes, miscellaneous and save a few dollars for emergencies. These items must be done regardless if you are at school or not. Get a copy of a budget in chapter 2.

- ***Paying Bills For Real;*** You will soon find out that when you start paying your own bills, the world can sometimes play cruel jokes. Translation: Lesson number one is, pay all of your bills early or on time to avoid late charges. If you get behind, it's hard to catch up. Ask any adult and they will confirm this for you. Next, stay in close contact with your creditors and utility companies. It's no fun to come home and be without hot water or electricity. When the main responsibility falls on your shoulders, sometimes you may get caught in a knot and owe out more than you actually have coming in. It happens to the best of us. Try to stay on top of your finances. * Read over Credit and Finances in chapter 2.

- ***Taxes;*** Once your parents stop claiming you as a dependent you can file your own taxes. Double check to make sure that they aren't claiming you before you do. You may want to check with your financial aid office to make sure that your filing will not affect your status and availability. This is subject to change, also consult with a tax professional.

5. Transportation to Your New Place

You and your parents must decide how you will move to your new college campus. Are you going to drive, take the bus, train or fly? You will probably need additional luggage and boxes if you are taking a lot of your personal items from home. Start planning and packing early, you will have limited space in your new dorm room. Have a contingency plan for moving, this means have a plan B, in case your flight gets cancelled. Find out your exact mailing address so that you can get things shipped to you when needed.

6. First Time Away From Home - Check Out Your New Location

This may be your first time away from home. You will need to check out your new area, living quarters, the distance to campus and safety. Familiarize yourself with campus security, learn food locations and more. Every city and state has their own unique ways, rules, and regulations. You may want to do some research about the town you are moving to, this will help you to adjust and fit in.

7. You Didn't Get a Scholarship to College?

If you don't get a scholarship to a college or university, there are other options you may want to pursue. Life educates us that "for every door that closes, another one opens." It may just be your destiny to take a temporary detour and go to a junior/two-year college and raise your GPA. You may have family issues or just need to save some money first. Everything usually happens for a reason. You have several other options such as: working at a job that will pay your way to college or working during the day and going to school at night. You wouldn't be the first person to do this. You can apply for grants and scholarships and possibly start going to college online, a junior college or trade school. If you are persistent, things usually have a way of working out.

8. Not Going To College - What's Next? Something's Gotta Be Next!

For whatever reason, you decided not to go to college or put it on hold. You can make a decision to go to a trade school to study; cosmetology, being a chef, mechanic or computer programmer. Don't panic, just have a plan. You may just want or need to get a job in the mean-time. You can't freeload off of your parents – unless they approve. It's time for you to start experiencing what responsibility and living on your own really means. If you decide to stay at home, you must pay your own way and help your parents out.

9. Getting Your Own Apartment or Campus Housing

Some of you will be living on campus, in apartments or living with others. You're kind of ready to get your own apartment and get away from Mom and Dad's rules. You're grown up, and now it's time for you to experience what adults have been talking about for years. *Freedom*. It's not easy out here in the big world where you'll have the responsibility of paying rent, the gas bill, light bill, water in some areas, and not to mention food, personal care and miscellaneous items. When you decide to move, make sure you do your monthly budget and make sure you have enough income to cover all of your bills. Include your cell phone bill, moving and truck deposits that may be required. Check your apartment or campus housing completely and take someone with you to make sure everything is up to par (the way it should be). This is new to you, so you must think safety at all times. You will also have to consider a room mate and new living arrangements that include another person that you do not know that well. The two of you must determine your boundaries, interests and how you will share a small space. If you are moving into your own apartment you must make sure that it is safe. Check the local police department blotter so that you can see if there is crime in the area.

10. Shopping, Cleaning & Decorating

You will be shopping, cleaning and decorating your own dorm or apartment. Take your time and don't feel like you have to do it all at once. Shop wisely, compare prices and don't be afraid to use coupons or look for sales. Clean up regularly and disinfect your delicate living spaces, bathroom and kitchen. Wash your laundry and your bedclothes weekly. If you're not sure about how to wash, cook or clean ask for help before you leave home. It helps to prepare a schedule and have a clean up day. Keep your apartment clean, neat and free from dust and debris. Ask your parents or family to help you, they can also advise you how to furnish and purchase everything you need to get started.

11. Medical & Dental

If you are still being covered by your parents' medical insurance, make sure you have your own medical card in case of an emergency. Ask your parents what kind of coverage you have, and which doctors and hospitals you're covered by. Investigate how you may go for medical treatment while you are out of town, on and off campus. If you don't have any medical insurance, ask the school for information and resources to get medical treatment.

12. I've got Kids!

If you have children, you must investigate the area so that you can accommodate their needs; from formula to clothes, medical and daycare. You must also investigate where you can purchase food and exhaust every possibility to make sure you have the best care and opportunities for your child. Doctors, hospitals, daycare and schools are the number one priority when moving to a new area, or making a major change in your location or living arrangements.

MY JOURNAL ENTRY

List 5 things you learned after reading ***life preparation***. Discuss them with a parent, teacher, mentor or friends.

Chapter Eight: Motivational Life Lessons

Notes:

12 LIFE LAWS – ENRICHMENT QUALITIES

We have 12 Life Laws that you should repeat daily. These are positive affirmations to change your behavior, center your life and keep you on track. Repeat these affirmations daily for positive behavior when dealing with parents, teachers, friends, co-workers and team mates. Take some time everyday without a cell phone, television, radio or computer and prepare yourself for your daily events. This will give you uninterrupted quiet time to reflect on challenges and life enrichment qualities.

12 LIFE LAWS FOR TEENS:

1. I will give my parents and all other adults respect, at all times.
Make a conscious effort to watch what you say around your parents, adult family members and while you are out in the universe. Make a change in the way you act and what you say whether you alone or with friends.

2. I will stay in school; respect my teachers and my education.
As you are growing up, your personality and priorities will change. Your educational goals will change between grammar and high school. Make time to study, and keep your eye on the prize. This world will always require some type of education to be at the party. If you don't want traditional education, prepare for a trade school or certificate program.

3. I will always cherish my friends; they are special gifts.
Your friends have been chosen. If you have good friends, cherish them and do whatever you can to keep them. Friendship goes both ways. You never know when you're going to need their shoulder or the shirt off their back. Learn to be forgiving it will be one of your best attributes.

4. I am confident and self-motivated to achieve anything I set my mind to.
You should make it a point to be more confident and motivate yourself from within. Train yourself to have confidence and project confidence in your work, education and daily life events. You can't buy confidence.

5. I will work as a team with my classmates and sports team members.
Team building skills are important; one person can not do it alone. When you try to be the entire team, everyone loses. There will be too much on your plate and you're letting someone else off the hook. You won't mind the first time, but eventually you will feel misused.

6. Money is my friend. I will be more financially educated and astute this year.
You must be financially savvy in the future. Learn and make a point to budget and save some of your money. If you spend every dime you get, you will always be broke. Start reading about stocks, bonds, money markets and CD's. Find out about retirement options. It's seems far away, but if you don't think time flies, just look how quick you got from eight grade graduation to now. In a few short years, you'll be grown and out on your own. Money is the fastest disappearing act around.

7. I am a leader; I will learn to follow in order to lead better.
The best leaders must also know how to follow. A good leader can see when there is a need and get it done. A great leader will get in the trenches and do the work without being asked. An old saying that is still true, *"Lead, follow or get out the way."*

8. I will recognize peer pressure that is not positive and head it off at the pass.
Peer pressure is what causes us to follow others. The good ones have a way of making you feel like you are really are out of step. Be aware of these people, and these situations, make your own program, then decide who you will let in.

9. I will take care of my body through proper sports, diet and exercise.
Engage in a sports or after-school program that works for you. Find an exercise or fitness program that fits you. Diet changes don't have to be drastic, drink more water, cut back on fried and fatty foods. Get regular check-ups and see a doctor if you think something is wrong.

10. I will do unto others as I would have them do unto me.
Treat your fellow man with kindness every day not just on special occasions. The nicer you are, and the more good you put into the universe, the more will come back to you. If you don't want people to argue with you, fight you or mistreat you, think of this when you are dealing with people.

11. I will use my creativity to make my own style. I am a Name Brand.
You must make your own style, and let them copy you. This includes clothing, hair style and accessories. Whatever you wear, wear it with confidence. Use your creative genius to be the best at everything you do. Success is a state of mind. Once you believe it, they will too!

12. I will make quiet time in my daily schedule to meditate and gain peace of mind and a spiritual center.
You must allow yourself at least five minutes a day …or more without a cell phone, television or any noise to meditate with your affirmations. This is time just for you to center yourself. Eventually, you will add more time. You should also use this time review challenges and the events that you will face. Seek balance in your life.

MY JOURNAL ENTRY
List 5 things you have learned about ***life laws***. Discuss them with a parent, teacher, mentor or friends.

____

____

____

____

____

12 STEPS FOR TEENAGERS TO BUILD CHARACTER

Teenagers can build character by perfecting these qualities. It is important for all teens to know how to build character to make them a better person, community leader, student, family member, child, team member and athlete. Most importantly, the way your character develops will also impact the way you operate in the world. Society needs teenagers to be honest, trustworthy, fair, integral, responsible, diligent, compassionate, strong, confident, caring and a good citizen. This chapter will help you to understand a little about character building skills.

12 STEPS FOR TEENAGERS TO BUILD CHARACTER:

1. Trust & Honesty
Always be trustworthy. You must tell the truth, do the right thing even when it's not the popular choice. Be as honest as possible, and do not tell lies. If someone loses something and you see them, stop them and give it back. Treat others as you would want to be treated. If someone loses a cell phone, wallet or purse, think about it as if it were yours.

2. Money
Money seems to be the root of evil. We all lend and borrow money from friends and family. You don't want to lose a friend or family member over money. So if you borrow money pay it back, if you lend money establish your rules of how you want it paid back. An old friend once told me, "if you can't afford to lose the money you lend, then don't do it". The moral is, people have great intentions, but they may not give the money back when you expect or need them to.

3. Fairness & Integrity
Being fair is not always easy. You may have to decide to be split between two friends. You must know the difference between justice (the right thing) and vengeance (getting back at someone). You must be open minded so that you weigh all the pieces of the puzzle and come out with the correct decision in a difficult situation. If you or someone is in an argument, listen to everyone before making judgments. To be a person with integrity you must do what's right. You must be able to do right when it's costly or very hard. This means you must refrain from giving in to temptation and be true to yourself. You must be ethical and know the difference between right and wrong and stand by the right decision.

4. Courage
Having courage as a teen means you are standing up for what you believe even when no one else stands up with you. Sometimes you may have to stand alone. You can't give in to negative peer pressure. Having courage means you aren't afraid to express

yourself. It takes a lot as a teenager to have courage and strength. You may have to not only stand up for yourself, but others that can't stand up for themselves. There's a popular quote that says, "if you don't stand for something, you'll fall for anything".

5. Responsibility

The world needs more responsible teenagers. This means doing what needs to be done, sometimes without being asked. You must be reliable, dependable and accountable for your actions. Do not make excuses for things you've done wrong or blame others. Use good judgment and always exercise self control.

6. Citizen

It is important to be a good citizen. To be a good citizen you must be responsible. You must do your part to make the world a better place. This includes your involvement in community service. You must conform to the rules of society. Your part includes; obeying laws and respecting authority. When you are of age you should vote. People have paved the way for you to vote and when you become old enough you will vote and pay taxes. Give some of your time to your church, local organization, school or your community. Most high schools have mandatory service learning hours that have to be completed before graduation. You must be involved in community service.

7. Diligence & Perseverance

When you are a diligent person, you strive for excellence at all times. You want the very best for yourself. You are self-disciplined and do what needs to be done with your education, sports and without being constantly reminded. Diligent teens strive for excellence and don't give up until they finish. Learn from your mistakes and failures and use them as determination to get to the next level.

8. Caring & Compassion

Teenagers that are caring and compassionate are not mean, cruel or insensitive. They are kind to everyone and possess in innate ability to empathize with humans in general. You openly lend helping hands to others. You are a very generous, charitable person and give for the benefit of others.

9. Reputation

Do you have a "rep"? This means, do you have a reputation that is good or bad? What do people think when they hear your name? You don't want a bad reputation to follow you. You may not care, but at point in life it may haunt you when you least expect it. If you can shed a bad reputation, do it now, before it's too late.

10. Team Building / Sports

You will be put into groups or teams at school, church or community events. You may be the smartest or most talented in the group. Everyone should pull their weight in the group. It's is up to you to make sure that everyone is involved. If you are a leader or team captain, it's up to you to be fair to everyone. You never know when you may need one of these others. Always consider others, your team members, referees and other teams you play. Be respectful, courteous and have compassion for others.

11. Strength & Confidence

Being able to be strong says a lot about who you are. This means you can take the challenges life dishes out. If you are strong, this means you have grown a thick skin and you don't let little things bother you. It's OK to be self-confident and feel good about yourself. Don't be arrogant or conceded. Be confident, secure and know who you are.

12. Thoughts For Discussion

When playing sports – do you play fair? Do you think that cheap shots and hits are all fair as long as you win? What do you say to people that don't get to play a lot? Are you caring or do you make fun of them? If you are a star do you think you can override the coach? If you find someone's wallet do you return it? Do you make fun of others that are less fortunate or do not dress fancy or have name brand clothes? Do you take responsibility for your actions?

MY JOURNAL ENTRY

List 5 things you have learned about ***character building***, and then discuss them with a parent, teacher, mentor or friends.

CHAPTER RE-CAP

Chapter I. – What's Happening Now!

- ***Parents*** are your best friends, don't misuse them. We love, usually give way too much, and keep making the same mistake even when you don't deserve us. We're the phone call that always answers!
- ***Friendships*** are for life. You can choose your friends even though you can't choose your family. Choose good friends so you only have to do it once. They can last you a lifetime. Friendships are good when you need a shoulder to cry on.
- ***Music & Hip Hop*** is up to you to listen and watch music videos with caution and maturity. You know what music lyrics are acceptable and which aren't. Show your parents that they can trust you. *Don't imitate bad behavior or what you heard on TV. It's all make believe and someone's getting paid big buck to make sure you believe it!*
- ***Everyday Etiquette*** is to remind you that there is a certain way you should carry yourself *"everyday"*, not just when you're dressed up. You want to eat properly at restaurants and formal events.
- ***Communication*** is important between parents, friends and family. How you are able to communicate with people tells a lot about you. This will be especially important when you start going on job interviews, going to outings, events and luncheons. You will want to know how to communicate for each different event. Be aware of your speech, how you react to questions and the gestures you use to communicate with people. You know what they say about first impressions, they are truly lasting.
- ***Conflict Resolution*** can be done within. If you see trouble brewing, take the high road; reason it out or simply "just walk away".
- The ***Internet*** is a resource for information. It's used to connect people and businesses across the universe. Make sure you don't give out any of your personal information or meet a stranger by yourself that you don't know.
- ***Preteen Life Preparation;*** is for the eleven and twelve year olds on their way to teenagership. Don't copy, start bad behavior or grow up too fast. Enjoy your life at the age you're supposed to be. It will go so quick. Peer pressure will make you do things you don't want to do, and you'll be sorry later. Take your time to grow up.
- ***Laws*** are something you must to abide by. Take care of your license, registration, and stay away from illegal acts and illegal acting friends. If you know drinking, using drugs or smoking in school is prohibited don't be around others that participate. If a fight breaks out at school, lose yourself in the crowd and walk away.
- Find a ***sport*** or ***activity*** that you like. You don't have to be the best, just good enough to enjoy it. It helps to build character and keeps you from being bored in the process.

Chapter II. - High School Stuff

- ***School*** and your education are of the most important things you'll ever do in life. Enjoy, learn and savor the experience, you'll wish for this later.

- ***Peer Pressure*** means someone is reflecting their views, feelings and actions onto you. Be a leader, and if you decide to follow someone, make sure that their intentions are worthy of your time.

- ***Dating & Relationships*** aren't the end of the world. If you find a nice honest person to date that is drama free, this can be a good thing especially with parental blessings. If it doesn't work, maybe it's not time yet. Remember, everything comes in time and when it's supposed to happen.

- ***The Prom*** will usually provide you with a once of a lifetime memory. Make it fun, memorable, safe and free of anything that you will regret. This means behavior, drugs, sex or any other things that people say should happen on the one and only "prom night." There is a life after "prom night."

- ***Graduation*** must be your "number one" priority as a senior. You need to be walking that stage. Many teens wait until it's too late to find out they won't graduate. From your freshman year throughout the rest, stay on top of your credits your GPA. Make it your priority to get on up outta there. You don't want to be in high school once all your friends leave.

- ***Driving*** is something every teen is eager to do. Be safe and follow all the rules of driving and for you car. Driving is a privilege and if it's ever taken away you'll regret it. One bad judgment or accident can change your life forever.

- ***Gangs, Gun Violence & Bullies*** are prevalent in our cities and among our youth. We can slow down the violence with your help. Remember guns kill, gangs kill and you can live without either of them. If you need a surrogate family or friends, join a positive youth group, church or community organization. Bullies are insecure and have no right to pick on anyone. Report bullies to school or police, they can be arrested.

Chapter III. - Money, Jobs & Entrepreneurship

- ***Checking & Savings Accounts*** are something that everyone should have as they approach young adult hood. You will be able to deposit and cash work checks, and save money for college. You will also have somewhere for your parents to deposit money for you to access while you're in college.

- ***Budget & Savings*** are the 2 golden rules of money. Budget your incoming money and outgoing expenses each month so that you can keep up with your finances. Save ten to fifteen percent of your income in a separate account that you don't touch it. This is your "rainy day" money. It always rains, eventually.

- ***College Scholarships*** will be on the mind of every high school senior. Start your search early so that you will have the benefit of every available scholarship available. Check with your school counselor, coach and the school you want to go to, for additional scholarships that are available. This is a very competitive and tedious process, so get to it a.s.a.p. www.fastweb.com

- ***Credit Cards*** are good to have for emergencies. To keep your credit in good order, you have to pay your credit card bills as soon as you get them. Keep your balances low and manageable. People that have excellent credit recommend that you pay them off to a zero balance each month. The better your credit score is, the easier it will be to get credit when you need it.

- ***Job Readiness*** will prepare you for getting a job. You need to know how to interview, what questions to expect from a hiring authority. Learn how to dress on an interview, what's acceptable and what's not? Learn what Human Resource Managers are looking for. If you think expensive sweatsuits are acceptable for job interviews, read this chapter thoroughly – twice.

- ***Keeping a Job*** is how you will be successful after you get the job. Many people can get a job, but can't keep it. Learn how to keep the job you have or advance in the job you currently have.

- ***Entrepreneurship 101*** is about owning your own business! Learn the basic steps to owning a business, and the terminology used for small business ownership. Many teens have started their own business and are very successful. Learn the key steps to getting started.

- ***Start Up Business Ideas*** will give you ideas of what kind of business to start. This chapter lists many businesses that teens have started and some new ideas. This is for teens that have gotten the bug and need that extra push!

- ***Your Special Talents & Gifts*** are unique to you. Make the best of it, perfect it and use it for your benefit while you're young. Later is sometimes too late. If you sing, fix cars, computers, draw or make pottery better than the next person, get busy now and don't procrastinate. Remember no one can take your gift from you.

- ***Sports Jobs*** are for athletes who want to make money doing what they love, we've included a list of sports jobs and their descriptions. This way you can have your cake and eat it with extra icing!

Chapter IV. – Health & Wellness

- ***Healthy Eating*** is important to pre-teens and teens. Our lives are constantly on the move and we eat more fast food now than ever. Try to slow down, eat some fruits, vegetables, salads and cut out the unhealthy snacks. Drink water everyday.

- ***Staying Healthy*** is number one on the minds of many teens. Get tips and ideas on how to staying healthy, eat healthy and live healthier lifestyles. You only have one life and it's your responsibility to live it to the fullest. This includes walking and exercising.

- ***Athletes Health*** is paramount for every teen that is playing sports. Learn how to prevent sports injuries from happening or recurring. Athletes should also learn other important facts they need to know about how to stay healthy.

- ***Stress & Anxiety Management*** is a major factor for teenagers. Peer Pressure, family and school pressure all contribute to stress and anxiety. Recognize signs and symptoms and when your body is calling out to you. You must learn ways to cope and redirect stress.

- ***Safety*** is learning how to stay safe in new environments. Safety is learning about date rape drugs, keeping your instincts together to recognize trouble that may be brewing. Daily inspection of your house, apartment, dorm or car is part of staying safe.

- ***Homeless Teens*** need resources, survival lessons and skills. Society needs to understand why and how they have gotten this way. We've explored some of the reasons why teens leave home or were forced out their parental environment. There are transitional living situations and resources for homeless teens.

- ***Advanced Etiquette*** is needed to advise you on the proper behavior and eating procedures at formal gatherings. Etiquette is a must before going to your first luncheon, wedding or upscale restaurant. You'll learn interesting things like which utensil and glass you should use first.

- ***Teen Person's with Disabilities*** will help you to become knowledgeable and sensitive to teens that have physically challenges.

- ***Self-Esteem*** can be positive, very high and if worked at, can be a character building experience. Individuals with low self-esteem need to know how to boost their self-esteem. If you don't know what outside and inner factors influence your self-esteem, then you won't know how to make positive changes. Stand tall, be positive, join sports, youth groups and don't focus on your weight – focus on being healthy.

- ***Teen Pregnancy*** is important and teen mothers and teen father should know what options are available. They should weigh all procedures, challenges and decisions when faced with this dilemma. This chapter gives them options and explain how to prevent teen pregnancy.

- ***Piercing*** along with tattoos is the new teen phenom (excitement). Piercing is being done in ears, eyebrows, navels and places we can't discuss. Know how to find a piercing specialist that's safe, clean, and sterile and is a professional. Learn how to prevent unnecessary infection.

- ***Tattoos*** along with piercing is the new teen phenom (excitement). Tattoos are in places we can't discuss in public. Know how to find a tattoo artist that's safe, clean, and sterile and is a professional. Learn how to prevent unnecessary infection.

Chapter V. – Just The Personal Stuff

- ***Sex & Abstinence*** is about sex, sexually transmitted diseases and abstinence. Birth control, oral sex, decisions, risks and peer pressure.

- ***Drugs*** are a major peer pressure challenge. Addictive drugs include; marijuana, LSD, PCP, amphetamines, and inhalants. Learn how not to do drugs so you won't fry your brain.

- ***Drinking & Smoking*** are both addictive and five times harder to quit than they are to start. There is disease and addiction linked to both drinking and smoking.

- ***For Girls Only*** deals with girls taking control of their life, their body and learning how to respect themselves. The importance of girls and their relationships with Mom, Dad, dating and self empowerment.

- ***For Boys Only*** deals with boys taking control of their life, their body, relationships and respect. The importance of boys their relationships with their fathers, mothers, dating and empowerment.

- ***Sexually Transmitted Diseases*** can kill. There are about seven major sexually transmitted diseases that need attention and prevention from. STD's can be prevented by the proper and consistent use of condoms or abstinence.

- ***Homosexuality*** is the relationship between individuals of the same sex. Learn about safe sex, prevention of STD's, learn how to deal with parents, friends and challenging issues. Teen homosexuality is an ancillary factor to homelessness, runaways and lack of proper parental communication.

Chapter VI. – Teen Testimonials

- ***Teen Dominique*** says about high school; freshman year is very important academically. You have to take more responsibilities for your actions. The teachers are stricter then in grammar school.

- ***Teen April*** says about life; Friends: I wish I would have known that true friends are there for you when you need them, not just when they need you. Infatuation is not love, just because you really have strong feelings for someone does not mean you are in love with them

- ***Teen Demi*** says boys; make better friends, don't tend to gossip as much and when it's a first date it doesn't hurt to go "Dutch. " Most cute boys already know they are cute. The more you fawn over him and tell him he's cute, the more girls flock to him. If you want a boy to respect you, don't exploit yourself as promiscuous.

- ***Teen Darius & Tom*** says about life's obstacles; Try to always surpass your limitations. Obstacles are put in your path to make you stronger. You can overcome any challenge in your life, just stay focused and determined. Obstacles inspire you to make changes and solve problems in your life.

- ***Spirituality, Religion & Faith Based Programs*** Many teens are involved in their church, community or a faith-based program. Once you are educated, you will be able to make your own decisions. Our goal is not to persuade you, but to inform you. Some teenagers follow or practice religion because it is part of their heritage, tribe, ethnicity or family culture.

Chapter VII. – Life After Teenagership – Entering the Real World

- ***College Preparation*** provides lists of what you need to take to college, what to expect when you get to college, your safety rules and getting a job. You really need to prepare yourself for college. You only have a few months to prepare after graduation.

- ***Life Preparation*** shares insight into the world after graduation. You must prepare for your real life transition to college, apartment life, dorm life or moving away from home. Important details that you will know about your medical and dental needs, moving away and paying your own bills.

Chapter VIII. - Motivational Life Lessons

- ***12 Life Laws*** should be repeated repeat daily. These are positive affirmations to change your behavior, center your life and keep you on track. Repeat these affirmations daily for positive behavior when dealing with parents, teachers, friends, co-workers and team mates.

- ***Steps For Teenagers to Build Character*** It is important for all teens to know how to build character to make them a better person, community leader, student, family member, child, team member and athlete.

- ***Chapter Re-Cap*** is the book at-a-glance, a quick overview of the book. When mentors, instructors and youth leaders are using this book for a specific group, they can use this review to decide which area to focus on. This area is also good for teens to who can't read the entire book to get an At-a-glance view of the book.

- ***Motivational Wisdoms*** for teenagers to have positive motivational sayings to use in their everyday life to uplift them. They are also good to have when writing papers or giving a speech.

Chapter IX. For Parent's Only

- ***For Parents Only*** has a few tips of how to effectively communicate with your teenager on the hard subjects; sex, drugs, schools and peer pressure. Learn how to understand and communicate with your teen. Find out what you can do to help them with life enrichment and facing difficult daily challenges. We have to teach them and re-teach them until they understand.

- ***12 More Secret Weapons for Parents*** has more information for parents only. Here you will find a few more techniques for parents to stay connected at all times; mentally, physically and emotionally. It's our holistic obligation to the universe and all teenagers will benefit.

Notes:

MOTIVATIONAL QUOTES

These quotes are for you to use when public speaking, writing, or just for entertainment. Expand your vocabulary. Having our favorite quotes at your fingertips will help you when you are making a speech and need a laugh or to spark an interesting discussion. Just remember….

Everyone Can't Be in Your Front Row...
Life is a theatre - invite your audience carefully. Not everyone should have a front row seat in our lives. There are some people in your life that need to be loved from a distance. It's amazing what you can accomplish when you let go, or at least minimize your time with draining, negative, incompatible, not-going-anywhere relationships, friendships, fellowships! **Observe the relationships around you.**

Pay attention to: Which ones lift and which ones lean? Which ones encourage and which ones discourage? Which ones are on a path of growth up hill, and which ones are going down hill? When you leave certain people, do you feel better or feel worse? Which ones always have drama or don't really understand, know and appreciate you and the gift that lies within you?

12 SUBJECTS OF MOTIVATIONAL QUOTES:

1. Life Quotes
- Truth is not always popular, but it is always right. ~Anonymous
- Appearances often are deceiving. Never trust the advice of a man in difficulty. ~Aesop
- Revenge is a dish that should be best served cold. ~ Anonymous
- Be civil to all, sociable to many, familiar with few, friend to one, enemy to none. ~Ben Franklin
- Never argue with a fool. People might not know the difference. ~Anonymous
- Reality is a crutch for people who can't cope with drugs. ~Lily Tomlin
- As far as my today is better than my yesterday, my tomorrow will be better than my today. ~ Abiodun Adegbite
- You can tell whether a man is clever by his answers. You can tell whether a man is wise by his questions. ~Anonymous

2. Teen Motivation
- Live in the present and the present only. For the past is done and over with and the future may never come. ~Anonymous
- You have to know when to accept rejection and reject acceptance. ~Ray Bradbury
- Life is what you make it, so make it amazing. ~K.W.
- What is extraordinary rarely begins in perfection. ~Anonymous
- There are no such things as problems, just the opportunity for solutions ~Anonymous
- It's easy to make a buck. It's a lot tougher to make a difference. ~Tom Brokaw
- No dreams come true until you get up and go to work on them. ~Anonymous
- Enthusiasm is the electricity of life. How do you get it.? You act enthusiastic until you make it a habit. ~ Gordon Parks

3. Wealth

- It isn't necessary to be rich and famous to be happy. It's only necessary to be rich. ~Alan Alda
- Lots of people want to ride with you in the limo, but what you want is someone who will take the bus with you when the limo breaks down. ~Oprah Winfrey
- You aren't wealthy until you have something money can't buy. ~Garth Brooks
- If you want to know what God thinks of money, just look at the people he gave it to. ~Dorothy Parker
- Lack of money is the root of all evil. ~ George Bernard Shaw
- Money is like manure. You have to spread it around or it smells. ~J. Paul Getty
- Finance is the art of passing currency from hand to hand until it finally disappears. ~Robert Sarnoff

4. Jobs / Entrepreneurship

- Everyone has a right to a university degree in America, even if it's in Hamburger technology. ~ Clive James
- New ideas pass through three periods; "It can't be done, It probably can be done, but it's not worth doing, I knew it was a good idea all along!" ~ Arthur Clarke
- Entrepreneurs are the forgotten heroes of America. ~ Ronald Regan
- Opportunity is missed by most people because it comes dressed in overalls and looks like work. ~ Thomas Edison
- Nothing is really work unless you would rather be doing something else. ~J.M. Barrie
- Forget past mistakes. Forget failures. Forget everything except what you are going to do now and do it. ~William Durant founder of General Motors

5. Education / Experience

- Experience is not what happens to you; it's what you do with what happens to you. ~Aldous Hexley
- Experience is one thing you can't get for nothing. ~Oscar Wilde
- Education is when when you read the fine print; Experience is what you get if you don't. ~Pete Seeger
- There are two types of education. One should teach us how to make a living. And the other how to live. ~ John Adams
- Good manners will open doors that the best education cannot. ~Clarence Thomas
- You can pay people to teach, but you can't pay them to care. ~Marva Collins
- Experience is sometimes, the worst teacher, it gives the test before the lesson. ~Vernon Law
- America's future will be determined by the home and the school. The child becomes largely what he is taught; hence we must watch what we teach, and how we live. ~Jane Addams
- Education is the power to think clearly, the power to act well in the world's work, and the power to appreciate life. ~Brigham Young
- Teachers open the door, but you must enter by yourself. ~Chinese Proverb

6. Success

- Recipe for success; Study while others are sleeping, work while others are loafing; prepare while others are playing; and dream while others are wishing. ~William A. Ward

- Success is not the key to happiness. Happiness is the key to success. If you love what you are doing, you will be successful. ~Albert Schweitzer
- The dictionary is the only place where success comes before work. ~Anonymous
- Listen a hundred times, ponder a thousand times. Speak once! ~~Anonymous
- Even if at first you do succeed, you still have to work hard to stay there. ~Richard C. Miller
- Things turn out best for people who make the best of the way things turn out. ~Anonymous
- Keep in mind that neither success nor failure is ever final. ~Roger W.Babson, Columnist
- The best way to predict your future is to create it. ~Anonymous

7. Friendship

- Life without friendship is like the sky without sun. ~Anonymous
- The secret to friendship is being a good listener. ~Anonymous
- A friend is one who knows you and loves you just the same. ~Elbert Hubbard
- He who has a thousand friends, has not a friend to spare, while he who has one enemy shall meet him everywhere. ~Ralph Waldo Emerson
- It is not true that nice guys finish last. Nice guys are winners before the game ever starts. ~Addison Walker
- A friend is someone who sees through you and still enjoys the view. ~Wilma Askinas
- In prosperity our friends know us; in adversity we know our friends. ~Anonymous

8. Parents

- Parents can tell but never teach, unless they practice what they preach. ~Arnold Glasgow
- God could not be everywhere and therefore he made mothers. ~Anonymous
- Role modeling is the most basic responsibility of parents. Parents are handing life's script so their children, scripts that in all likelihood will be acted out for the rest of the children's lives. ~Steven Covey
- The most important thing a father can do for his children is to love their mother. ~Henry Ward Beecher

9. Motivational

- A lot of people have gone farther they thought they could because someone else thought they could. ~Zig Ziglar
- To the world you might be one person, but to one person you might be the world. ~Anonymous
- You have to meet all of the challenges, big and small because how you start is how you finish. ~Bernie Mac
- Everyday is a good day, some days are just better than others. ~Anonymous
- If we want to change for the better, we have to be the miracle. ~Ralph Lauren
- Every charitable act is a stepping stone toward heaven. ~Howard Beecher
- Nobody ever died of laughter. ~Max Beerbolm

10. Spiritual

- If you can't feed a hundred people, then feed just one. ~Mother Teresa
- All things are either Blessings or Blessings in Disguise. ~Rahul. S.
- For many are called, but few are chosen. ~Matthew: 22:14
- To know the road ahead, ask those coming back. ~Chinese Proverb
- He who is ashamed of asking is ashamed of learning. ~Danish Proverb
- It's only those who do nothing who make no mistakes. ~Joseph Conrad
- It is less of a problem to be poor, than to be dishonest. ~American Indian
- Never sit while your seniors stand. ~Anonymous
- Knowledge that is not used is abused. ~Anonymous
- You already possess everything necessary to be great. ~Anonymous

11. Leadership / Teamwork

- Every time I close the door on reality it comes in through the windows. ~Jennifer
- Humor is just another defense against the universe. ~Mel Brooks
- A man's go to do what a man's got to do. A woman must do what he can't. ~Rhonda handsome
- Alone we can do so little; together we can do so much. ~Helen Keller
- A real leader faces the music, even when he doesn't like the tune. ~Anonymous
- Leadership is the art of getting someone else to do something you want done because he wants to do it. ~Dwight D. Eisenhower
- In simplest terms, a leader is one who knows where he wants to go, and gets up and goes. ~John Erskine
- One of the the tests of leadership is the ability to recognize a problem before it becomes an emergency. ~Arnold Glasgow
- A good objective of leadership is to help those who are doing poorly to do well and to help those who are doing well to do even better. ~Jim Rohn
- You will never be a leader unless you first learn to follow and be led. ~Tiorio
- Integrity is the most valuable and respected quality of leadership. Always keep your word. ~Jim Rohn
- Do not follow where the path may lead. Go instead where there is no path and leave a trail. ~Harold McAlindon
- Sometimes a player's greatest challenge is coming to grips with his role on the team. ~Scottie Pippen

12. Encouragement

- Don't let life discourage you; everyone who got where he is had to begin where he was. ~Richard Evans
- Who has confidence in himself will gain the confidence of others. ~Leib Lazarow
- Happiness is a choice that requires effort at times. ~Anonymous
- Good, better, best. Never let it rest. Until your good is better and your better is best. ~Tim Duncan
- I can accept failure, but I can't accept not trying. ~Michael Jordan
- Do not let what you cannot do interfere with what you can do. ~John Wooden
- He who is ashamed of asking is ashamed of learning. ~Danish Proverb

Notes:

Chapter Nine: For Parent's Only Understanding Your Teen

FOR PARENTS ONLY!

Here are a few tips of how to effectively communicate with your teenager on the hard subjects; sex, drugs, schools and peer pressure. My fellow parents, as hard as it is to admit, we are partly responsible for some of the indulgences we have allowed our teenagers. To prevent them from the struggles we had, coupled with giving them things we could not afford growing up, we give them a lot. To some degree we enjoyed watching them have these things. Some days it's like watching a fast moving technology train wreck of endless electronic toys; CD players, MP3 players, palm pilots, video games, computers, digital this and that. Just when you think they have everything, the world throws something else on you. So in an effort to take them speeding into the 21st century, our teens have cell phones and cars with televisions, cable in every room on plasma televisions and gym shoes that cost a phone bill. This is the short list. Now that we have indulged them, and given them everything; we're looking at the monsters we've made. Smile. Some are out of control; others are just happy enjoying the *indulgence ride*. Below are some suggestions on how to understand and communicate with your teen Find out what you can do to help them with life enrichment and facing difficult and daily challenges.

12 TIPS FOR PARENTS ONLY!

1. Parent – Teen Communication
Communicating with your teen sometimes sounds like they are speaking a foreign language that you can't understand. What is really happening is they are trying to get your attention. Teens have a way of discussing ***A*** by using ***B***, and they may not always speak candidly and discuss their feelings and problems. They are growing up and trying to express their own individuality. Unfortunately, we have to read in front, in back, above *and* between the lines. They have to start being mature and working out some of their own issues. You must be direct, ask questions but know when to back off. Never feel like a subject can't be discussed, regardless of how delicate or hard it is. Try to not to holler at them in front of others or curse them out. This sometime makes them shut down. Let them know you're there when they need you. They will eventually come around.

2. Love Your Teen
Love your kids unconditionally, however you can. Some parents (me) are touchy feely types who believe that "a hug a day, keeps the bad spirits away". Obviously this does not describe every parental or guardian situation. Although our teens sometimes act like adults, they really want your love and your attention. This doesn't mean they want slobbery kisses while their friends are watching, but a hug here and there can be worth a million dollars. They will rarely say "mom, dad I need a hug, but trust me they do. Love is not clothes, shoes or money. It's affection, caring, security and showing it. It means going to their sports games to support them even when you know they may warm the bench. They want to feel safe, secure and protected. Love is something you show, and your teen must feel it. Hopefully, it's reciprocal and they will love you back.

3. R.E.S.P.E.C.T. *"Find Out What It Means To Me!"*
A song that teens are really singing. Most adults in our genre were raised that respect

comes automatically with being an adult. If we saw a young person disrespecting an adult we would check them and they would probably stop right away. If they thought you were going to tell there parents, they would really straighten up. Today…hmmm, the kids may tell you off, and then bring the parent back to tell you off even more and in some cases start an altercation. This is due to several factors in the rearing of children along with different value systems; our youth possess more relaxed attitudes. Society blames media, music, video and younger parents as some of the reasons for this breakdown. *What Now?* We have to make changes in our children, so as they become responsible young adults they will be able to lead by example. It's up to you to spend time guiding them and showing them techniques on how to handle respect of adults, teachers and their peers. We are role models whether we want the job or not. We have to teach them and re-teach them until they understand.

4. Language University

Where do we start? Somewhere between "we taught them better", "where did they learn to speak like that" and then we "blame the rest on the music videos, rock music and hip hop". How do we get them under control so that we can take them out in public? First, we start by correcting them when appropriate and show them how to speak proper English. The music media may have started it, but we have to finish it. When you hear something really disgusting, you should check them on it - it's how you do it that's important. Call them to the side and let them know it was disrespectful and young kids are around, or you don't care for it. Explain the reasons why to them, that usually works well with these young adults. Try to curb the adults cursing in your household. You are still part of "the village", all the teens in the universe. Have some fun with them in between. Remember this is their world and our future generation.

5. Teens Smoking, or Using Drugs & Alcohol

If your teen is using alcohol or drugs, the first step is to talk with them. Try to find the underlying source. It may be stress, peer pressure or some other factor. Next try an older young adult family friend or sibling. If this doesn't work, counseling or therapy is next. There are also teen support groups they can join. We are scared of this because it says failure, but that's really not true. There are specialists for everything, use them. Teens will confide in others what they will NOT tell you. If you have to consider rehab or support groups don't hesitate. Seek advice, because your child only has one life, which is the one you started. It goes so quickly. Lastly, a little birdie told me that some parents introduce their kids to liquor, drugs and *"get high with them." WOW!* What a horrible message and a horrific example to set. If you can, discourage your teen from smoking; we're one more step toward keeping them healthy and living longer lives. It is also a fact that children raised in the households of smokers also have a greater chance of becoming a smoker as well. Also, it's now proven that second hand smoke is damaging to the health of non-smokers. Whatever can be done to help to your teen or prevent them from smoking, drinking or using drugs should be done. If they need a physician's assistance or support group, you must do everything you can to assist them.

6. Your Teen Has Lack Of Interest In School

If you have noticed that your teenager has a lack of interest in school - you can do several things. First always talk to the teen and see if there is a particular reason. You may be surprised it could be a bully at school, a class that is not going well, a teacher or project that's not going well. Your teen may need help or tutoring in a particular subject and are afraid or embarrassed to ask. You must get to the root of the problem. It could be drugs, a medical problem, or you may have a child that does not prosper in a traditional school setting. After you find out why, then you must decide the next step; you may decide on home schooling, alternative schools or your teen may just tough it out until graduation. Then you will decide on a trade school or certificate program as an alternative to traditional college. Keep your mind open as you approach this subject and the manner in which you choose deal with it.

7. T.V. & Music and Violent Games are Ruining My Teen!

Today's music seems to have taken over the world. It has crossed all boundaries, race, music styles and age. If that's not enough, by the time our kids are two years old they can sing the words of any x-rated song before they can read or form real sentences. If we could put lessons to rap music we would be in business. We're up against the songs lyrics, music videos, games and it keeps on coming. Our youth are mimicking this behavior. Then the rap stars are multi billion dollar business owners thus adding on to their heroism and stardom. Not begrudging the rap industry, we're actually in awe of their business acumen. We just have to choose our HEroes and SHEroes carefully. The answer is staying on top of it, even though it feels like a part time job. What are your kids watching, listening to and participating in? We have to be the ambassador's of parenting keeping it all in perspective. You shouldn't take their music away from them, they know how to get it, but start early letting them know you're listening and watching. If they are preteens, buy the censored version of CD's labeled *"Parental Advisory"*. Find another young adult to tell you what the songs are really about. Watch the music video's and limit the cable channels and time they can watch. Finally, if you allow your kids to watch and listen to certain music, have a mature dialog that explains that these rap artists and musicians are getting paid hundreds to entertain them and its make believe. Talk intelligently about what it means to be responsible about what they are watching and listening to.

8. Peer Pressure

Combating what happens at school with what you are teaching them is another full time job. As a parent you will hear *"everyone's doing it,* and *everyone's wearing it"* about one hundred times. Don't cave in. Time will show that you can be "cool" with your teenager without giving into every single request. Actually, the truth is that they want the discipline and want to know you care. It's hard to give them everything we couldn't have at their age. We try to give them everything their peers have and then some. We should reward our teens for good behavior and positive actions.

9. Sex

Talk to your teen about sex, no exceptions! If you don't someone else will and you can't be sure they will be telling them the right thing. You would be surprised how many teens are uneducated about using protection and getting pregnant. You would be surprised how many girls get pregnant because they have birth control pills and don't take them regularly. Many of them seem to think they can't pregnant the first time. You need to discuss the whole enchilada; birth control, safe sex, peer pressure and relationship pressure. Every small detail counts. Frighteningly preteens are having sex very early in the fifth and sixth grade. They are having oral sex and not classifying it as sex. Scary but true. We need to educate them as much as we can. When it's too late it doesn't count.

10. Sports/Hobbies/Clubs/Activities

Keeping your teen busy should be your part time job. For my teen this has been very successful. It takes some juggling; but it's really worth it in the end. Your child should always have sports, hobbies or extra curricular activities to participate in. Teens have plenty of energy and it's up to us to channel it in a positive direction. Some teens are very focused and know exactly what they want to do. Others will need a little nudging and you may have to spend a few dollars while they join different types of dance groups, singing groups, sports or basket weaving. Support them anyway, whether they start on the team or warm the bench. They will remember you for it. Keep them busy and expose them to as much as you can.

11. Jobs & Entrepreneurship

Your teen will be soon looking for a job. They will need your guidance to decide, if they are mature enough to juggle work and school. Where they work, what type of job they will have, location and how much they will make are important factors. Entrepreneurship is also a consideration. More teens are starting their own small business in schools, at home or in other locations. Safety is a very important issue to consider because some jobs may cause them to get off late at night. Your teen should start with a summer job and then take it one step at a time deciding on if they are able to work during the week. If their grades are suffering they may have to give up the job, even if they need the money. Entrepreneurship is now being taught in many schools, organizations and Faith-Based programs. Teens have dozens of opportunities to start small businesses and make thousands of dollars. They need strong support systems from parents, family and friends. See our chapter on entrepreneurship.

12. Stuff !

- *Punishment;* How do you punish your kids? Some say take away things such as cell phones, extra curricular activities and privileges. The key to getting their attention is…you must do something! Footnote: negative punishment does not work for all kids.

- *Spirituality, Religion;* The million dollar question is, should you encourage your children to practice your family beliefs, or do you let them choose their own spiritual path?

- *Trust Factor;* Make sure you develop a trust factor with your teen. If you establish a trust factor, it will make your conversations and communication easier because they will be honest and sincere.

- *School;* School is an important factor in your child's life. The teachers are overworked and dealing with a new generation. Keep up with what's going on with your teens. It's your responsibility, because they may not tell us the entire production. They sometimes leave part of the movie out.

MY JOURNAL ENTRY

List 5 things you learned by reading ***For Parents Only***.

PARENT'S SECRET WEAPONS

Here's a few more secret weapon techniques for us parents. These are small reminders about things you probably already know. Since, life deals us such a busy lifestyle that we sometimes just don't have time for every little thing. Our teenagers look mature like they have it all under control; we're impressed and extremely happy. While we're glancing left, something on the right may fall off and we've missed it. It's up to us to keep them organized and on track. We have to stay connected at all times, mentally, physically and emotionally.

I have a sweet, dynamic, beautiful, multi-talented, bright, hard working energetic teenager who is the love of my life. She's got it all going on, but occasionally, she misses a step and that's where I come in. That's my job. And I work very hard at it. We have to do this for all teenagers, even the ones that do not belong to us biologically. It's our holistic obligation to the universe to *help* all teenagers.

12 SECRET WEAPONS FOR PARENTS OF TEENAGERS:

1. Listen To Everything They Have To Say
Many times your teens are giving hints as to what is going on in their life, and for whatever reason we may not being pay attention. We must listen – they may not repeat it. Remember they are still kids, ours or someone's.

2. Make a Date With Your Teen
Spend as much time as you can with your teen, even if this means making a date to get on their calendar. If you have more than one child, carve out times for them individually. This way they will all feel special and that they have your undivided attention and love. Suggestions for dates include dinner, shopping, the museum or a cultural trip.

3. Support
You should support your teen in every any endeavor they have. Even if it's basket weaving. I know parents that have never been to one game of their children, one choir performance or one event that their child has participated in. There is no excuse for this; you are saying their interests don't matter to you. They may not tell you, but it hurts their feelings.

4. When You Are Both Parents
When you have to be both parents, wait until they're old enough to understand why the other parent drives you crazy. They may never need to know, every situation is different. This must be handled with care. If not, they will surprise you and give you the stomach ache of your life when they decide the other parent is their hero and want to go live with them. Being both parents is hard enough, so just do your very best and celebrate being both. Don't restrict yourself to one type of domestic or sport activity. They should know the responsibility from both sides.

5. Get To Know The Teachers

Once your teens are in high school and they have their own agenda, they distance themselves and we kind of let them. Keep control of what's going on and this means keeping up with your child's teachers. You may contact them by phone, email, in person or anyway you can. Don't take anything for granted with your child's grades. Once you know the teachers, and they see your interest, they will be more inclined to contact you if your teen is not meeting standards or something is going wrong. You don't want to be the last person to know that your child may need summer school or they need credits to graduate. One other thing that bugs me to the end, is when teachers say that your child has done something wrong, and parents blast the teacher and assume their child is not at fault. It is to our benefit as parents, and our duty – to at least investigate first before placing blame. This will eliminate our child getting alienated later – especially when we find out they actually may have been at fault.

6. Dating

Teen dating is a really sticky situation. If we have girls, we don't want to hear the word. If you have a boy, you don't mind, but you don't want it to get out of control. When they're listening, we can try to encourage them to slow down, have a lot of friends and go out on as many group outings as they can stand. However, time and maturity will eventually catch up with us and they will start doing their own thing. Most importantly, communicate with your teen. Make sure they know what they should and shouldn't do when dating. Review the gifts they buy, or receive and make sure they are appropriate. Keep your ears and eyes open so you won't be the last to know about whatever is going on.

7. Reward Your Children

When your teenagers have done well, they should be rewarded. It can be small or large, but they do appreciate your acknowledgement. Some teenagers respond better with positive reinforcement. This could be an educational accomplishment, sports, church or an entertainment program. You may want to take them out after a performance and spend time with them or buy flowers. You may want to give them a card or other gift. The important part is that you acknowledge them.

8. Keep Them Busy - Positive Energy

This is the number one key to raising a teenager. Keep them busy with sports, faith-based programs or other activities. If they want to work and their grades are good, let them get a job. It will teach them discipline, responsibility, team building and give them independence. If their time is occupied with positive energy, the less time they have for negative experiences.

9. Sex With Minors

Many teens are having sex with older individuals. Older women are having sex with very young men. We must educate our teens that these kinds of "curiosity sessions" can come with long term problems. Years go, this was looked at as a right of passage for young men. It's a big no-no for a grown adult to date a 16 year old. We must be parents and explain what consequences can come of these types of relationships. It is illegal and considered statutory rape.

10. Discipline
Our teens and pre-teens need discipline. They may not want it, but they need it. When they resist, pull them back. It doesn't always seem like it, but when you stick to your principles they appreciate it later. When you make rules, standards and guidelines, it shows that you care what happens to them. If you don't set any, they will run over you and ultimately lose respect for you, others and themselves.

11. Domesticate Your Teen; Including Cooking
Teach your teen to wash, clean, cook or at least make a few healthy meals. We don't have to turn them into cooks, but we want them to be able to feed themselves. Your teen should be self-sufficient and know the basics of taking care of themselves. This will be beneficial when they get home from school or go off to college. Your menus can be a series of easy salads, baked or broiled ideas. There are many easy-to-do recipes or quick food ideas that are not that high in calorie or fat content.

12. Responsibility and Prioritizing
Responsibility and prioritizing is extremely important for our new young adults. A scheduling system is needed in order to effectively balance school, work, sports, activities and major events that affect their life. If you train them early by using calendars, planners or palm pilots organization will be ingrained in their daily behavior forever through young adult hood. As they start to mature they will start to do things their own way, but usually some of it will rub off.

MY JOURNAL ENTRY
List 5 things you learned by reading ***Parents Secret Weapons***.

___

___

___

___

___

___

___

___

___

___

Appendix I.

1100 Website Resources

African American Resources
Aawc.com
africana.com
blackamericaweb.com
blackfamilynet.net
everythingblack.com
blackvoices.com
blackkplanet.com
melanet.com
netnoir.com
thekingcenter.com
politicallyblack.com

Alcohol
adca.org.au
aacap.org
goaskalice.columbia.edu
naadd.org
alcoholscreening.org
alcoholfreechildren.org
collegedrinkingprevention.gov
alcoholalert.com
apas.org
adca.org.au
.potsdam.edu/hansondj/FAS/FAS.html
icadts.org
alcohol411.info
talkingwithkids.org/alcohol.html
puberty101.com/d_alcohol.shtml
rand.org/publications
visionsteen.com
questdiagnostics.com
enotes.com/teens-alcohol-article
accessexcellence.org
stopaddiction.com/news
teenink.com
egrinder.com/teenalcohol
sober-teens.com
alcoholfreechildren.org

Athletes
mirror-mirror.org/athlete.htm
edreferral.com/athletes_and_ed.htm
teenagerstoday.com
dietplanet.info
focusas.com/BodyImage.html
schools.shorelineschools.org
dietplanet.info
youthdevelopment.org
Work-Outs.net
SportsWorkout.com
carlette.com/teencoach.htm
nutritionathome.com

Boys Only
teenpuberty.com
Puberty 101
abuseintervention.org
thebody.com
menstuff.org
tpronline.org
oneyoungparent.com
icbe.org
counseling.org
teenpuberty.com

Bullies
ncpc.org
Bullying.org
cwfa.org
10meters.com/teens
naesp.org
bullyonline.org
stopbullyingnow.hrsa.gov
StopABully.com
safechild.org
bullybeware.com
bullyfreekids.com
no-bully.com/high_school.html
bouldenpublishing.com
youbigbully.com
safeschoolscoalition.org
coastkid.org
fastdefenseprograms.com
HealthPolitics.com
bridges4kids.org
kidshealth.org
comskills.com
helpmyteen.com

Business Etiquette
seasons-of-life.com
essentialetiquette.ca
biz-ewomen.com
themannersclub.com
etiquettesurvival.com
ravenwerks.com executiveplanet.com
businessculture.com
etiquettesurvival.com
coachbiz.org
worldbiz.com
cyborlink.com
ryangrpinc.com
babyboomers.com
etiquettehell.com
sellingselling.com
corsinet.com
icbe.org
enquirer.com
epinions.com
alletiquette.com
emailreplies.com
social-graces.com

Business Financing
hjventures.com
blackenterprise.com/teenpreneur.asp
blackenterrprise.com
blackmoney.com
businesscenter.ibm..com
kipbusinessreport.com
nbmbaa.org
tnj.com

Career Development
asee.org
black-collegian.com
guru.com
monster.com
tbwcareers.com
urbanrecruiters.com
theetiquetteinstitute.com
FabJob.com/EtiquetteConsultant
worldbiz.com
forbes.com

Careers
Monster.com
youthrules.dol.gov
career-education.com
payscale.com
hotjobs.com
Tunu.com
JobsSearch.org
teens4hire.org
CareerTest.us
jobsonline.com
rileyguide.com
quintcareers.com/teens.html
stepfour.com/jobs
dictionary-occupationaltitles.net
fedquest.com
jobbankusa.com
salary.com
salaryexpert.com
doli.state.mn.us/childlbr.html

Checking And Savings for Teens
bankingkids.com getchecking.org
cuu.com
bankrate.com
spcu.org
deseretnews.com
wmtcu.com
capcomfcu.com
fnbsm.com
thesolutionsite.com
ilo.org
ccutx.org
student-manual.com
pagenation.com

newcomersguideusa.com
bankingessentials101.com
youngbiz.com
kidsway.com
cuna.org

College & ACT Information
collegeview.com
greatoaks.com/pages
act.com
exampleessays.com
fafsa.ed.gov
ACTCA.Org
testprepreview.com
Act.com
act-secrets.com
act.org
powerprep.com/
4tests.com
gocollege.com
saab.org
act-sat-prep.com
freevocabulary.com
test-preparation.net
college-scholarships.com
act-sat-prep.com
freevocabulary.com
test-preparation.net
college-scholarships.com

College Preparation
collegeprep.okstate.edu
ClassesUSA.com
collegeispossible.org
petersons.com
ecampustours.com
sayplanning.com
offtocollege.com
choiceprog.com
ccymcablackachievers.org
teensarenotadisease.com/school.html
mootney.org
parent-teen.com
parentsoup.com
nextstepmagazine.com
teen.apl.org/college.html
800canlearn.com/p-links.php
teenchannel.net
aboutcollege.com
freep.com
collegeconfidential.com
dorm.org

College Scholarships
teens.geoportals.com
fastweb.com
fcps.edu
thesavvyclick.com
blackexcel.org
blackstudents.com
Essayedge.com
college-scholarships.com
collegeview.com
ImmediateScholarships.com
college-scholarships.com
hbcu-central.com/
UnitedStatesGrants.Org
palomar.edu/aasf/
collegedata.com
coca-colascholars.org
hsf.net
littleafrica.com/scholarship
FreeScholarshipGuide.com
blackrefer.com
microsoft.com/college/scholarships
usagovernmentgrants.org
fastaid.com
college-athletic-scholarships.com
usgrantsguide.com
upromise.com
thesalliemaefund.org
fafsa.ed.gov
hispanicbusiness.com
shpe.org
chci.org
hispanicfund.org
findtuition.com
government-grant.101soho.com
disabledperson.com
hacu.net
fedmoney.org
aachac.org
afrotc.com
uncf.org
scholarship.tylenol.com

Communication
ncrel.org
scanews.com
diaryproject.com
teachingteens.com
onestionline.com/communication_skills
child.net
wvi.com
studentinsight.com
disciplestoday.com
broward.com
focusas.com/ListeningSkills.html
parent-teens.com
schooltree.org
conversation-magic.com
msucares.com
youthwork.com
couplescompany.com
americantrailswest.com
tobacco.org
teenlifeministries.com
dynamicyouthspeaker.com
thelegacyforchildren.org
brettell.org
comskills.com

Conflict Resolution
ncjrs.org
angrykids.com
urbantech.org
strugglingteens.us
goodcharacter.com
whatkidscando.org
bcparent.com
tenresolutions.org
teencontact.org
conflictsolvers.com
conflict-resolution.net
teensolutions.com
afsc.org
mimediation.org
takeastand.com
ycwa.org
fastdefenseprograms.com
worldfitforkids.org
teensupport.org
wholechild.net
angeronline.com
mediate.com
waynesbooks.net
bruderhof.com

Credit & Credit Cards
ftc.gov
cardratings.com
bluesuitmom.com
smartconceptbooks.com
find-credit-card.com
financialfitnesscoach
ndcu.org/fit/teen/money/credit.htm
nebankers.org
targetbest.com
southern.org
stretcher.com
parent.umn.edu
cyberbeggar.org
bmoawheelsofdreams.org
parentsforchrist.com
cusucceed.net
instantcreditnow.com

Dating & Relationships
teenadviceonline.com
young-expressions.com
goromance.com
christianteens.about.com
cherish.com
inspirationpoint.com
home.fuse.net
loveisnotabuse.com
mpoweryouth.org
teengrowth.com
mutedfaith.com
teenrelationships.org

kiwibox.net
relationshiphq.com

Teen Person with Disabilities

ldanatl.org
disabilitycentral.com
Ada.gov
ldresources.com
ala.org/parents/index.html
disabilitycentral.com/activteen
familyfunabilities.com
cdipage.com
ncld.org
interdys.org
disabilityworld.org
latebloomerpublishing.com
couragecamps.org
beliefnet.com/story/145/story_14597_1.html
winsfoundation.org
familyeducation.com
stonemountainschool.org
unicef.org
disabilityworld.org
thewheelchairsite.com
wheelchair-guide.net
bizwiz.com
americasathletes.org
greyhouse.com/sports.htm
womenssportslink.com
thesportscorp.org
nyc.gov

Driving

roadreadyteens.org
drivehomesafe.com
teendriving.com
carfax.com/teen
safedrives.com
tell-my-mom.com
teendriving.com
drivingportal.com
safeamerica.org
ipromiseprogram.com
teenarrivealive.com
newcomersguideusa.com

Drugs

drug-rehabs.org
drugs.com
streetdrugs.org
clubdrugs.org
health.org
talktofrank.com
theantidrug.com
drugfree.org
freevibe.com
jointogether.org
perinatology.com
druglibrary.org/
urban75.com/Drugs
whitehousedrugpolicy.gov/streetterms
travel.state.gov
4woman.gov/faq/rohypnol.htm
homeoffice.gov.uk/drugs
focusas.com/SubstanceAbuse
talkingwithkids.org/drugs.html
drugabuse.gov
howstuffworks.com/athletic-drug-test.htm
drugsbite.com
naadd.org
lifebytes.gov

Education:

aauw.org
bigchalk.com
education-world.com
enc.org/classroom
fastweb.com

Entrepreneurship

iiee.org
eplace.org
kidpreneur.org
teenink.com
youngbiz.com
kidsway.com
teen.stanford.edu
youngentrepreneur.com
cjonline.com/teen
cyborlink.com/
sba.gov/teens
kidauthors.com
ye.entreworld.org
youthventure.org
entrepreneur.com
cybi.org.au
entrenuity.org
iiee.org
kidsway.com
kauffman.org
abcsmallbiz.com
aspira.org/entrepreneurship/Intro.pdf
familymatterschicago.org/teenprograms.html
yes-inc.org
library.thinkquest.org
highschoolstartups.com
nfte.com
netpreneur.org
raisingourkids.com
youthtaskforce.org
eplace.org
uhea.org/convention/ teen
kidsfirst.org
childtrends.org
bgclub.org/main
inroads.org
entrepreneurialsecrets.com
dbedc.com
vcs.k12.nc.us/nvhs/career
uwci.org/yar/links.htm
entrepreneurs.com
ardd.org/service_entrepreneurs.htm
usasbe.org

Etiquette 101

bixxo.com/npa/10_com.html
etiquettesaintlouis.com
thefamilycorner.com
rudebusters.com
taranstreehouse.net
true-teen.com
politechild.com
biz-ewomen.com
magnificentmanners.com
schoolbug.org
themannersclub.com
etiquettesurvival.com
online.sfsu.edu
family-daily.com
kidsturncentral.com
joansue.com

Finances

ntrbonline.org
bluesuitmom.com
teenanalyst.com
nclnet.org/moneyandcredit
ucanr.org
nclnet.org/finances/teensurvey1
US-Finance4u.com
nefe.org
kidscashmanagement.com
teenadvice.about.com/cs/savingmoneyciti-
group/financialeducation/curriculum/teens.htm
secu.org/boom/faq.html
breakingnewsblog.com
Teen_Life/Advice/Business_and_Finances
bootcampsforteens.com
teenagerstoday.com
fool.com/teens/teens11.htm
theezine.net
youthspecialties.com
mvelopes.com
desjardins.com/teen

Friendships

links2love.com
secretexpressions.com
friendship.com
theacorn.com
goldbamboo.com
kavitanjali.com
queendom.com
lifetimetv.com
myjellybean.com
quiz.teenmag.com
yournewromance.com
hometown.aol.com
outdoorshub.com
anguillian.com

teenangels.org

Gangs & Violence
ctprevention.com
hopefs.org
papercamp.com
streetgangs.com
safeyouth.org
teenzone101.net
youthwork.com
racematters.org
ngcrc.com
shutitdown.net
csun.edu
gangresearch.net
safestate.org
streetgangs.com
gangwar.com
gang-busters.com

General
Habitat for Humanity
suicide-helplines.org/
way2hope.org
parenthood.com
nrscrisisline.org
true-teen.com
larcc.org
familytlc.net/teens
teenfashion.about.com
shykids.com
teenink.com
astc.org/resource/youth
teen-scene.com
dancesafe.org
fitteen.95mb.com
useekandufind.com
teenadvice.about.com
teenspoint.org
helpyourteens.com

Girls Only
girltech.com
girlscouts.org
womenswork.org
teenpuberty.com
girlsite.org
Puberty 101
Teenvoices.com
girlzone.com
gurl.com
agirlsworld.com
girlsinc.org
sistagirls.org
beinggirl.com
girlspace.com
smartgirl.org
thisismeinc.org
estronaut.com
girlynation.com

counseling.org
teenpuberty.com
girlhealth.org
bygirlsforgirls.org
notmenotnow.org
thebody.com

Graduation
rexanne.com
promslide.com
graduationparty.com
education.umn.edu
operationgraduation.com
wastelandmag.net
kidspartyfun.com
airsho.com
pluk.org

Healthy Teens
teenagerstoday.com/resources/articles/he
althyteens kidshealth.org/teen
extension.iastate.edu/teen
slimkids.com
4teenweightloss.com
healthyteensmarin.org
bridge-comm.com/site/review.htm
teencentral.net
teenhealthfx.com
teenshealth.org
tenspeed.com
healthscout.com
girlhealth.org
teengrowth.com
nicozan.com
teengrowth.com
teenhealthfx.com
DBSAlliance.org
SleeplessinAmerica.org
Teensforteens.net
fitteen.95mb.com
yourskindoctor.com
Theinsite.org
teengrowth.com
teenhealthissues.org
estronaut.com

Homeless Teens
cbel.com/teen_life
rmcumc.org
crisisclinic.org
mail-archive.com
windyouth.org
safeplaceservices.org
guide2homelessness.blogspot.com
homelesssurvival.com
homeless123.blogspot.com
homeaid.org
solutionsatwork.org
gatesfoundation.org
teenshelter.org
teenliving.org
propeople.org
avillagewetrust.com
lifeworksweb.org
nrscrisisline.org
streetteens.org
standupforkids.org
nationalhomeless.org
aidforteens.com
ehsd.org
nhi.org
lambda.org
streetkids.net
donrearic.com/homeless.htm

Homework & School
andovertownsman.com
Teenreads.com
familyfirstaid.org
nextstepmagazine.com
refdesk.com
aolatschool.com
syvum.com
riteofpassage.com
classbrain.com
schoolwork.org
starbright.org
ireallyhateschool.com
ala.org/teenhoopla
ipl.org/div/teen
homeschoolteenscollege.com

History & Politics:
cnn.com
blackfacts.com
cyndlist.com
embark.com

Internet
ajkids.com
cyberteenscom
teenmag.com
safeteens.com
netsmartz.org
isafe.org
kidskonnect.com
kidshealth.org
kidgrid.com
Safe2Read.Com
chiff.com
kidproof.blogs.com

ISP's
aol.com
yahoo.com
netscape.com

Jobs for Teens
Campandstyle.com
teenjobs.org

snagajob.com/teenjobs
quintcareers.com/teen_jobs
nclnet.org/childlabor
gotajob.com
coolworks.com/teen-jobs
groovejob.com/resources/teen-jobs-legal
jobammo.com
theparentreport.com
resources/ages/teen/safety
spankmag.com
CollegeBoard.com
kidzworld.com
lplonline.org/teen/tjobs
fhyouth.org
mysummercamps.com
misterpoll.com
kidshealth.org/teen/school_jobs
interlocken.org
campjobs.com
allensguide.com
promsplus.com
jobdoggy.com
quintcareers.com/teen_jobs
4teachers.org/kidspeak/careers
coolworks.com
barrfoundation.org
fabjob.com
mysummercamps.com
teenresources.studentcenter.org
ehso.com/oshateen
teens4hire.org/resources
theparentreport.com
disabilitycentral.com
talentdevelop.com
americaconnects.net
sexualharassmentpolicy.com
outdoored.com
parenting.ivillage.com
jobshopdepot.com
government.jobsearch.com

Kids Only

coolmath.com
discoverengineering.org
discoverykids.com
pbskids.org
thetech.org
tryscience.org
yahooligans.com

Media & Entertainment

aficaonline.com
bookwire.com
cushcity.com
106park.com

Magazines

essence.com
vibe.com
teenmag.com
ym.com
seventeen.com

Music/Hip-Hop/Rap

daveyd.com
rap.about.com
yale.edu
oldschoolhiphop.com
africanhiphop.com
jam2dis.com
multirace.org
youngpop.com
nbufront.org
vanillafudge.com
epinions.com
freerepublic.com
aap.org
mediascope.org
democracynow.org
vicnet.net.au
theroc.org
ericnuzum.com
music-critic.com
harmful.org
a-teens.com
pluggedin.org
freevibe.com
teenmusic.com
rap.about.com
youthcommunication-vox.org
tolerance.org

Parents

beaconstreetgirls.com
parentsjournal.com
bigislandforum.org
family.org
wholefamily.com
ncfy.com
gang-busters.com
urbantech.org
singleparent.lifetips.com
girlsandboystown.org
houseparent.net
pluk.org
family.org
larcc.org
Parenting.aol.com
Teenhelp.
parenting.ivillage.com

Peer Pressure

Teenhelp.org
just-4-teens.com
teenpuberty.com
worththewait.org
iwannaknow.org
hooah4health.com
keepkidshealthy.com
counseling.org
clearinghouse.adhl.org
kidzworld.com
madd.org
cfoc.org
notmenotnow.org
communityintervention.org
rainbowbabies.org
HelpYourTeenagerCopeWithPeerPressure
christophers.org
teencontact.org
thepoint.org
whatsdrivingyou.org

Piercing

safepiercing.org
tribalectic.com
body-piercing.com.
planetthree.com
youngwomenshealth.org
personalmd.com
gentleparent.com
immunize.org
pitt.edu
tonguerings.net
piercinglife.com
body-piercing-secrets.com
tonguestud.com
bodypiercingguide.com
belly-rings.net
bodymodification.com
pacificbodyjewellery.com
bybenjamin.com
floss.com
thedoctorsdoctor.com

Preteens

beaconstreetgirls.com
washington.edu
familiesaretalking.org
preteenagerstoday.com
canikissyou.com
chrysaliswomen.org
houseparent.net
nutritionforkids.com/emlnews
greatschools.net
ileadyouth.com
ahwg.net
youthdevelopment.org
cac.washington.edu
theparentreport.com

Prom

promspot.com
largerteens.com
roadreadyteens.org
promspot.com
beautybuzz.com
310online.com
stives.com

beauty.about.com
African-pride.com
naturallycurly.com
alternahempshampoo
kidzworld.com
sydneyscloset.com
promdress.net
jewishfamily.com/families
perfectproms.com
teenagerstoday.com
teenadvice.about.com/cs/promnight
teenhealthcentre.com
limousines.com
promsplus.com

Safety & Crime Prevention
safeteens.com
osha.gov
catssafecommunities.org
mypreciouskid.com
massgeneral.org
womanmotorist.com
foodsafety.gov
lessonplanspage.com
teenweb.org
safety1st.org
compeace.org
cdc.gov
wiredteens.org
cdipage.com
protectkids.com
safekids.com
4j.lane.edu
missingkids.com
drivehomesafe.com
ipromiseprogram.com
crime.org
ycwa.org
preventviolence.org
enn2.com/crime.htm
ncjrs.org/txtfiles/curfew.txt
preventviolence.org
ncpc.org
attleboropolice.org/teendating.htm
training.ncjfcj.org/Crime%20Violence.htm
thejobspider.com
stopviolence.com
jointogether.org
fluidpowersafety.com/sfty_teen1.html
compeace.org
weprevent.org
traviscase.org
fathersforlife.org
violentkids.com
tamucc.edu
ncpa.org/pi/crime/pd082599g.html

Savings Accounts & Budget
dcu.com
kuoks.com
agriculturefcu.org
christianhelps.org
nls.org/teen/budget.pdf
financialplan.about.com
themint.org
kidsmoney.org
italladdsup.org
foxway.com
thebeehive.org
budgeting-order.com
jumpstart.org
cents-ability.org
nefe.org
ye.entreworld.org
thesoonersclub.com
seriousliving.net
onestionline.com
younginvestor.com
byparents-forparents.com
nonempty.com
free-financial-advice.net
mgv.mim.edu.my

Self Esteem
recreationtherapy.com
selfesteem4women.com
more-selfesteem.com
self-esteem-nase.org
kidsource.com
selfesteem.org
confidencewithdating.com
parentsandgirls.com/article1003_2.shtml
teenshope.com/HelpSelfEsteem.htm
parentsandgirls.com
rense.com
aidforteens.com
depressionissues.com
suwsyouth.com
apa.org
parentmagic.com
Self-Esteem-Building.com
self-esteem.ws/sitemap.html
gutsforteens.org
teenacademy.org
bridges4kids.org
kidshealth.org/teen/question/emotions
self_esteem.html

SEX & Abstinence
allaboutsex.org
sxetc.org
worththewait.org
teenpuberty.com
teen-aid.org
aimforsuccess.org
choosingthebest.org
advocatesforyouth.org
abstinence.net
basicdecisions.com
gravityteen.com/abstinence
sexrespect.com
abednet.org
friendsfirst.org
notmenotnow.org
safeinc.org
ywwf.org
share-program.com
my.webmd.com/content/article/1739.50140
cfoc.org

Smoking
Notobacco.org
Be-Health-Smart.com
tobaccofree.com
Nicotine-Anonymous.org
keepkidsfromsmoking.com
lungusa.org
no-smoking.org
cancer.org
smoking.go.ro
notobacco.org
ash.org
4woman.org
tobaccofreekids.org
ama-assn.org
americanheart.org
physicseq.com/teenage-smoking.htm
weights.com/teenage-smoking-statistics.htm
tobacco.org
quia.com/rr/97763.html
ncc.uidaho.edu/teenageissues.html
nicotinefreekids.com
quitsmoking.com
mobileyouth.org
impacteen.org
ritobaccocontrolnet.com
lungusa.org

Spirituality & Religion
biblestudytools.net
musalman.com
beliefnet.com
religioustolerance.org/nataspir.htm
Meaning-of-life.info
interfaithcalendar.org
amazingbible.org
spiritualityhealth.com
spirituality.com
spirithome.com

Sports / Jobs
blackathlete.com
espn.com
SportsInterns.com
jobsinsports.com
womensportsjobs.com
sportmanagementclub.com
sportsemploymentnews.com
sportscareers.com

sportsemployment.com
sports-management.com
workinsports.com
CollegeSportsCareers.com
Internship-USA.com
stlsports.org
sportsinternjobs.com
internsearch.com
onlinesports.com
vault.com/employment/MajorLeagueBaseball.html
SportsManagementWorldwide.com
baseballjobs.net
coachfinder.com
hscoaches.org
jobsinsports.com
basketballjobs.com

STD's/AIDS
aids.about.com
YourSexualDiagnosis.com
teensource.org
mihivnews.com
avert.org
herpes.com
freeteens.org
teenadvice.about.com/library/101/bl_101_sex.htm
teenawareness.org
waifaction.org
worththewait.org
iwannaknow.org
preventaids.net
herpes-coldsores.com
aidspartnership.org
tbdhu.com
kidzworld.com/site/p3009.htm
lovesmarts.org
familydoctor.org/x5414.xml
bodyteen.com
condomhall-condoms.org
ashastd.org
avert.org

Stress
teachhealth.com
adviceforallages.org
stress.org
teen-depression.info
stressbusting.co.uk
trauma-pages.com
mindtools.com
isabelperez.com
ivf.com
lifepositive.com
livizi.com
ppmhc.org
teen-matters.com
cyc-net.org
gutsforteens.org
thehealthcenter.info adaa.org
nmha.org
twu565.org
stressdiagnosis.com
copingtoday.com

Tattoos
tattoos.com
everytattoo.com
safe-tattoos.com/faq.htm
vanishingtattoo.com
tattoodesign.com
tattoo100.com
supercoolstuff.com
colormybody.com
bodymodification.com
tattoosbysage.com
tattoos.com/safe.htm
bodymodification.com
tattoosguide.com/wingtattoos
gurl.com
k12.nf.ca/roncallips/2002/journalism/Kristel/teen_tattoos3.ht
ypress.org
darksidetattoo.com
faqs.org/qa/qa-818.html
silkcitytattoo.com/faq.html

Technology
blackengineer.com
eweek.com
getnetwise.org
iaaec.org
nacme.org
tnj.com

Teen Pregnancy
ppgg.org
pregnancy.org
teenparents.org
teendads.org
noappp.org
medscape.com
itsuptome.org
plannedparenthood.org
americanadoptions.com
nationallifecenter.com
gotmepregnant.com
thebody.com
teenwire.com
standupgirl.com
parentingteens.about.com
teenpregnancy.org
yppo.com
oneyoungparent.com/dad2
inwoodhouse.com
20ishparents.com
womenclique.com
joe.org
parentteen.com
unplannedbaby.com
letsgetreal.org
parenting.com
advocatesforyouth.org

Troubled Teens Resources
drugtestyourteen.com
bootcampsforteens.com
nationalyouth.com
focusonyourchild.com
tell-my-mom.com
teenhelp.us
discoveryacademy.com
suite101.com
parentlink.act.gov
naturalfamilyonline.com
safeparents.com
familymanagement.com
whyteensneedtobesafe.com
bidstrup.com
familymanagement.com
psychologyinfo.com/depression/teens.htm
theparentreport.com
troubledteen.us
familyeducation.com
parentingteens.about.com/od/promresources
madd.org
girlspace.com

Youth Empowerment & Motivation
Christian-Entrepreneurs.com
helpmyteen.com
youthempowerment.com
ritesofpassageonline.org
gyeonline.org
youthactivism.com
ftcc.fsu.edu/resreports/july99/index.html
nllc.org
yess.co.nz
cywd.org
youthempowermentscheme.org
girlsblossom.org
empowertheyouth.org
aypf.org/pubs.htm
hopeworldwide.org
SuperCamp.com
teenprogram.info
volunteersolutions.com
youthempowerment.org
yealliance.org
centerforempowerment.org
yedcin.org

RESUMÈ

Demi Lobo
100 Demi Q Avenue
Chicago, IL 60666
(773) 222-2222
Email: forteenz@aol.com

Demi Lobo

OBJECTIVE	To gain the knowledge and experience needed to become a professional in the television and broadcasting field.
EXPERIENCE	**Cold Stone Creamery** - Chicago, IL 8/2005–Present **Crew Leader** • Supervise and train other store employees • Manage and close store without supervision • Prepare sales reports, count registers, re-stock store, bake items and service customers
	Girl's Sports World/GSW - Chicago, IL 2003–Present **Coach/Coordinator** • Coach youth sports camps • Register children for camps and collect registration fees • Assist in fan club mailings for Jalen Rose and other professional athletes
	Professional Entertainment Experience - Chicago, IL 1999–Present **Model** • Cover model for teenage book, "For Teens Who Think They Know Everything" • Book model for children entertainers, "Cutie In Commercials" • 1st Illinois Best Actress in National Beauty Pageant in Orlando Florida **Singer** • Accomplished vocalist currently in production of music CD • Annual featured vocalist at Danny Davis' Black History Month Event • Perform at various social and sporting events
	People's Gas – Chicago, IL Summer '04
SPORTS	Chicago High School Girls Basketball Team (Captain/Starting Guard) 2002-06 Dance Team 2003-06 Girls Volleyball Team 2005 Girls Track Team 2004
ACTIVITIES	Member of Trinity United Church of Christ (Drill Team, Choir, Athletes for Christ Youth Ministry).

Appendix II.

MODELS, AUTHORS AND BUSINESS PARTNERS INFORMATION

Models

Dominique Jones, 16 – Cover Photo, Author,Teen Testimonials. Dominique is a print model, who works as a manager at ColdStone Creamery in Beverly Hills and Oak Lawn Illinois. She is a junior, she plays basketball and has other extracurricular interests. She can be reached for modeling jobs at: forteenz@aol.com.

Demi Lobo, 17 – Cover Photo, Author,Teen Testimonials. Demi is a print model, semi-professional singer and motivational youth speaker. She is currently working on the release of her C.D. Demi, a senior at the Chicago High School, captain of her school basketball team, and she also participates in her church drill team. Demi also works as a manager at ColdStone Creamery in Beverly Hills Chicago and Oak Lawn, Illinois. She can be reached for modeling, singing or youth speaking engagements at forteenz@aol.com.

April Miller – 16, Model, Author, Teen Testimonial Chapter. April Miller is a senior in high school and she performs in several performance dance teams around the city of Chicago. She is planning on a career in fashion merchandising. She can be reached at forteenz@aol.com.

Brittany Williams – 15, Model, Brittany is in our preteen chapter and is a high school sophomore in Chicago. She enjoys volleyball, reading and shopping. Nakiah, Dominique, and Stacey are models in our friends chapter.

Business Partners Network

- GSW Publishing, Life Skills U., Kandias Conda – forteenz@aol.com, goddesskandi@aol.com
- Psychodrama Graphic Design and Web Services, Brian JA Kelly – psychodrama@hotmail.com
- DAE Communications, a Hump Dyddi Cyti Co. Deborah Evans – mystfaith1@aol.com
- 360Beyond Photography, Cedic "Pharoah" Pope, Co-Founder, Build Today Lead Tomorrow, e:contact_360@yahoo.com
- Michelle Ruscitti – Author, Sports Jobs, Co-Author, Music Hip-Hop – vip_ me2@yahoo.com VIP Marketing and Entertainment, Exposing Very Important People to the Public with style
- Dr. Angela Wheeler – Author, Avoiding Sports Injuries, Healthy Teens
- LaConda Mines, Transitional Living Career Institute – www.tlciwecare.com
- Nicole Cabell, Speaker, Radio Personality WVON 1450, Mahogany Blue Inc., cabelln@yahoo.com
- Gargoyle Creative Services & Design, Sean Hicks – grgoyl1@aol.com

INDEX

D

Order Form

GSW Publishing

For Teens Who "Think" They Know Everything

12 Tips for Teens on Life Skills, Parents, Peer Pressure,
Sex, Health & Everything Else!

By: Kandias Conda

www.forteens.biz

Price: $17.95 each

Visa, MasterCard and American Express accepted

Mail Order: **GSW / Attn: Order Department**
3400 W. 111th Street, #142
Chicago, IL 60655

E-Mail Requests: info@forteens.biz or ForTeenz@aol.com

Telephone Requests: (773) 495-5585 (Orders/Workshops Requests)
(773) 341-4243 (Fax)

To order books, schedule speaking engagements or workshops, email or call the numbers listed above.

Please send me ____ copies of "For Teens Who Think They Know Everything"

Company:			
Name:			
Address:			
City:		State:	Zip:

Shipping and Handling: Enclose $5.00 for the first book and $1.00 for each additional book. (Please allow 5 to 10 days for shipping)

PAYMENT METHOD :	_____Checks made payable to "GSW" _____Money Orders made payable to "GSW"

Credit Card:

____Visa _____MasterCard _____American Express

Card Number:

Name on Card:	Expiration Date:

Order Form

GSW Publishing

For Teens Who "Think" They Know Everything

12 Tips for Teens on Life Skills, Parents, Peer Pressure, Sex, Health & Everything Else!

By: Kandias Conda

www.forteens.biz

Price: $17.95 each

Visa, MasterCard and American Express accepted

Mail Order: **GSW / Attn: Order Department**
3400 W. 111th Street, #142
Chicago, IL 60655

E-Mail Requests: info@forteens.biz or ForTeenz@aol.com

Telephone Requests: (773) 495-5585 (Orders/Workshops Requests)
(773) 341-4243 (Fax)

To order books, schedule speaking engagements or workshops, email or call the numbers listed above.

Please send me ____ copies of "For Teens Who Think They Know Everything"

Company:			
Name:			
Address:			
City:		State:	Zip:

Shipping and Handling: Enclose $5.00 for the first book and $1.00 for each additional book. (Please allow 5 to 10 days for shipping)

PAYMENT METHOD :	_____Checks made payable to "GSW" _____Money Orders made payable to "GSW"

Credit Card:

____Visa _____MasterCard _____American Express

Card Number:

Name on Card:	Expiration Date:

Author's Bio

For Teens Who "Think" They Know Everything is another brainchild from three time successful author Kandias Conda. "Kandi" is an author, speaker, trainer, and entrepreneur who shares her expertise in this hard hitting self-help guide for teenagers. For the past ten years she has been speaking to hundreds of teenagers and young adults teaching life skills, personal enrichment, entrepreneurship and team building. She has developed sports and mentoring programs to help teenagers develop leadership skills and cope with self-esteem, peer pressure and personal challenges.

"Kandi" is currently the Director of Youth Conferences and After School Programs for the Illinois Institute for Entrepreneurship Education in Chicago. She is instrumental in development, planning and organization of youth entrepreneurship conferences and after school programs in the city of Chicago. She taught Life Skills for 5 years to athletes in the Chicago Bulls/Chicago Park District Men and Women's basketball league. She is a graduate of Southern Illinois University, and she also served in the United States Air Force for 11 years.

Her client list includes; DCFS transitioning youth, Chicago Public Schools, alternative schools, Chicago Park Districts, churches, and community programs around the country. Kandi was honored in 1995 by the Naismith Basketball Hall of Fame for her contribution to women's professional basketball. Kandi has attended Trinity United Church in Chicago, IL. for the past twelve years. She is the Chairperson of the Athletes For Christ ministry which organizes sports programs for youth and young adults. Kandi also has a teenage daughter that is dynamic, beautiful, athletic, smart, successful and very talented - she knows what it takes to make it all happen. She continues to encourage and empower teens and young adults around the country, one book at a time.